Fun with Digital Imaging: The Official Hewlett-Packard® Guide

Fun with Digital Imaging: The Official Hewlett-Packard® Guide

Lisa Price and Jonathan Price

IDG Books Worldwide, Inc.
An International Data Group Company

Foster City, CA ■ Chicago, IL ■ Indianapolis, IN ■ New York, NY

Fun with Digital Imaging:
The Official Hewlett-Packard® Guide

Published by
IDG Books Worldwide, Inc.
An International Data Group Company
919 E. Hillsdale Blvd., Suite 400
Foster City, CA 94404
www.idgbooks.com (IDG Books Worldwide Web site)

ISBN: 0-7645-3307-X

Printed in the United States of America

10 9 8 7 6 5 4 3 2 1

1O/QS/QW/ZZ/FC

Distributed in the United States by IDG Books Worldwide, Inc.

Distributed by CDG Books Canada Inc. for Canada; by Transworld Publishers Limited in the United Kingdom; by IDG Norge Books for Norway; by IDG Sweden Books for Sweden; by IDG Books Australia Publishing Corporation Pty. Ltd. for Australia and New Zealand; by TransQuest Publishers Pte Ltd. for Singapore, Malaysia, Thailand, Indonesia, and Hong Kong; by Gotop Information Inc. for Taiwan; by ICG Muse, Inc. for Japan; by Norma Comunicaciones S.A. for Colombia; by Intersoft for South Africa; by Eyrolles for France; by International Thomson Publishing for Germany, Austria and Switzerland; by Distribuidora Cuspide for Argentina; by Livraria Cultura for Brazil; by Ediciones ZETA S.C.R. Ltda. for Peru; by WS Computer Publishing Corporation, Inc., for the Philippines; by Contemporanea de Ediciones for Venezuela; by Express Computer Distributors for the Caribbean and West Indies; by Micronesia Media Distributor, Inc. for Micronesia; by Grupo Editorial Norma S.A. for Guatemala; by Chips Computadoras S.A. de C.V. for Mexico; by Editorial Norma de Panama S.A. for Panama; by American Bookshops for Finland. Authorized Sales Agent: Anthony Rudkin Associates for the Middle East and North Africa.

For general information on IDG Books Worldwide's books in the U.S., please call our Consumer Customer Service department at 800-762-2974. For reseller information, including discounts and premium sales, please call our Reseller Customer Service department at 800-434-3422.

For information on where to purchase IDG Books Worldwide's books outside the U.S., please contact our International Sales department at 317-596-5530 or fax 317-596-5692.

For consumer information on foreign language translations, please contact our Customer Service department at 800-434-3422, fax 317-596-5692, or e-mail rights@idgbooks.com.

For information on licensing foreign or domestic rights, please phone +1-650-655-3109.

For sales inquiries and special prices for bulk quantities, please contact our Sales department at 650-655-3200 or write to the address above.

For information on using IDG Books Worldwide's books in the classroom or for ordering examination copies, please contact our Educational Sales department at 800-434-2086 or fax 317-596-5499.

For press review copies, author interviews, or other publicity information, please contact our Public Relations department at 650-655-3000 or fax 650-655-3299.

For authorization to photocopy items for corporate, personal, or educational use, please contact Copyright Clearance Center, 222 Rosewood Drive, Danvers, MA 01923, or fax 978-750-4470.

Library of Congress Cataloging-in Publication Data

Price, Jonathan, [DATE]
    Fun with digital imaging : the official Hewlett-Packard guide / Jonathan Price and Lisa Price.
        p. cm.
    ISBN 0-7645-3307-X (alk. paper)
    1. Photography–Digital techniques. 2. Image processing–Digital techniques. I. Price, Lisa, [DATE] II. Title.
TR267.P75   1999
006.6–dc21   99-25397
                                                         CIP

ABOUT IDG BOOKS WORLDWIDE

Welcome to the world of IDG Books Worldwide.

IDG Books Worldwide, Inc., is a subsidiary of International Data Group, the world's largest publisher of computer-related information and the leading global provider of information services on information technology. IDG was founded more than 30 years ago by Patrick J. McGovern and now employs more than 9,000 people worldwide. IDG publishes more than 290 computer publications in over 75 countries. More than 90 million people read one or more IDG publications each month.

Launched in 1990, IDG Books Worldwide is today the #1 publisher of best-selling computer books in the United States. We are proud to have received eight awards from the Computer Press Association in recognition of editorial excellence and three from Computer Currents' First Annual Readers' Choice Awards. Our best-selling ...For Dummies® series has more than 50 million copies in print with translations in 31 languages. IDG Books Worldwide, through a joint venture with IDG's Hi-Tech Beijing, became the first U.S. publisher to publish a computer book in the People's Republic of China. In record time, IDG Books Worldwide has become the first choice for millions of readers around the world who want to learn how to better manage their businesses.

Our mission is simple: Every one of our books is designed to bring extra value and skill-building instructions to the reader. Our books are written by experts who understand and care about our readers. The knowledge base of our editorial staff comes from years of experience in publishing, education, and journalism — experience we use to produce books to carry us into the new millennium. In short, we care about books, so we attract the best people. We devote special attention to details such as audience, interior design, use of icons, and illustrations. And because we use an efficient process of authoring, editing, and desktop publishing our books electronically, we can spend more time ensuring superior content and less time on the technicalities of making books.

You can count on our commitment to deliver high-quality books at competitive prices on topics you want to read about. At IDG Books Worldwide, we continue in the IDG tradition of delivering quality for more than 30 years. You'll find no better book on a subject than one from IDG Books Worldwide.

John Kilcullen
Chairman and CEO
IDG Books Worldwide, Inc.

Steven Berkowitz
President and Publisher
IDG Books Worldwide, Inc.

Eighth Annual
Computer Press
Awards ≥1992

Ninth Annual
Computer Press
Awards ≥1993

Tenth Annual
Computer Press
Awards ≥1994

Eleventh Annual
Computer Press
Awards ≥1995

IDG is the world's leading IT media, research and exposition company. Founded in 1964, IDG had 1997 revenues of $2.05 billion and has more than 9,000 employees worldwide. IDG offers the widest range of media options that reach IT buyers in 75 countries representing 95% of worldwide IT spending. IDG's diverse product and services portfolio spans six key areas including print publishing, online publishing, expositions and conferences, market research, education and training, and global marketing services. More than 90 million people read one or more of IDG's 290 magazines and newspapers, including IDG's leading global brands — Computerworld, PC World, Network World, Macworld and the Channel World family of publications. IDG Books Worldwide is one of the fastest-growing computer book publishers in the world, with more than 700 titles in 36 languages. The "...For Dummies®" series alone has more than 50 million copies in print. IDG offers online users the largest network of technology-specific Web sites around the world through IDG.net (http://www.idg.net), which comprises more than 225 targeted Web sites in 55 countries worldwide. International Data Corporation (IDC) is the world's largest provider of information technology data, analysis and consulting, with research centers in over 41 countries and more than 400 research analysts worldwide. IDG World Expo is a leading producer of more than 168 globally branded conferences and expositions in 35 countries including E3 (Electronic Entertainment Expo), Macworld Expo, ComNet, Windows World Expo, ICE (Internet Commerce Expo), Agenda, DEMO, and Spotlight. IDG's training subsidiary, ExecuTrain, is the world's largest computer training company, with more than 230 locations worldwide and 785 training courses. IDG Marketing Services helps industry-leading IT companies build international brand recognition by developing global integrated marketing programs via IDG's print, online and exposition products worldwide. Further information about the company can be found at www.idg.com.   1/24/99

Credits

Acquisitions Editor
Martine Edwards

Development Editors
Philip Wescott
Kenyon Brown

Technical Editor
Susan Glinert Stevens

Copy Editors
Luann Rouff
Anne Friedman
Amanda Kaufmann
Corey Cohen

Book Design
Kurt Krames
Cátálin Dulfu

Production
IDG Books Worldwide Production

Proofreading and Indexing
York Production Services

About the Authors

Lisa Price and **Jonathan Price** have written many articles about family software for *Family PC*, *MacWorld*, and *Home Office Computing*, as well as books on Microsoft home essentials and Windows for kids and families. Lisa is features editor for Brainplay.com, a webzine dealing with children's software, toys, and videos. Jonathan has displayed his art in major museums and galleries in New York and around the world; he has also written two dozen books about art, video, theater, writing, and computers. The Prices' Web site is at http://www.theprices.com.

To Toby and Summer

Foreword

Fun with Digital Imaging is a very different kind of computer book: it's a book that shows you an extraordinary world of possibilities using the variety of computer and computer-related tools available today. If you have a souped-up multimedia computer, digital camera, scanner and high-end color printer, great: you'll find projects in here that use that equipment in new and interesting ways. But if you are like me, you're more likely to have only a computer and scanner; or a digital camera and computer but not a color printer. Doesn't matter: You can still get a lot out of this book. Instead of scanning a photograph or taking a digital photo, you can use public domain images you download from the Web or a CD to complete exactly the same projects. And, if you're shy one color printer, there's always your local copy shop down the street.

You see, today, there are numerous ways to get and manipulate images and to create dazzling output, no matter which computer you own, and what great digital toys you may have assembled. And the best part is that anyone can do these projects: folks who don't have a fortune to spend on computer equipment, kids, retirees, and everybody in between. Oh, and that's something else that makes this book special: it's not aimed at digital imaging professionals (whoever they are!); it's aimed at you and me, our kids, parents, and friends.

One thing is for sure: this book is going to give you lots of terrific ideas — ideas about personal and community projects; ideas about creating impressive looking materials for your home or small business; ideas about family projects like starting that genealogy record you've been thinking about for years. There's no time like the present to get these projects going, and this is the perfect book to take along. Enjoy!

Rick Smolan
Creator of *A Day in the Life* photography book series

Preface

If you've been intrigued with the possibility of printing in color, here's a book that lets you take advantage of the new gear, such as digital cameras, scanners, and color printers.

If you always enjoyed making pictures, working with crafts, or just generally showing off, this book will help you add colorful graphics to every project, thanks to your personal computer.

If you want to bring your family closer together, or just get close to friends, making bright, colorful images on your computer can amuse, intrigue, and draw everyone together around the electronic hearth. This book shows you how.

If you want to publicize community activities such as fund drives, or sporting events, use this book to make your newsletter, brochures, and posters stand out. And, finally, if you want to wow your sweetie with a romantic message, you'll find the secret inside.

Helpful Icons

This book uses four types of icons as visual cues to annotate the contents of the text:

Warning

The warning icon warns you when to watch out or when to take particular care when performing a procedure.

Cross-Reference

Most people won't read this book from cover to cover, instead zeroing in on the chapter or information they need. The Cross-Reference icon tells you that information relevant to the topic you're reading about is located elsewhere in this book.

Note

The Note icon offers an aside or extra information about a topic.

Tip

The Tip icon is perhaps the most important icon. It signals the kind of information that saves you time, money, and aggravation.

How to Use This Book

This book is focused on creating projects with digital images that you either scan from photographs or grab from a digital camera. Most of the material in this book provides ideas to help you get started. Before you begin, however, you need to know how to acquire and manipulate digital images. The first three chapters should help you get up to speed.

Part I: Getting Started covers the basics of digital images — what they are, why they're important, and how you make them. You'll also find exactly the types of hardware and software you need to use scanners, digital cameras, and printers, how to configure and calibrate these tools.

Part II: Projects discusses how you can put your new knowledge to work. You'll get ideas for projects for the home, work, school, or the community.

Acknowledgments

We would like to acknowledge the great support given by Martine Edwards, Chip Wescott, and Anne Friedman of IDG Books Worldwide, and by Pat Pekary at Hewlett-Packard, whose vision launched this book, and saw it through to publication.

Contents at a Glance

Foreword ix
Preface xi
Acknowledgments xiii

Part I: Getting Started 1
   Chapter 1: Why Now? 3
   Chapter 2: How Pictures Go Electronic 17
   Chapter 3: Sharing Your Pictures with Others 49

Part II: Projects 59
   Chapter 4: Projects at Home 61
   Chapter 5: Projects at Work and School 189
   Chapter 6: Community Activities 269

   Appendix: Troubleshooting 309

   Index 331

Contents

Foreword ix

Preface xi

Acknowledgments xiii

Part I: Getting Started   1

Chapter 1: Why Now? 3

Pictures R Us 4

    Why do they call these images digital? 7

    Why electronic imaging has taken off 8

    What you can produce using digital images 14

Chapter 2: How Pictures Go Electronic 17

At the Center — Your Computer 18

    Enter the Macintosh 18

Scanning an Existing Picture 19

    How scanning works 20

    What you may be able to do with your scanner 21

Snapping a New Picture with Your Digital Camera 29

    How digital cameras work 30

Using Your Old Camera and Having the Photos Digitized by a Developer . 34

Plugging Your Video Camera, VCR, or DVD Player into Your Computer . . 35

Using Software to Create Electronic Pictures from Scratch 36

    Mapping those bits 37

    Drawing onscreen 39

    Manipulating photos 41

    Printing with project software 46

    Starting points 47

Chapter 3: Sharing Your Pictures with Others 49

Printing Your Pictures 50

    How printing works 50

How paper affects the look of your pictures. 50
Loading paper — that's the trick. 52
It's a setup 53
E-mailing Your Pictures 55
Posting Pictures on Your Web Site. 56

Part II: Projects   59

Chapter 4: Projects at Home 61

Making Your Own Greeting Cards 62
Remembering Mom with a card 62
Getting into the holiday spirit. 69
Becoming a postcard magnate 76
Party Time. 77
Turning an invitation into a conversation. 78
Drawing guests to your house 80
Waving hello 83
Leading the way to the party — with signs galore 85
Decorating the door with banners 89
Wrapping up a gift with homemade papers 92
Creating special bags to hold party favors 96
Creating a lightweight box for a little gift 98
Envisioning Your Garden and Yard 101
Getting picky about your flowers or veggies 105
Mapping out the land. 108
Using photos to sharpen your vision of the yard to come 110
Hobby-Rama 114
Beating the post office at the stamp game 114
Tracking your triumphs. 120
Labeling your collection with images 122
Watching the skies 125
Ironing your life into a quilt. 127
Cooking Up Images in the Kitchen. 129
Drawing up a little shopping list. 129
Sticking to your diet. 132
Labeling your best Preserves 132
Concocting very special calendars 136
Providing recipes even a new cook can follow. 139
Creating personalized aprons. 143

Pet Pals 144
   Putting together pet memorabilia 144
   Taking your pet on an imaginary flight 147
   Boasting about your goat 151
   Finding that lost pet 153
   Putting your pet on a pedestal 154
Making Genealogy Graphic 157
   Documenting what it was like 157
   Making a map of the old sod 160
   Using software to dramatize your genealogy 164
   Surfing for information and images 167
   Creating a family newsletter 171
   Posting a family Web page 172
Expressing Love 175
   Remembering that cruise 176
   Starting with a poem 178
   Dreaming of you 180
   Edible love 181
   Appealing scents 184
   Invitation to a special dinner for two 186
   Valentine's Day 186

Chapter 5: Projects at Work and School 189
Showing Off Your Home Business 190
   Saying who you are with your letter paper 190
   Making postcards for announcements and thank-you's 200
   Letting folks know — with a newsletter 202
   Creating certificates and awards 212
Polishing Health Care 213
   Creating personal reminders 213
   Making instructions easy to follow 216
   Relaxing your patients 219
   Activities for restless fingers 221
   Rewarding good behavior 223
Brightening the Classroom 223
Marketing Your Organization 246
   Picking your colors, font, and symbol 249
   Creating posters 255
   Report and proposal covers 258
   Catalogs 260
   Creating a portfolio of successes 263
   Succeeding at direct mail 266

Chapter 6: Community Activities 269

Volunteering 270
    Making sure meetings are attended 270
    Announcing events and work sessions 272
    Fund-raising can be fun 275
    Campaigning 277
    Livening up a newsletter 279
Celebrating Sports 281
    Making your own sports cards 281
    Celebrating the whole team 284
    Morphing into a big leaguer 285
    Getting ready for the big game 287
    Making mini-posters 289
Exploring Neighborhood 292
    Advertising your garage sale 292
    Setting up a treasure hunt 296
    Making a map of your block 298
    Making a game out of local real estate 301

Appendix: Troubleshooting 309

Index 331

Getting Started

1   **Why Now?**

2   **How Pictures Go Electronic**

3   **Sharing Your Pictures with Others**

Why Now?

IN THIS CHAPTER

- Why graphics have such deep appeal
- Why making electronic images has taken off
- Materials you can brighten up using these new digital images

Pictures R Us

People love pictures. Which do you look at first — Figure 1.1 or 1.2?

Figure 1.1

The roadway takes off into the distance, two dirt tracks going through the weeds, next to the ditch. The cottonwoods crowd in from the sides of the road. Sunflowers rise up out of the tumbleweeds and willows along the edge of the road. We can tell from the tracks that cars and trucks pass through here occasionally, crushing the seedlings of any weeds that might take over.

Figure 1.2

The text describing a scene may get all the details, but it doesn't attract our attention until we have looked at the picture. Looking at an image has always been a lot more fun than reading about it. The shapes, the lines, the perspective; all offer more for our eye to play with, and for our mind to explore.

We soak up more information from a picture than from text. A dramatic image communicates a whole message all at once, rather than presenting one idea after another, as text does. We see how different parts of the scene interact with one another; we discern relationships right away. The picture's message sinks in quickly, evoking memories and emotions, as in Figure 1.3. In a moment, we absorb the whole picture, and feel its impact. In this case, the eye and mind recognize the scene, putting together trees, colonnade, and tulips to come up with a whole message that says more than the mere words "White House" can.

And once we've seen a graphic, we recall it more than twice as well as words. In fact, according to research, if the image is striking or distinct, we recognize it with almost 100 percent accuracy.

Figure 1.3 *Image from Print Artist from Sierra.*

Many of us think in images before we can put our concepts into words. Creative scientists like Albert Einstein report their thinking processes as primarily working with visual images long before they come to write anything down. Nikola Tesla used to design complex electrical devices in his mind, setting them to run and then taking them apart in his head, to see where the worn parts were — all without a word spoken.

So images are a way of thinking. But you would hardly know that if you attended the average school, where words are king, numbers are queen, and pictures are for kindergartners. Most of us are not encouraged to use imagery to work through our ideas, or to express ourselves. "Put that in writing!" we are told.

So we enjoy images, but feel shy about using them. We remember in our fingers the shame we felt when our first attempts at drawing a flower or a house came out badly. Many of us — most of us — believe firmly that we cannot draw a straight line. We have learned that text is important, whereas pictures are, well, just decoration (as in Figure 1.4), or amusement. Graphics, we feel, "illustrate" what the text says. But we rarely recognize that graphics can carry the main load of our expression, with words acting as mere notes, as in Figure 1.5.

The Dutch painter Rembrandt van Rijn often did self portraits, dressing up in theatrical costumes, but in this painting we see him as he might have looked after work, his white handkerchief still protecting and warming his head, a thick coat against the cold, his hair brushed back. But what strikes us most acutely is his glance, knowing, almost cynical, a bit doubtful, unblinking--a painter's eye.

Figure 1.4 *Image from ClickArt from Broderbund.*

Figure 1.5 *Image from ClickArt from Broderbund.*

The computer changes our relationship with images. It does the hard work. If we want a perfect circle, the computer can make it for us in a second or two. The computer gives us the facility our hands never had, letting us draw elaborate diagrams, make beautiful and complex pictures, modify photographs, and seize on just the right image to modify slightly, to express our feelings, guide our viewers, or provoke someone into action.

Why do they call these images digital?

An electronic approach is also known as a digital approach, in contrast to the old-fashioned way (analog). Instead of using oil paint on a brush, and waving that across some canvas to create a rough analogy to the scene we are painting, the computer works by turning individual dots on and off, and assigning each one a particular color. Instead of working with a wash of paint, we are working with numerically coded patterns — a lot of digits. The resulting precision means that your manipulation of the image can be more exact, and the results can be reproduced more accurately; in effect, you have greater control because the images themselves are collections of electrons, not variable swatches of ink, paint, and veneer.

Now that we have mature software, relatively cheap digital cameras, high speed scanners, and color printers, we can play with images, think with images, and communicate with images. We are moving from a thousand words to a vision.

Why electronic imaging has taken off

Making pictures electronically, rather than using paintbrushes, pencils, glue, and scissors, offers you many advantages. No more splashes. Making images like Figure 1.6 with electrons is cleaner. You don't get paint on the rug or smell glue on your sleeve.

Figure 1.6 *From ClickArt from Broderbund.*

Figure 1.7 *From ClickArt from Broderbund.*

Making images electronically is also cheaper (you can even print money from clip art, as in Figure 1.7). Instead of buying supplies, you use electrons. Sure, the computer costs more than canvas for a few good-size paintings, but you already decided to buy the computer for games, word processing, budgeting, and what not. In almost half of American households, a personal computer is a given. You also need a printer, and these days, that might as well be a color printer, because color does not cost much more than black ink. With these tools, all you need to add is software to manipulate the images — at less than the cost of a lush brush for oil painting. Of course, you may want to add a color scanner, and a digital camera, for another five or six hundred dollars, but you don't have to. You can do a lot with what you already have.

Figure 1.8 *From ClickArt from Broderbund.*

Electronic imaging is faster. With a computer, you design something, and in a few minutes you have a print. You don't have to wait until you reach the end of a roll of film, take it to the camera store, wait a day or longer for developing, and then pick up the prints.

The images you create electronically are more integrated, like blocks in an arch or tiles in a mosaic, because all the pieces are just electrons, or dots (see Figure 1.9). The computer pulls every element together. On the screen, you can put together a photo, a drawing, and splotches of color and text; and when you print, they all come out on the same sheet. What would have been a pile of pasted-on paper before is now a single image, because all the parts are electronic, and have been synthesized before you print.

Figure 1.09 *From ClickArt from Broderbund.*

Working electronically gives you more flexibility. With software, you can quickly change the contrast, brightness, and tint of a photograph (see Figure 1.10). You can put two photographs together to create something that never happened, like a pet flying over the coastline. You have the services of a professional airbrusher to get rid of embarrassing moles, scars, and pimples on the faces of your subjects. And speaking of that...

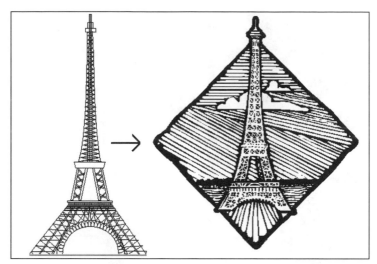

Figure 1.10 *From ClickArt from Broderbund.*

Work created electronically looks as if it came from a professional (as in Figure 1.11) compared with those sketches you used to do with pencils and correction fluid. Like a real artist, software can make perfect circles, squares, ovals, and patterns. The software does what pros used to do — letting you improve your photos, cut and paste, blend, and tip images upside down and sideways. What used to take an expert three hours with wax and light box, you can now do in a few clicks. You may not have the vast taste and aesthetic experience of a real artist, but with the software, you can fake it pretty well, because those skills have been built into the applications you use to make your work look great.

Figure 1.11 *From ClickArt from Broderbund.*

Working electronically lets you grab art from many sources (see Figure 1.12). The electronic nature of graphic files means they can come to you, ready to use, from all over the world, and from every century. If you have a regular camera, you can have your pictures digitized — made into computer files — when they are developed. Or, if you have paper prints or slides, you can scan those, emerging with electronic files. You can pick up pictures off your TV, if you plug your VCR or antenna into your computer, or if your computer comes with a built-in TV receiver. You can go into the World Wide Web and pick up images for private use. As long as you do not resell the images, using them only for your personal amusement or that of your friends, you have not violated the copyright of the original owners.

Figure 1.12 *From ClickArt from Broderbund.*

Working electronically also means you can display your images more widely, in many locations, where a traditional artist had to be content with using different media, all within the same gallery space (see Figure 1.13). Because your image is electronic, you can publish it on your Web site, send it along with your e-mail to your family, print it out as a poster, and shrink it down and print it in a letter. The same picture can show up in half a dozen media, depending on how ambitious you are. You can, for instance, print on a dozen different kinds of paper, plus some forms of cloth, plastic, and glass. Like an ad agency, you can publish the same image everywhere.

Figure 1.13 *From ClickArt from Broderbund.*

What you can produce using digital images

Once you begin to think graphically, you see ways to liven up almost every document you already produce, such as the following:

- Letters
- Reports
- Proposals
- Marketing brochures
- Flyers

But you also begin to recognize that you yourself can produce new materials — items you have never or rarely turned out, because you always felt you needed a professional artist's help, or a specialized printer:

- Posters
- Advertising postcards
- T-shirts, aprons, and pillowcases
- Banners
- Signs
- Web pages

If you turn to our Color Sampler, you'll see that the possibilities go way beyond these examples, as you find ways to brighten up your home, spruce up your small business, draw in the whole family, or work as a volunteer in community projects.

How Pictures Go Electronic

IN THIS CHAPTER

- Using a new approach to making pictures

- Turning a picture into an electronic image

- Using a digital camera to snap an electronic picture

- Digitizing your new slides or prints

- Stealing images off the TV

- Using graphic software to create electronic images

At the Center — Your Computer

In the ancient days of computers — fifteen years ago, say — we took it for granted that all one could see on a computer screen would be letters and numbers. Some crazed souls spent hours using x's and o's to build images, such as the Christmas tree shown in Figure 2.1, but these pictures were so crude that most people shuddered at their ugliness.

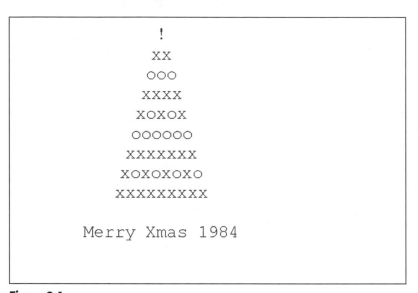

Figure 2.1

Enter the Macintosh

Suddenly, with the arrival of the Macintosh in the mid-1980s, you could make pictures on the screen. A little program called MacPaint struck with the force of an explosion, changing what we thought was possible to do on a computer. In a few minutes you could build a respectable-looking house or sketch cartoon figures like those shown in Figure 2.2, just by moving your mouse. The computer had become a graphics machine.

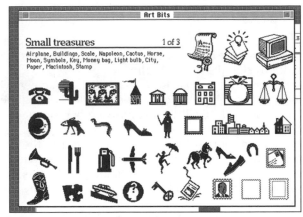

Figure 2.2 *HyperCard from Apple.*

Eventually, Microsoft adopted the idea of a graphical user interface, and now its operating system offers pictures instead of text—icons, toolbars, colors, and the ability to create and manipulate dozens of different kinds of images. In the last 15 years of uneasy cooperation and competition within the computer industry, hundreds of programs, and thousands of gizmos, have come to market, all designed to help us make pictures.

By now it's common for professional artists to use computers to make startling graphics and intriguing photos. And as the hardware and software trickles gradually down the market from professionals to the rest of us, we are now able to pull off effects that even the pros couldn't manage back when MacPaint arrived. Of course, nothing is as easy as the marketing people say, and until we practice making images for several years, the rest of us will lack an intuitive sense of what works and what won't—the learned taste of a professional. But a lot of that good taste has been quietly packed into the latest generation of equipment, and many of the tasks a pro used to labor over have been made instantaneous with the current software. So now, thanks to the computer, the rest of us can make images that amuse our friends, wow our relatives, and win over our customers, colleagues, and neighbors.

Scanning an Existing Picture

Scanners make it possible to get an image off paper and into your computer, so you can fix it up, put a border around it, print it, or post it on the Web.

How scanning works

Basically, a scanner works like a photocopier. You lay a picture on the glass, or feed it into a chute, and the machine moves a beam of very bright light across the picture, picking up, dot by dot, the colors in the image.

Imagine a grid like the metal mesh we use for screen doors or screen windows. The scanner is looking through each hole in the grid, identifying the color and recording that color in code — basically, using one number for each color it recognizes.

You can tell one scanner from another by the number of slots in the grid (or, looking at it another way, by the number of dots it examines). The higher the number, the better the resolution, because if you use a lot of little dots, you get very precise pictures. Low resolution would be 72 dots per inch, compared to 300 dots per inch, or higher.

Also, once a scanner spots a particular dot, the scanner's software can collect and store a lot of information about that dot, in code. Inside the computer, these codes are recorded by setting a series of switches. Each switch can be either on or off. In computer terms, the switch is called a *bit,* and its value can be either 1 or 0. So a code that is one bit long can contain only two possible values: yes or no, on or off, one or zero. Not much information there, but enough to record that a dot is black or white.

Once you ask for color, you need a lot more switches with which to record information. If the scanner team decides that the machine will recognize 256 different colors (barely enough for a crummy photo), the software will need eight slots to store the code (that's two raised to the eighth power, for you mathematicians; or 8-bit color, in computer jargon). So the more bits of color info a scanner can register and store, the more subtle variations in color will emerge, including a range of hues, brightnesses, and degrees of gray. Your scanner advertises its excellence in terms of 16-bit color, 24-bit color, and so on. Those terms can be mathematically translated into the number of colors the scanner is able to see and record, as described in Table 2-1.

Table 2.1 **Bit-depth and colors**	
32-bit	16.7 million or more colors, with 256 levels of gray
24-bit	16.7 million or more colors
16-bit	65.5 thousand colors
8-bit	256 colors
7-bit	128 colors
6-bit	64 colors
5-bit	32 colors
4-bit	16 colors
3-bit	8 colors
2-bit	4 colors
1-bit	2 colors (black and white)

With anything more than 1-bit color but less than 8-bit color, you can make simple colored designs. Once you have 16-bit color, you begin to get photographs that are recognizable, without too many garish effects. At 24-bit color and above, you are able to match or surpass a regular photograph. Most current scanners can handle 16-bit color or better; you know you are in good shape when your scanner boasts of handling "millions" of colors.

What you may be able to do with your scanner

Each scanner offers a different combination of tools with which you can control the process. Sure, you can always fix up an image after it is in electronic form. But you can have the scanning software make a lot of adjustments before it records the image — so you don't have to mess with it later.

When you first launch the scanner, you often get a thumbnail view of the whole image, and a larger view, showing what will be scanned, as shown in Figure 2.3. The following sections describe some of the adjustments you can make to your image.

Figure 2.3 *HP PhotoSmart Photo Scanner.*

Rotating

You may have dropped that old magazine cover on the glass without thinking. Now it appears upside down on your screen. If you want to be able to look at the picture objectively and make further changes, you need it right side up.

No, you don't have to cancel this scan and start over, guessing which way is up. Just use the software to turn it around. As with the HP Photo Smart Photo Scanner shown in Figure 2.4, most scanning software lets you turn the image 90 degrees at a click, or tilt it a few degrees with each click.

Figure 2.4 *From HP PhotoSmart Photo Scanner.*

That's usually enough unless you placed the image at an angle, or fed it through the middle of a grinder that gradually increased the odd tilt. If you're faced with a picture on a slant, you might have software that lets you actually grab a handle and twist it — or do so later with the photo-finishing software.

Mirroring

If for some reason you would like a mirror image of the original, no problem. You can do that. (But watch out for any pictures that have numbers or text in them, because mirror imaging turns numbers or names into gibberish, as you can see in Figure 2.5.)

Figure 2.5 *From HP PhotoSmart Photo Scanner.*

Cropping

You may not like part of the original image—such as the title of a magazine, or a half of someone's head, intruding into the edge. With most scanning software, you can slice off an unwanted top, bottom, or side, as long as you end up with a rectangle.

You can also ask the software for a list of possible dimensions, such as 3" × 5", or 4" × 6" (see Figure 2.6), and the software will throw up a light rectangle in those proportions, so you can drag it around the image to frame just the part you want. At the same time, you may be offered the opportunity to set the resolution, and told how much room the file will take, if you store all the information acquired at that resolution.

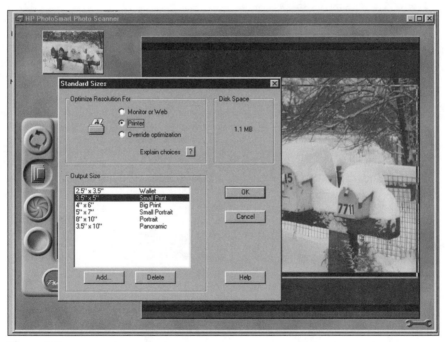

Figure 2.6 *From HP PhotoSmart Photo Scanner.*

When you finish cropping the picture, the image onscreen adapts to show you what the resulting image will look like. In Figure 2-7, for instance, we made the picture 3" × 10" — a wide panorama, but not very tall. The entire original still appears in the thumbnail view at the top left, but you can see the image as it will look after scanning, in the middle of the window.

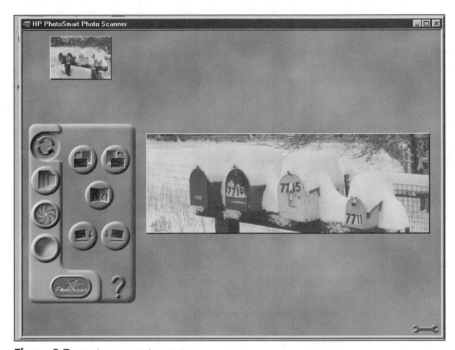

Figure 2.7 *HP PhotoSmart Photo Scanner.*

Of course, because the alterations have not been recorded, you can always change your mind, trying out different rectangles to see which best captures what you want.

Tip

Remember that you don't have to live with the original orientation of the picture. Even if it started out in landscape orientation—wider than it is tall—you can crop the picture so it ends up in portrait orientation—taller than it is wide, as shown in Figure 2.8.

Figure 2.8 *HP PhotoSmart Photo Scanner.*

Adjusting exposure

How much light is there on the mailboxes in the middle? How much light fell on the areas in the shade? That's what photographers mean by *exposure*.

If there were any problems with exposure in the original picture, you can make some small adjustments now. You can brighten up the picture as a whole by dragging a slider that affects the areas that are not pure white or pure black—the middle range. That's often the best you can do to cheer up a gloomy or overcast picture.

You're also usually offered the opportunity to make the light areas even brighter, and the dark areas even darker. These two settings can be treacherous, however. If you adjust them too much, the results are lurid. Play with brightening the light areas first, if you must, and then tweak the darks just a little. One false move with the dark controls, though, and the whole image turns to a fog, or a daytime picture begins to look like night. Pushing brightness or darkness to the limits also results in the loss of subtle details, as shown in Figure 2-9. (If you have an expensive photo editor such as Photoshop, you can just accept the picture as is, in the scanner, and then tweak the contrast and brightness; but if you have a low-end or relatively inexpensive photo editor, it won't do much better than your scanning software).

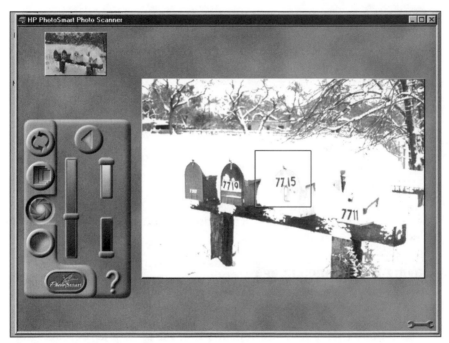

Figure 2.9 *HP PhotoSmart Photo Scanner.*

Tinting

You can usually cast a tint over the whole picture as you scan. With a winter scene, you can make it seem even colder by emphasizing the blues. You can turn clay into sand, and a dull sky into a vivid sunset. Or you can leach all color out of the image, producing a black-and-white image. The tools that allow these transformations, shown in Figure 2.10, result in dramatic, but very unrealistic, images when overused. A little tinting goes a long way. Extremes look ghastly on paper, and incompetent onscreen.

Figure 2.10 *HP PhotoSmart Photo Scanner.*

Click anywhere on the color wheel to tint the picture, and then drag the slider below to saturate the image with that tint, or reduce it to nothing—resulting in a black-and-white picture.

Saving the scanned image

You can save the same image in one of several different file formats. Which format you choose depends on what you want to do with the image.

■ **Bitmap (BMP).** If you're not sure, save the picture as a bitmap. This is the most common format, and almost any photo-editing and painting software can read it. It earned its name in the earliest days of computer graphics. The idea is that the screen has an imaginary grid on it and, to make a map of the image, you record what goes in each cell. Originally, when the images were just black and white, you only had to record one bit per dot— that is, one on or one off, to indicate black or white. But as color came in, the number of bits needed to record each dot grew, as mentioned earlier, to 8, 16, 24, and more. Naturally, when you start using 24 bits per dot, and you have 800 × 600 dots to keep track of, your file grows quite large—with some files taking up millions of bits, or, as we usually encounter these file sizes, 2 to 4 megabytes (a byte is eight bits).

- **TIFF**: To reduce the size of these files, various other formats were invented. TIFF (tagged image file format) saves every bit of information, but compresses the file by noting whenever two neighboring dots have the same color. TIFF does not lose any information, so it is called *lossless* by engineers.

- **JPEG**: This format, invented by the Joint Photographic Experts Group, throws away details you can't see in order to make dramatic reductions in file size. So this format is fine for photos you are going to use right away on the Web, where lost detail won't be noticed. But if you want to edit the picture, you can't be sure you will have preserved all the information you need; for example, if you want to print the image in a large size or pull detail out of the shadows. Pronounced "J-Peg," this format is very common, and very useful because the compression is 200:1, so the resulting file is one two-hundredth of the size it would have been without compression, as in a pure bitmap.

- **FlashPix**: An intriguing format, this puts several kinds of images into the same file—a large, fully detailed image for reworking, and smaller, compressed pictures that can be used for instant display onscreen or on the Web, or as thumbnail pictures in a program that you use to skim through a whole bunch of files, to spot the one you want. The image is also stored as a series of pieces, and then fitted together like tiles on a bathroom wall; a program can quickly display a low-resolution version of one tile, and then, as it gets additional detail, fill that in, so a viewer can see the image become clearer, gaining resolution. On the Web, this means that the viewer can often anticipate what the picture is going to be, without having to wait, and wait some more, to see anything. If you anticipate extensive reworking, FlashPix is an excellent format.

In addition to saving the scanned image, you can choose to print it. If you aren't sure whether you like your settings, save the image and then print it to see how it turns out. If you print without saving, you may never recapture the exact settings you had before you sent the picture off to the printer.

Snapping a New Picture with Your Digital Camera

Most of us remember film—that shiny black ribbon of plastic that sticks out of a cylinder, hooks onto some kind of ratchet, and gets advanced through the camera each time we take a picture—as long as we haven't stripped the holes or plugged it in wrong. Wave good-bye to film.

Instead of film, we can use electrons now. The digital camera acts like your scanner, recording information about each dot in its imaginary grid. Just like the scanner, the size of the dots tells you how precise the detail will be: the smaller the dots—the more of them in an inch—the better. Similarly, the amount of information about each dot, from a few bits to 32 bits per dot, tells you how many colors will appear in the final picture — again, the more the better.

Professional journalists use digital cameras costing $15,000 to $30,000. They pay that much to get resolution and color that's as good as a 35mm camera with an assortment of lenses costing about $1,000. Why do they bother? Because they can look over the images right away on the computer, with no developing time, pick the best three, and send those over the phone lines back to the magazine, newspaper, TV show, or Web site, so their work can be published within the hour. When it comes to speed, electronics beats paper by a day and a half.

With a digital camera you can afford, you probably won't get the same quality as the pros manage in fast-action, high-resolution images in low-light stadiums or on super-bright beaches at noon. But, frankly, that's OK. Digital cameras work great in medium light, on subjects that are not as fast as a baseball player's bat. Digital cameras produce somewhat softer images than regular film does, and the colors tend toward the pastel, rather than the hard; the overall impression may be, well, a bit more impressionistic than a 35mm camera can provide. But if you have been using really low-end cameras, you'll see a noticeable improvement in detail.

You'll also be able to manipulate the images like crazy afterward — cropping out unimportant detail, moving the star elf to the center of the picture, brightening things up. So even without a dark room or a professional at your side, you can "improve" your pictures after they are taken, thanks to the computer. That's a real plus, once you get the hang of the photo-finishing software.

How digital cameras work

Basically, you point and shoot. You look through a tiny viewer, find your subject, and click. Yes, you have a lot of other options, but basically the camera works like the box camera you once got from the cereal company.

But most digital cameras offer a lot more functionality than snapping a shot. Here are a few of the most common options.

Previewing a picture

On the back of the camera there's a rectangular screen. So if you find you are squinting when you look through the regular little viewer at the top, you can have the camera display whatever it sees, in that panel set into the back. Often, the display shows you icons standing for any other options you have set, so you know, for instance, that you asked that the date be stamped on every image, or a particular border be put around the picture.

Getting your distance

You may be able to zoom in on the picture, too. Some cameras offer a close-up setting, so you can get a head shot of a friend, as shown in Figure 2.11, or a full-frame image of your mother's favorite silver box. If the camera lets you get close, it probably also offers a distant or infinite focus, so you can take landscapes like that shown in Figure 2.12 without the woods seeming more like mist than trees.

Figure 2.11

Figure 2.12

If you want to get in the picture yourself, most cameras offer a timer. You set the picture up, with everyone else in it, and then tell the camera, "Wait ten seconds before you take the picture!" Then all you have to do is rush over, squeeze into the crowd, and adopt a fixed smile, while you wonder if the camera has already taken the picture.

Deleting mistakes

If you don't like a picture you just took and decide it was a mistake, you can get rid of it right away. The advantage? Having discarded the bad picture, you now have room for another shot.

Some cameras allow you to delete any image you've taken if you realize, "Hey, I got a much better shot of that just now, and I want to make some room for more pictures." You can also delete every picture you've taken. (You usually do this after you have transferred all your pictures from the camera to the computer and want to clear out the memory to take more pictures. But if you just hate the pictures you've taken, you can erase them all, usually with a few clicks of a button, using the menu that shows up in the LCD panel or viewfinder.)

Overcoming excessive light and shadows

Most digital cameras have trouble with the kind of shadows you see before nine in the morning or after five. That nice flower on the shady bank becomes a dark blob, as shown in Figure 2.13.

Figure 2.13

And similarly, if you pose a person in front of a brightly lit area, such as water at noon on a sunny day, the camera will take its light reading from the background, and your friend's face will end up as a shadowy, colorless shape.

To overcome these limitations, the cameras usually offer you a way to adjust the exposure, so you "expose" the "film" longer or less than normal.

■ If the scene has shadows in it, you'll want to compensate for that by increasing the exposure, so the camera sops up more light during the picture taking.

■ If you are looking directly into the sun, or you see a very bright background behind your real subject, you should first move your subject, if possible, so that brilliance disappears. If you can't move your subject, then increase the exposure so that the sky or background is overexposed, but your subject shows up.

■ If your entire subject is the brightly lit material, then you need to reduce the amount of time you "expose" the "film," so that less light comes in.

Choosing quality

Most digital cameras offer you three options mislabeled "quality." Actually, each setting makes perfectly good pictures. But the ultimate destination of those pictures differs.

■ **Good**. If you are making a picture that will only be shown onscreen, as on a Web site, you do not need a lot of detail. The average person's monitor only shows 72 dots per inch, so you do not need to record a lot more than that to get an image that looks fine, particularly if you keep it small. For these purposes, the Good or Basic setting is fine.

■ **Best**. At the other end of the spectrum is the Best or Advanced setting. This captures much more detail, but takes a lot more room in memory. Why bother? Well, you would use this setting if you intended to make a gigantic poster, or enlarge a picture beyond a postcard size and then print it on paper. To compete with *National Geographic*, you'll need the best possible setting.

■ **Medium**. The in-between setting captures enough information for you to blow the picture up to 5" × 7" with no problem, and to 8" × 10" without noticeable fuzziness on paper. But you won't get crystal clarity at the larger sizes. Your picture will look fine onscreen, but because it has more information than the Good or Basic setting, the OK or Medium picture takes up more room on your hard disk, and takes longer to load on a Web site.

Picking and preserving

Because each image is just a file, once you've captured it, you can treat it the way you do a file on your hard disk. You can delete it. You can protect it so someone else doesn't accidentally delete it. You can transfer it to the computer. You can select certain images and print them directly from the camera.

Some systems allow you to get rid of pictures from the computer. Others insist that you use the camera's controls — basically a series of menus that show up in the panel on the back of the camera. You click through many options to get the one you want, such as Erase Pictures, and then you have to choose whether to delete the current picture or all of them, and then, just to make sure, the camera software asks for just one more confirmation that you really, really want to go ahead and make the erasure.

Viewing what you've taken

You can usually have the camera run a slide show, displaying each image for a few seconds in the panel on the back of the camera. You can hook up to a TV and do the same thing on your TV. And you can show the pictures on your computer monitor to decide which ones you really want to save or print and which you feel like discarding.

Using Your Old Camera and Having the Photos Digitized by a Developer

Most camera stores and photo developers offer this service now. They develop your regular film and, if you want, give you a floppy disk or CD-ROM with electronic versions of every picture, along with the paper prints or slides. The quality is usually excellent; in fact, if you order several different resolutions, the higher-resolution pictures may have better detail than anything you could manage with a home scanner.

And if you already use a 35mm camera, the original images will be sharper overall, and particularly detailed in shaded areas, so that your digitized versions will offer more flexibility than pictures taken with a consumer digital camera — you'll be able to blow them up to a larger size without losing detail; crop out a small section and blow that up; and pull details out of areas that at first seem too dark or too light.

The biggest disadvantage of this approach is that you are paying a fee to have every image digitized, even if some pictures stink. And the fee is quite high through regular development shops. Seattle Filmworks is cheaper; you buy their film, use it, send it in, and get digitized images for a lot less than the neighborhood camera store charges. Again, though, you are committed to paying for every image.

Also, these services take a long time, compared to the instantaneity of a digital camera or scanner. You often have to wait several weeks while the developer sends the film out of state to a special lab.

Cannier photographers get everything developed the old-fashioned way, and then pick out their very best and have those digitized. This way, you know you are paying only for the images you really want to use. But having someone else digitize your images is more expensive than buying your own scanner, if you have more than a hundred or so images.

Plugging Your Video Camera, VCR, or DVD Player into Your Computer

If your computer is fairly new (bought within the last few years), you can display short clips of video onscreen. If your computer has a video jack (or a card that you install to receive a video cable), you can import video from a video recorder or camera and show it on the screen. With software such as Adobe's Premiere, you can edit the video, too; adding titles, cutting dull parts, and splicing together a new sequence.

Of course, raw video takes a lot of room. A single still picture that fills your screen as a bitmap image may take 2.5 megabytes to store. Now imagine 30 of those pictures every second, the rate of normal video. You can easily fill up a 100-megabyte hard disk in less than two seconds if you don't use some form of compression, squeezing the information down to manageable size.

Therefore, you will probably want to run video until you see a shot you like, and then capture that as a still such as the one shown in Figure 2.14, a frame showing Mount Fuji. In effect, you will grab a frame here and there. You can save the still in the formats your graphic software can use: BMP, JPEG, or TIF.

Figure 2.14 *From Mount Fuji, Spiritual Earth, DVD from Pioneer.*

If you have software to display a TV image, you can save a frame, or a whole series of frames if you are brave and have an enormous hard disk. Or you can freeze the frame and take a picture of the screen, saving the screen capture (in Windows, by pressing PrintScreen, opening a paint program, and pasting the picture in; on the Mac by pressing Command-Shift-3, which saves the image as Picture 1 to Picture 9 in whatever folder contains your System Folder).

If your computer has a DVD (digital video) drive, or if you can plug your DVD player into the computer, your video is already digitized, and somewhat compressed, so you will get high-quality stills.

Using Software to Create Electronic Pictures from Scratch

You can create plenty of great pictures — and decorate clip art or photos — using graphics programs that range from simple-minded to so complex you have to watch a video before you can use some functions. The following sections brief you on what you can dowith different kinds of graphics programs.

- **Paint software** manipulates dots to make a picture, which the program considers a map of bits (a bitmap)

- **Drawing software** makes images on the fly by calculating the curves, straight lines, and so on, tracing the way each line follows a series of directions, or vectors; because the image is stored as a series of equations, not a map of bits, the picture can be easily reproduced at 600 dots per inch on a laser printer, 2,400 dots per inch on a typesetter, and 72 dots per inch on your screen, without losing its resolution or smoothness.

- **Photo-finishing software** adjusts the brightness, tint, and individual dots of a photograph (a photograph is actually considered a very big bitmap).

- **Project software** helps you prepare cards, posters, or brochures using prepared designs, clip art, and a little imagination.

Mapping those bits

Paint programs let you create images one dot at a time. Using tools that let you draw a straight line, rectangle, square, oval, or circle, you just click in the white space and drag for instant results, as shown in Figure 2.15. Miraculous enough while you're playing, but after you release the mouse button, the magical lines fall back into the imaginary grid. Each dot lives alone. You can no longer click the straight line, for instance, and thereby select the whole thing. It is just a set of individual dots now — a map of bits.

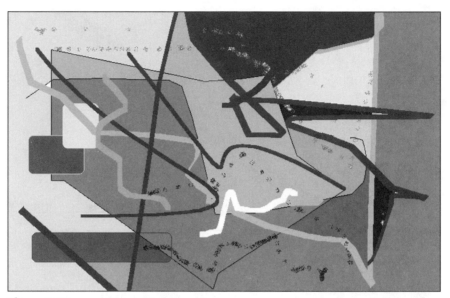

Figure 2.15 *Created in Paint from Microsoft.*

Bitmap programs are fun to fool around with, but hell if you want to make changes. Yes, you can erase a chunk, or select a rectangular region and move it, flip it, or delete it. You can even select an irregular section and get rid of it. But to edit precisely this way, you have to zoom way in, so that you can literally see every bit, as shown in Figure 2.16. On the screen, each bit is known as a *pixel,* because each is a *picture element.* Once you spot a pixel, you can erase it, change its color, or leave it alone.

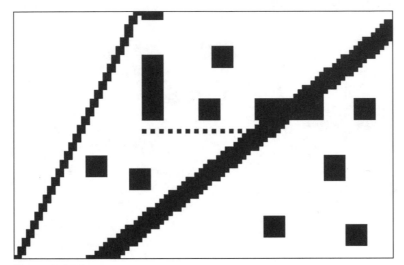

Figure 2.16 *Created in Paint from Microsoft.*

If you haven't used a program like MacPaint or Microsoft Paint, you'll get a kick out of the paint bucket, which lets you pour a color into any area that has a line around it; the paintbrush, which lets you draw big squiggly lines almost anywhere; and the spraycan or airbrush, which lets you puff a color on, as if it came out of an aerosol can.

Examples of bitmap or painting programs include the following:

- ■ MacPaint from Apple
- ■ Paint from Microsoft
- ■ Fractal Painter

Drawing onscreen

On the computer, drawing is different from painting. As you've just seen, paint programs let you create pictures that are known as bitmaps. Drawing programs, on the other hand, produce *vector graphics*. With drawing programs, you create whole objects that continue their existence as wholes even after you finish drawing one. This is because each one consists not of a map of where the dots are, but a set of formulas that allow the computer to reconstruct the object as a whole by tracing the vector (or direction) of the lines needed to create it. For instance, you can draw a rectangle in Paint and it ends up as a set of dots that happen to look like a rectangle, but in a program such as Corel Draw or Windows Draw, you can draw the rectangle, go on to do something else, and then come back and click on the rectangle, which selects the entire rectangle, so you can move it, resize it, even reshape it. In a drawing program, you work with objects that just happen to be made up of any dots available.

Most of what you can create in a drawing program looks, at first glance, like what you can do in a painting program, as shown in Figure 2.17. The difference, though, is in the way you can edit elements. Because each object can be manipulated separately, you can make small and large adjustments quickly, without accidentally erasing something else. The results may not be a lot better, but at least they don't eat up nearly as much time. Figure 2.18, for instance, shows the results of 30 seconds of editing to the image shown in Figure 2.17.

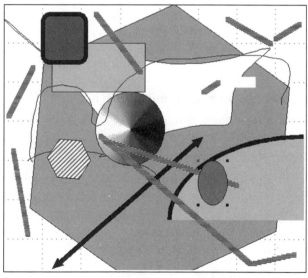

Figure 2.17 *Created in ClarisWorks, now renamed AppleWorks, from Apple.*

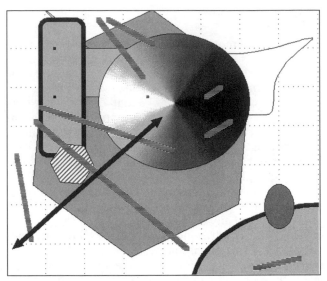

Figure 2.18 *Created in ClarisWorks, now renamed AppleWorks, from Apple.*

Because you're working with whole objects, you get to do tricks like the following:

- Move an object to the front, or tuck one object behind another (without destroying either one)
- Adjust the size of an object
- Change the shape of an object
- Change the lines used, the color fill, or the pattern filling an object
- Copy and paste an object without worrying that you might accidentally select part of the background and copy that as well
- Flip the whole object without its surroundings
- Group a set of objects into a larger module, and then manipulate that as an object

Products that offer drawing include the following:

- Corel Draw from Corel
- Windows Draw from Micrografx
- Illustrator from Adobe
- KidPix from Broderbund

Increasingly, products for children and grownups offer *both* drawing and painting in one package. We particularly like Deneba's Canvas because it lets you switch between drawing and painting as if they were on different transparent layers. Other products that offer both drawing and painting include:

- AppleWorks from Apple
- Orly's Draw a Story
- PaintShop Pro from Jasc

Manipulating photos

Technically, photographs are bitmaps, but such complicated ones that an ordinary paint program can hardly do them justice. Starting with the great granddaddy of all photo-finishing programs, Adobe's Photoshop, these programs let you do what in the past a professional might do in the darkroom. You can, for instance, start with an ordinary photo like the one shown in Figure 2.19 and then perform any of the following:

- Increase the brightness, as in Figure 2.20, or darken the whole image at once
- Tint the whole image with a color
- Increase the apparent sharpness, or soften the whole with a blur
- Soften the edges so the picture seems to fade into the surroundings
- Make parts of the image transparent, so it floats above something else you can see below
- Cut out a section
- Rotate or flip the whole picture, or a selected part
- Trace a subject and make a copy, as shown in Figure 2.21
- Take the color out of one part of the sky and apply it to another portion of the sky
- Change the color of a roof so it stands out from the shadows behind it or from the trees in front
- Paste one subject's head on another subject's body
- Frame the image or put a fancy border around it, as shown in Figure 2.22
- Drop your picture into a prearranged setting, as shown in Figure 2.23
- Invert the colors in the original, creating a startling new image, as when we invert the photo of Mount Fuji to create the image shown in Figure 2.24

Figure 2.19 *Created with HP PhotoSmart C20 camera..*

Figure 2.20 *Created in Picture It! from Microsoft.*

Figure 2.21 *Created in Picture It! from Microsoft.*

Figure 2.22 *Created in Picture It! from Microsoft.*

Figure 2.23 *Created in Picture It! from Microsoft.*

Figure 2.24 *Image from Mount Fuji, Spiritual Earth, DVD from Pioneer, manipulated in Picutre It! from Microsoft.*

Products that offer photo-retouching include the following:

- Canvas from Deneba
- Complete Publisher from Sierra and Micrografx
- MGI Photo Suite from MGI
- PhotoCreations from Creative Wonders
- PhotoDeluxe from Adobe
- PhotoDraw 2000 from Microsoft
- PhotoMagic from Micrografx
- Photoshop from Adobe
- PowerGoo from Kai
- Snapshot Digital Imaging Software from Sierra and Micrografx

Printing with project software

Some programs take advantage of painting, drawing, and photo-manipulation to offer a combo-pack designed to make it easy to turn out projects such as greeting cards, calendars, and posters. Broderbund's PrintShop is the oldest and most famous program, starting out as a way for people to make banners, and now expanded into a sophisticated program capable of almost any print job, as indicated by its window full of projects (see Figure 2.25).

Figure 2.25 *PrintShop from Broderbund.*

Most of these programs come with an ample supply of clip art — predrawn cartoons, existing photos, ready-made illustrations. Many come with partially created projects you can edit for your own purposes. And most offer templates for you to create newsletters, brochures, flyers, greeting cards, posters, and banners from scratch.

Project software includes the following:

- Complete Publisher from Sierra and Micrografx
- Crayola Print Factory from IBM
- Print Artist from Sierra
- Print Artist Craft Factory from Knowledge Adventure
- PrintShop from Broderbund
- Print Studio from Disney
- Printable Expressions from Hewlett-Packard

Starting points

You start with what you have. If you have none of the hardware or software we've mentioned, what should you buy? That depends on what you want to do most, or first.

- If you would like to work with that box full of old family pictures, then your top priority should be getting a scanner and, if it does not already come with it, some photo-editing software.

- If you have a fine camera already and are going to take more pictures, consider using your photo developing store for getting electronic versions of your best slides and prints, and then manipulating those in paint, photo-editing, or project software.

- If you like the idea of snapping a picture and then manipulating it right away, get a digital camera, which probably comes with some photo-editing software.

- For graphics that don't depend on photos, consider the paint, draw, and project software.

- If you are going to print graphics, but not photos, any inkjet printer that handles color will be OK. But if you want to print photos, move up the scale to something like the HP PhotoSmart printers, which do a fantastic job with both graphics and photos.

CHAPTER

3

Sharing Your Pictures with Others

IN THIS CHAPTER

- Printing your pictures
- E-mailing images
- Posting your images on the Web

Printing Your Pictures

Printing lets us share our pictures. We can give a print to a relative to put up on the wall, or we can post a reminder image on the refrigerator. We can turn out a ten-foot-long banner, a postcard to send to our customers, a newsletter for our Parent Teacher Association, or a brochure for our new business. Paper makes the image solid, letting us circulate it, and, if the printer is up to the task, it appeals to the eye.

The picture on your screen is brighter because it is made out of light. The picture on paper, though, lasts longer. If someone puts it up on the wall, the image makes an impression each time someone glances at it, picks it up, uses the information in it, or experiences some emotion about it. Printing preserves and distributes your message.

How printing works

The printers of today work via the same basic mechanism as paint programs: their incredibly complex software, and strenuously simplified machinery, figure out what color each dot should be and where it should go, and then quickly lay those dots down on paper. The smaller the dots, the more precise your image will be. So printers are advertised for the number of dots they can print per inch: 300 dpi is good, 600 is fine, and more than that enables some pretty spectacular effects.

The different physical mechanisms used determine the size of those dots. Lasers, for instance, can be more precise than a spray, or a jet of ink. But most of us do not need a laser printer to enjoy the results of our work on electronic images.

If you bought your color printer in the last few years, it can do an amazing job on graphics (art made out of colors and lines), and a surprisingly good job on photos. Photographs, though, are a tougher challenge because in order to be convincing, they need really tiny dots, and paper that can receive and smoothly integrate all of them, in either a glossy or matte surface. Some recently evolved printers concentrate on photographs, such as the Hewlett-Packard Photo Smart line. Output from these printers matches or beats anything your local developer can manage.

If you've just been using your printer for letters and reports, you may be astonished by how many different kinds of paper it can handle and how many different options it offers for making pictures or incorporating pictures into your documents.

How paper affects the look of your pictures

You've no doubt noticed the different impression you get from holding a newspaper and a glossy magazine. Well, now you can print on a range of papers, too — although you don't have quite as many options as a professional printing operation does. They can choose from thousands, whereas you can choose from a dozen or so, depending on the vendor.

- **Regular plain paper.** Good for text, and OK for graphics, it makes photos look a little pale. It's the least expensive option.

- **Premium and heavyweight paper.** Gives your document dignity and absorbs ink well, but may sop up ink and bleed if you have large solid patches of color, as in simple clip art . More expensive than regular paper, but not as expensive as the special-purpose papers, covered below.

- **Bright white paper.** Great for documents you want to present to a boss or a customer. Shows off your colors well in graphics, and makes photos look a little crisper. This is just a little more expensive than regular paper.

- **Transparency film.** Used for making presentations with overhead projectors. OK as long as you make each one simple, with big text, and just one image. More expensive than regular paper.

- **Photo paper.** Ranges from regular through premium, in glossy or matte surfaces. Specifically designed to handle the mass of little dots needed, and to integrate them all on a smooth surface. Expensive, compared to regular paper.

- **Greeting card paper — glossy or matte.** Designed to be a card, with a crease already in the paper, so you can print, fold, and mail. The glossy paper is photographic and takes an image well. Expensive, compared to regular paper.

- **Note-size photographic paper — glossy or matte.** Designed for small images (4" × 6"). It just takes a little fiddling with the manual feed mechanism or the paper tray to get these small sheets in the right position. Expensive, compared to regular paper

- **Postcard paper.** Photographic paper for photographic postcards, with one side glossy, the other matte, in a fairly heavy weight. The least expensive of photo papers.

- **Calendar paper.** A glossy surface on one side for the photo, and a plain surface for the calendar on the other. Expensive, but you aren't going to need very much.

- **Labels.** You can print labels, complete with an image, in your printer. Very low cost for a lot of labels.

- **Business cards.** Print a dozen or more per sheet, and then tear them apart on the perforations. Good for instant cards. If you get them from a paper vendor, these sheets can come with preprinted color images, to which you can add your own. Much less expensive than having these printed for you.

- **Mailers.** Three-fold heavy stock that you can fold along the creases and press together, because it is self-sealing. Ready to mail. A bargain.

- **T-Shirt transfer paper.** Takes the image and acts as a transfer medium to your T-shirt, apron, pillowcase, and so on, by ironing. Moderate cost.

- **Tyvek.** A waterfast, tough material that you may have encountered as an envelope around documents sent via FedEx. Suitable for signs, inside and out. Very specialized, so it costs more than other large-size surfaces.

■ **Large-size heavyweight paper — coated, glossy, or semi-gloss**. Available in rolls from two feet to 54 inches wide, and 100 feet long, this paper works with giant printers like the HP DesignJet at your local copy center, for posters, signs, and murals.

Check your printer manual if you think you might want to try anything stiffer than regular and extra-bright papers, because the way the printer feeds paper through its various rollers and gears may get hung up on thick paper, transparency sheets, or even the T-shirt transfer paper. Generally, the newer your printer, the more likely it will be handle a wide range of materials. Some can, for instance, print on paper bags; and some even handle cloth. But don't risk making a mess. Open that manual first.

Loading paper — that's the trick

Loading regular paper — that's no problem. You just shove it in between the guides and maybe tuck a little lever in, to make sure the paper is snug. But as soon as you work with paper that's glossy on only one side, or small-size papers or labels...well, you may find you need to experiment a bit.

The problem is that you often can't easily tell which side should be up, which end is going to be the top, or which side of the tray the little papers should go in. Interestingly, the "right" way changes from one vendor to another, which is why the people who package the paper conveniently forget to give you a diagram or instructions. Alas, it is time to turn to the printer manual, and even with that you will want to try out a few test strips.

One way you can figure out what's right for your own printer is to run a semi-scientific test:

1. Take a piece of plain paper.

2. Mark one end of it to show the surface facing up, nearest to you, as you put it into the printer.

3. Print something.

4. Analyze the results, answering the following questions:

   ● Does your printer print on the side of the paper that is facing up when you load or not? (Now you know whether to put the glossy side up or down.)

   ● Is the end that was nearest you when you loaded the top, or the bottom, on the printout? (Now you now which labels are considered "the top.")

Try to imagine how the paper goes through the various grinders, ratchets, and rollers, so you can figure out which end of the paper it grabs hold of, to start. (This becomes crucial when you are putting in small pieces of paper that don't reach each end of the tray.)

For small sheets of paper, use both sets of guides within the paper tray, nudging the paper in whatever direction they want to go. Generally, if you end up with the guides close to the paper (but not jamming it) you will be OK. But you may have to tell the printer that you are using small paper — and in some cases, you have to tell it this twice. Your application often knows that you are working in a small format, but when you choose to print, the dialog box acts as if it has no idea what size your project is. That's a danger sign. You should set the size there and then go to the options in the dialog box called Properties, Printer, or Setup to tell the system, again, that you are using a small size. This second dialog box is more permanent than the others — that is, it saves these settings, and expects that you will be using the small paper forever after. So there is a third time you have to change the settings: whenever you stop using small paper. (If your printer comes with a good manual, it might actually tell you how to handle the settings in the Properties dialog box when you change sizes.)

It's a setup

Normally, you don't have to mess with the dialog boxes that let you tell your printer how you are going to operate. But once you start playing with images, papers, and special effects, you may have to explore these options a bit more.

If you are changing the way you feed paper in (from the paper tray to manual feed, for instance), or if you are going to use an odd-sized paper, or if you have a picture that is wider than it is tall (such as a landscape of a mountain chain), you need to alert the printer through the Print Setup dialog box. The File menu usually offers a Print Setup command, which brings you to the dialog box shown in Figure 3.1. The Print Setup dialog box lets you set the size, orientation, and feed mechanism for your paper — and change printers, if you are lucky enough to have more than one.

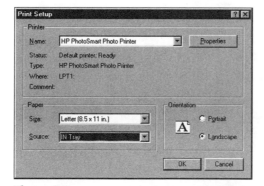

Figure 3.1 *Print Setup dialog box from MGI Photo, from MGI.*

Following are four circumstances in which you should use this dialog box:

■ If you have two printers, use the drop-down menu at the top to pick the printer that's best for the work you are about to print. For instance, if you have an HP PhotoSmart printer in addition to a DeskJet, you might switch to the PhotoSmart printer for photos.

■ If you are using any paper size other than 8"   10", pick the dimensions from the Size list.

■ If you're going to feed the paper manually, choose that option from the Source list.

■ If your picture is wider than it is tall, choose Landscape orientation; otherwise, leave the setting at Portrait.

Note the little Properties button in the Print Setup dialog box. That leads to new depths — and, in many cases, the same settings you just set. Given the way the Windows operating system works, you may want to use the Properties dialog box (shown in Figure 3.2) as well as the Print Setup, just so you are sending the same message to the printer every time. If you leave the properties set as is, the standard settings there may override the ones you choose in Print Setup — or vice versa. Yes, we know this does not make sense. But remember that Microsoft builds operating systems by adding feature after feature, incorporating multiple ways of doing the same thing without deleting the earlier features, so the opportunity for mixed signals grows with each release.

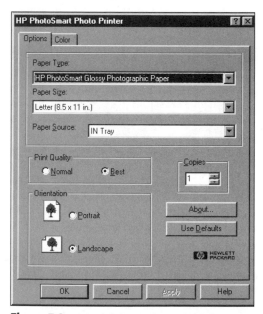

Figure 3.2 *Dialog box for Hewlett-Packard PhotoSmart Photo Printer.*

The Properties dialog box lets you define paper type, size, source, and orientation, as well as the standard quality and number of copies you want your printer to make from now on — until you change your mind again. Technically, the Properties dialog box is longer-lasting than any other, because its settings are in effect each time you launch the computer. So you could say it is a bit more durable than others, more influential — though never determinative.

Aside from the options already mentioned, the Properties dialog box lets you specify the kind of paper you are using (photographic, notecard, and so on), the quality of printing job you want (basically, how much detail you insist on), and other options that depend on what the printer can do. Use this dialog box each time you change papers or job types (going, for example, from printing a report that is mostly text to printing a photo).

E-mailing Your Pictures

Increasingly, families stay in touch by sending pictures back and forth over the Internet. In this way, grandparents get to see the latest hijinks from their namesakes, and cousins get to see one another grow up, even if they live on opposite coasts.

If you and the recipient are both using the same software, such as America Online or Outlook 98, you may be able to drop an image right into your message and send the text and picture as one message. Try it and see.

If you aren't using the same software as the recipient, send the art as an attachment to the text of your message. But here, too, you need to make sure that your recipient has software that can read the file containing your picture. Generally, they will be able to open one of the following:

- A bitmap file (with the suffix .bmp, pcx, or tif in Windows), such as that created in a paint program.

- A JPEG (ending in .jpg) file, another image made as a bitmap, but one that is usually a photograph and can be opened by any Internet browser such as Netscape, America Online, or Internet Explorer, or in a photo-finishing program.

- A GIF, or Graphic Image Format, file (ending in .gif), best for graphic images that are not photos; openable in any Internet browser.

- If you and your recipient use a Mac, you can also use the MacPaint version of a bitmap, a TIFF (Tagged Image File Format) or PICT (Picture) file, if the recipient has painting or drawing software like your own, plus the JPEG and GIF formats, if the recipient has an Internet browser. (Windows recognizes TIFF files, too, but hardly anyone uses them in that environment.)

One caution: Don't try to embed a huge image file, or the receiving site may choke. Try small pictures first.

Posting Pictures on Your Web Site

If you already have a family Web site, you may want to post your images there, in just the way that you put up other pages. If you don't already have a Web site, but are pondering making one, the following products can help:

- **AppleWorks from Apple** (http://www.apple.com). Formerly called ClarisWorks, this is a simple product, and a bit limited, but good if you aren't trying to do anything fancy. Web pages are just one of the things this multipurpose program does. (Mac and PC)

- **Complete Publisher from Sierra and Micrografx** (http://www.sierra.com). A bundle of products that work with one another and with Microsoft Office, so you can make drawings, 3-D images, photos, and pages for your Web site. Not primarily a Web publishing program, but has templates for Web pages. (PC)

- **FrontPage from Microsoft** (http://www.microsoft.com/products). An extension of the Office suite, this product is built for business, but works fine at home. Lets you see what you are building as you build it. (PC and Mac)

- **Home Page from FileMaker** (http://www.filemaker.com). A very popular program for building Web pages without having to know secret codes in the Hypertext Markup Language (HTML). Works well with the popular database FileMaker. (Mac and PC)

- **Internet/Intranet Design Shop Gold from Boomerang** (http://www.mosaiccom.com). Lots of power, and probably better if you are already familiar with building Web pages, because navigation leaves a bit to be desired. (PC)

- **PageMill from Adobe** (http://www.adobe.com/prodindex/pagemill/main.html). Great for graphics, this is an excellent product, particularly if you are already familiar with other Adobe products such as Photoshop and PageMaker. Not recommended for absolute beginners. (Mac and PC)

- **Visual Page from Symantec** (http://www.symantec.com/vpage/prodinfo.html). Good clip art, plenty of features, but a bit heavy-duty if all you want is a quick family page. If you intend to create a serious Web site, take a look. (PC and Mac)

- **Web Easy from Ixla** (http://www.ixla.com/products/webeasy/webeasy.htm). Very easy to use, with tons of clip art. You won't want to use this for your home business, but if you just want to post pictures of your pets, or make a family site quickly, start here. (PC)

- **Web Express from Microvision Development** (http://www.mvd.com/webexpress/index.htm). This product has most of the features of Front Page, at half the cost. A good starter kit. (PC)

■ **Web Studio from Sierra** (http://www.sierra.com). Lots of clip art for buttons and backgrounds, along with animations and sounds so you can make a lively site quickly. (PC)

■ **Word for Office 97 and Word for Office 98** allow you to include the tags for Web pages crudely, but when Office 2000 ships, you can use Word much more easily to create Web pages, and then, using the Web Page Publisher, transfer them to your site. (PC, Mac)

First you make a page, and then you drop the graphic in, save it, and send it to your site. Most of these programs will do the sending for you, which is good, because that's often the hardest part of putting up and maintaining your Web site.

For the Web, use the JPEG format for all your photos, and the GIF format for everything else. Your Web page editor may be able to bring in images with other formats and convert them to these two, which are the most common on the Web. Anyone's browser can read these two.

If you scan the image in, scan for 72 dots per inch (dpi), which is the resolution on most monitors; that way you don't build a huge file, and the picture looks fine on the screen. (While 72 dots per inch may be fine for displaying pictures on-screen, you need more dots per inch if you intend to print. Check your printer manual to find out how many dpi it can handle, and tell the scanner to scan at that rate. Remember, too, that dots per inch matter more on-screen than on paper; two printers with the same dots per inch differ in the way they lay the ink on the paper, and the precision with which the dots are placed.)

Pictures look great on the Web, but most home users don't have high speed lines, so as a courtesy, use only one small image per page, or perhaps two, so people can quickly see what you are offering, and escape if they want. Avoid trapping people in endless downloads. (Many folks do not realize they can interrupt a download with a click of the Stop icon.)

To speed downloading time (the average time it takes for a person to get the picture off the Web), keep each image small—certainly no bigger than 4" × 6", or 30K in file size. You can make the image small in your graphic software—that's the best way. Or you can have your Web editor make it small, which sometimes works, but sometimes just sends the whole massive file and then shrinks it to fit into a small frame after all that time.

So the hardest thing about putting your electronic images up on the Web is restraining yourself. If you just can't resist putting up an 8" × 10" picture of your baby, at least warn people in advance by putting a smaller version up, and announcing that a larger version is available. Tell visitors how big the larger version is (how many kilobytes [KB] the file takes up) and how long it takes to download for an average home user. This way, users can decide whether they want to spend all that time or not. That's Web courtesy.

PART

II

Projects

4 **Projects at Home**

5 **Projects at Work and School**

6 **Community Activities**

CHAPTER

4

Projects at Home

IN THIS CHAPTER

■ Making your own greeting cards

■ Leading the way to the party—with signs galore

■ Wrapping up a gift with homemade paper

■ Getting picky about your flowers and veggies

■ Mapping out the land

■ Beating the post office at the stamp game

■ Ironing yourself into your quilt

■ Drawing up a little shopping list

■ Sticking to your diet

■ Concocting very special calendars

■ Making recipes even a new cook can follow

■ Keeping your pet's biography

■ Showing where everyone came from, with maps

■ Celebrating Valentine's Day

Making Your Own Greeting Cards

As children, we used to haul out construction paper, paint, and glue to make cards for our moms, decorate monthly calendars, and produce enough Valentine's Day cards for everyone in the class to get one. The whole year seemed to hang like cards on a string, hitched from one holiday to the next.

Now we are too busy to get all those supplies, clear a space on the dining room table, and assemble one or two cards — or more than a dozen. So we go down to the mall.

The racks of greeting cards stretch out to the far end of the store, sorted by category and subcategory; and you may even be able to find a Get Well card for your nephew who likes fish, and a Congratulations card for your grandparents, still on the family farm, on their fiftieth wedding anniversary. But even with all this specialization, the eight cards you find just don't seem quite right for you and the people you want to surprise and please.

So make it yourself — with the computer! The computer doesn't leave your fingers sticky with white paste, and you can make great cards and calendars without spilling any paint or maneuvering scissors along a curving dotted line. Surprisingly, you can make each card personal yet colorful, so each one becomes a real gift.

Remembering Mom with a card

Of course you should remember your mom every single day, but on Mother's Day, you have to be sure to send a card — with or without flowers — or else she may feel neglected; after all, every other mother is getting cards that day. If you're a dad, you may want to help your children fashion special cards for their mom. If you're old enough to read this book, you can do it yourself, making a card that will cheer your mom, and show off your color printer at the same time!

Coaching your kid

If you have a child who's not old enough to type at high speed or read all the words on the screen, you may want to help. When kids are old enough to grasp and click the mouse, they can make their mark, and as for the words — they can dictate while you type the message. Here's how to coach your child through the process:

1. Launch any painting or drawing program.

Tip

If you don't have anything else, turn to Paint (in Accessories on Windows machines) or MacPaint, the first, and still one of the most fun, of the painting programs; these products generally come with your machine. Other good programs for kids are Canvas from Deneba, ClarisWorks from Apple (there is a special version called ClarisWorks for Kids, and the original ClarisWorks has recently been renamed AppleWorks), Crayola Print Factory and Crayola Magic 3D Coloring Book from IBM, Magic Artist from Disney, Photo-Paint from Corel, KidPix from Broderbund, and PaintShop Pro from Jasc.

2. Open a new document.

3. Select a tool such as the Straight Line or the Oval, and have your child practice using it for a while (see Figure 4.1), "just to see." Encourage play.

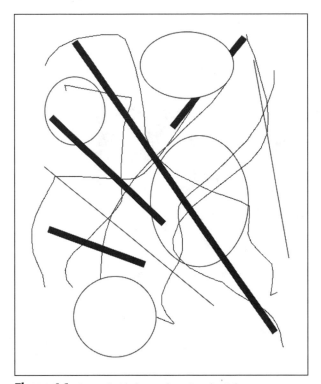

Figure 4.1 *Created with Canvas from Deneba Software.*

Kids who've never used paint software before are likely to experiment over and over. Be patient. They learn a lot from experimenting — like how moving the mouse affects the picture on the screen, what clicking means, and how the computer allows them to make perfect lines without using a big fat pencil.

4. When one line of play slows down, change the colors for lines and *fill* — the color that gets poured into any contained shape, filling it up to the edge of the boundary lines.

5. Save frequently, so if your child inadvertently wipes out the image, you can resurrect it.

6. Try filled ovals and rectangles, the brush, and — above all — the eraser (see Figure 4.2).

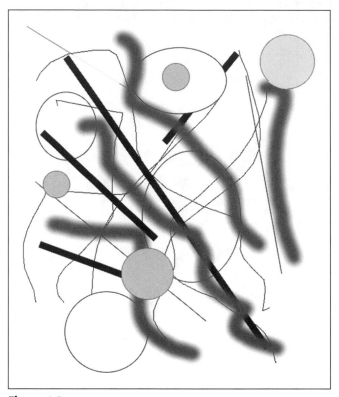

Figure 4.2

Kids love the eraser. Destroying is just as fun as creating, and you have to be stoic when they wipe out something good.

7. If you have an electronic version of a picture of your child, bring that in on top of what the child has done, without blocking too much (see Figure 4.3).

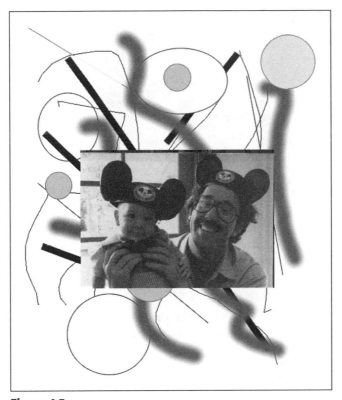

Figure 4.3

8. Take over the mouse and keyboard, and record a short message from your child.

9. Print! And deliver with breakfast.

For your own mom

You know how corny the store cards can be, and you know what your mom likes. So take a moment to consider what kind of pictures she would get a kick out of — what personal photos you could include, or what clip art might recall some of your childhood exploits. You could draw your own picture, planting your photo right in the middle of it as suggested above; or you could start with a photograph of yourself when you were younger.

1. Use a scanner or photo store to bring an electronic version of the old photo into your computer (see Figure 4.4).

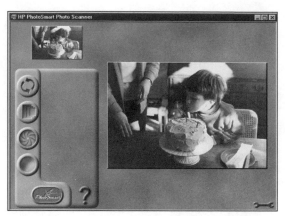

Figure 4.4 *Scanned using Hewlett-Packard's PhotoSmart Photo Scanner.*

2. Crop the picture to get rid of interfering furniture or odd elbows that may intrude. Save the cropped version.

   In photo editing software, use the Crop tool to select the part of the picture you want to save. In a paint program, use the Rectangular Selection tool to grab the part you like, and then choose File ➪ Copy, open a new document, and paste the best part of the photo into that new document (see Figure 4.5).

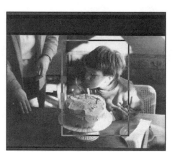

Figure 4.5

3. If your picture editing software offers frames, pick one your mom might like.

   Many painting programs offer premade frames. If you don't find any in your software, you can make one in a paint program, and then paste your edited picture on top, as shown in Figure 4.6.

Figure 4.6 *Frame from Microsoft Picture It!*

4. Add a message, as shown in Figure 4.7.

Tip

If your photo editing software does not offer text, you may need to save the picture and then reopen it in a general-purpose paint program. Usually, the Text tool is a giant A.

Figure 4.7 *Text made possible by Paint Shop Pro, from Jasc Software.*

Automating Your Cards

Want to turn out cards en masse? Check out some of the software that lets you pick a picture, a sentiment, and a multiplicity of extras to turn out a somewhat personalized card for everyone on your list. You can edit the text and modify the imagery these programs offer.

■ Photo Creations from Creative Wonders lets you use an original photo of your own, enhancing its brightness and colors, blurring it, or turning it into a fuzzy sketch, and then add a clip art image and surround the imagery with a prepared page design, frame, or border.

■ Printable Expressions from Hewlett-Packard offers a whole series of greeting cards in kits, each containing blank cards and envelopes; a CD-ROM with a hundred greetings you can modify; and two dozen pieces of artwork or photos. The collections follow themes such as holidays, seasons, flowers, and landscapes, with a few dedicated to individual watercolorists. Available in card and grocery stores, each kit puts everything you need into one package.

From Printable Expressions, Greeting Card Collection, from Hewlett-Packard.

- Print Artist Platinum from Sierra Home offers more than 7,000 photos, more than 30,000 clip art graphics to play with, and a few thousand layouts to fit them into.

- PrintShop Signature Greetings from Broderbund enables you to frame photographs, put together cards for a particular theme (a holiday, for example, or a birthday), and make greeting cards and postcards, plus envelopes and address labels.

If you just want to send a card to someone online, you can grab an image off the Web from one of the biggest collections of photos, engravings, and paintings in the world — the Corbis collection, which is based on the Bettmann Archives. At `http://pix.corbis.com/postcard/` you can pick an image, add your own text, and send it to anyone who gets e-mail. Note, however, that some e-mail systems make it hard for images to get through attached to an e-mail message, so there is a small possibility that the person you send this online postcard to may get the text but not the picture. But what the heck — you can't beat the cost, which is free. The postcards serve as a way of publicizing Corbis' for-fee products such as prints and posters.

Getting into the holiday spirit

Every family has its own favorite holidays. In Jonathan's family, the Fourth of July is celebrated as if a few of his great-great-greats had won the Revolution single-handedly. In our house, Halloween is big because the kids have just spent three or four months watering the pumpkins and now they get to carve eyes and teeth in the pumpkins, and set the jack o'lanterns out in front of the house with candles inside. But of course we have to hang spider webs and pictures of goblins, too. We've found that with a color printer we can make great cards and decorations for those holidays our family really cares about. You can too!

Putting your heart into your cards

Love blooms in February with Valentine's Day — but how can you make a card that's special for someone you love? Playing with clip art and your own original designs can produce a much more personal, and fun, card than anything you could find at the store. In fact, on whatever occasion the culture urges an exchange of cards — for Kwanza, say, or Christmas, or Hanukkah — you can use your computer to add a personal touch, to brighten the spirits of the person you are reaching out to.

■ Use a lot of tiny clip art images to outline a shape such as a heart.

This way, people can see the overall image from a distance, discovering up close the extra details. If possible, color the clip art images the color of your shape; if you can't change the line color, then try filling in the holes in the picture with that color, as was done in Figure 4.8, to blend the clipart in.

Figure 4.8 *Original images from Print Artist from Sierra Home.*

■ Paint a picture or decorate a clip art image at the bottom half of your page, or make sure there is something interesting there, and then print that page. When you fold the paper in half, vertically, you can put the image on the front, as in Figure 4.9. Flip the paper over and put it back in the printer, and make a new image with your text — your message — and then print that. When people lift up the image, they see the invitation underneath (see Figure 4.10). Now fold the paper so the recipient sees the image first, and then lifts the paper up and reads the message.

You may have to try this a few times to figure out which way to insert the paper you've got the image on.

Figure 4.9

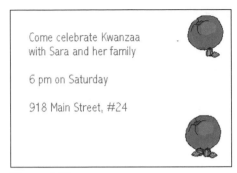

Figure 4.10

■ A little tougher to accomplish but fun: Cut a hole in the image, so the recipient can spy the message underneath. Or put a tiny image underneath the image, like a witch inside a pumpkin, as in Figure 4.11, or a candle inside a window.

Figure 4.11 *Images from Print Artist from Sierra Home.*

People love discovering what is inside, as in Figure 4.12. Of course, you may need to experiment a few times to get the locations right. You can cheat by making the hole somewhere near the bottom left or right corner of the first page, and putting the mouse or candle, or whatever image goes underneath, on the other side, at the bottom of the second document. If your software offers to show you rulers, you can use them to place the images in mirror locations. Another idea: Put a picture of your face underneath, so you seem to be waving from inside the card.

Figure 4.12 *Images from Print Artist from Sierra Home.*

Tip

Print a page-size graphic of a pumpkin, cut out its eyes, and attach a string so your child can wear it as a mask. To masquerade as the Great Pumpkin, use paper that is as thick as your printer can handle, or paste the graphic onto flexible cardboard.

■ Make an original image or borrow some clip art, but keep the whole picture small — maybe 2" × 2". When it is complete, select the image and an equal amount of blank space above it, choose Edit ➪ Copy, and then paste, paste, paste, leaving a quarter-inch or so between the pastes. Go ahead and paste up the whole page — just be sure you leave the equal amounts of white space above (see Figure 4.13). Now print and cut out.

Figure 4.13 *Image from Print Artist from Sierra Home.*

You have a set of personalized gift tags. You can write the TO and FROM inside when you fold the top part behind the image.

Tip

If possible, use slightly thicker paper than usual. Then the tag can hold up to rough usage, including being crushed under other presents or having its string pulled by accident. (Seal between plastic laminate and use an erasable marker and you've got reusable tags.)

■ Take nine clip art images that are appropriate to the season, make sure each is about 2" × 2" in size, and then lay them out on your page so they are evenly spaced, left to right and top to bottom. Add your message underneath one of the images, in fairly small type. Print the page on the front and back of a single sheet of paper, fold in thirds from top to bottom, and then fold in thirds from left to right.

The result is a tightly folded piece of paper that explodes with images of the season when opened (see Figure 4.14). Kids love unfolding and refolding to get the effect. Follow the color scheme of the season if you can add color to the images, so that the whole page has that set of colors, but each image seems different. Also, you may want to use Page Setup on the File menu to set the orientation to landscape (wider than it is tall) if your images tend to be wide, rather than tall.

Figure 4.14 *Images from Print Artist from Sierra Home.*

Turning the house into a fiesta

In October, pumpkins and ghosts set the tone for Halloween—and you may feel the impulse to decorate your house or office with scary orange-and-black images. At Thanksgiving, company is coming for dinner or the weekend—and you begin to wonder what you can hang on the walls to set the tone for that holiday. And at the end of the year, you may want to make sugar cookies, potato pancakes, or cheese blintzes to get the family in the spirit for Christmas or Hanukkah with some seasonal decorations. Here are some ideas you can work on with or without kids:

■ Start with a piece of clip art, make it big, and add several colors. Print that one, and then start over, using different colors. Print a series, with varying colors, so that you can put up a whole bunch of pictures on the same theme, but with each one looking a little different.

At Christmas, you can put up a bunch of trees, each with its own colored decorations. At Hanukkah, many different colors and shapes of menorahs (see Figure 4.15 and Figure 4.16). At Thanksgiving, the cornucopia can have wildly different colored fruits and vegetables. Who cares if your pears end up looking like eggplants?

Figure 4.15

Figure 4.16 *Image from Print Artist from Sierra Home.*

■ Resize a clip art image so it has to be printed on several pages, and then tape it together as a banner.

Some programs call this *tiling*. The idea is that the picture ends up on a series of tiles, like those in a bathroom. Taped together, they make a giant picture, such as the one shown in Figure 4.17.

Figure 4.17

■ Now try the reverse: Take a picture anyone can recognize even when smaller than your hand, enclose it in a circle, rectangle, or star, and then copy it and paste it as many times as you can fit on the page (see Figure 4.18). Print several pages' worth using the thickest colored paper you can get through your printer. Cut the images out and use them as ornaments on a Christmas tree, tack them up as a border around the room, tape them to your window, or hang them like a chandelier over the center of your dining-room table.

Figure 4.18

These decorations catch the eye and emphasize that you've changed the way the house looks. Use ordinary thread and tacks to put them up.

■ Take a very simple image such as an Easter egg, pumpkin, heart, or flag, make it fill the page, and then print it. Now select the image and, if the software allows, flip it so you are looking at the mirror image (see Figure 4.19). Print that. Now tape the bottom edges together, stuff the thing with crumpled newspaper, and tape the top edges together.

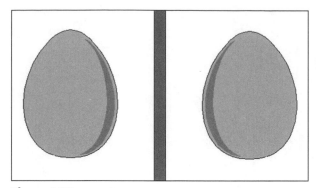

Figure 4.19 *Image from Print Artist from Sierra Home.*

Result: a stuffed object. You can run a threaded needle through the top, and string it from the ceiling. Floating there, it advertises the season to whoever walks by as the breeze spins it around.

Tip

Regardless of where you live or your cultural background, you can teach your kids how to whack a piñata: Fill your seasonal object with candy, string it up, and give them a broomstick to see who can break it open first.

Becoming a postcard magnate

If you want to send cards to a lot of folks all at once, consider creating a postcard. You can use special postcard paper (so it's stiff enough to send through the mail), or you can use ordinary paper and just tuck the thing in an envelope. Most fun is something that feels like a real postcard.

1. In your software, set up an area that is 4" × 6" or a little less.

   In many programs with predefined templates, you can say you want to create a postcard; in other image-editing programs, you can choose 4" × 6" for printing or canvas size, or you may have to experiment a bit to get the dimensions just right, using a rectangle to guide your hand.

2. Locate a photograph or clip art that matches the mood of the season, such as the one shown in Figure 4.20, which advertises Iris Day. Or improvise a drawing inside your rectangle.

3. Print and perfect (after all, you are going to make a dozen or more postcards, right?)

Figure 4.20

4. In the same program or a word processor, create the text for a greeting over on the left. (Leave room on the right for the address and stamp).

   In the word processor, set the left and right margins at 1.25 inches, and the top and bottom margins at 3.5 inches, to block out that size. This assumes your other program prints the postcard right in the center. If that assumption isn't correct, you will have to adjust the margins to get the spacing right.

5. Put the postcard back in the printer, image side up, and print your message on the back of the card (see Figure 4.21).

6. Make gummed labels for the addresses.

   You can use the sheets of self-stick labels, which you peel off after printing. Follow the directions that come with the labels for setting your margins and font size.

Figure 4.21

Party Time

The party begins as soon as the invitation arrives — or at least, you can set the tone for the whole shebang if you send an interesting, personal invitation. You can use your color images to do just that, for each person you want to invite.

Turning an invitation into a conversation

In Noah's school, certain months are birthday months. Half a dozen kids are competing to invite everyone to their parties, but there are only so many afternoons when the other kids are free. Sadly, some invitations get ignored. Parents forget to call to say their little darling won't be able to come. The birthday girl or boy expects 25 kids, but only 10 show up. Even if this hasn't happened in your neighborhood, you still want to make darn sure your invitation gets noticed. One way to do so is to make each invitation special by putting a face on the front. If you're creating invitations for your child's birthday party, your kid will seem to be asking the other kid directly.

1. Start by cutting your child's face out of the background, as shown in Figure 4.22. Use a freehand cropping tool, if possible, and don't sweat jagged edges.

Figure 4.22 *Image scanned with HP PhotoSmart Photo Scanner. Cropped in PaintShop Pro, from Jasc Software.*

You don't have to cut precisely. In fact, it's fine to include a little background.

2. Paste the cut-out picture of the face onto a blank electronic page (see Figure 4.23).

For the program you paste the picture into, use an application that lets you draw lines and add text.

Figure 4.23 *Cropped in PaintShop Pro, from Jasc Software.*

3. If the picture of the face was large before, shrink it so it only takes up a quarter or a third of the page. You'll need room for some text above it.

4. Above your child's head, write an invitation, as if your child were speaking.

5. Surround the text with a rectangle with rounded edges or a loose circle.

6. Attach the speech balloon to your child's face (or mouth) with two more lines, as shown in Figure 4.24.

Figure 4.24

Drawing guests to your house

A few weeks ago, our son Ben invited his high school football team over for dinner the evening before a game. Ben said that the players would be coming from north, south, east, and west, and some didn't know our neighborhood. Could we make a map?

We did. We used Visio Home because it has a lot of map symbols in it, but you can make do with any program that lets you draw lines with labels, and drop in graphics. Here's how:

1. Start with a landmark everyone knows.

   For us, that was the Rio Grande River, which flows by about a block away, on its way south to the Mexican border (see Figure 4.25). Your landmark might be a park, a big building, or a major intersection. See if you can find a graphic that suggests the nature of the landmark — and then put a label on it, just in case somebody still can't figure it out.

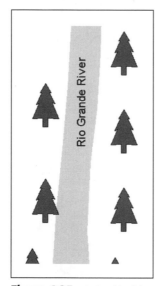

Figure 4.25 *Made with Visio Home, from Visio Corporation.*

2. Include any major streets people might take to get to your house from all over town.

   The point is that people need to be able to spot something they recognize to get oriented. For us, there are major thoroughfares to the north, south, east, and west, as shown in Figure 4.26. (Our block is a short dead end, so nobody has ever heard of it).

Figure 4.26 *Made with Visio Home, from Visio Corporation.*

3. Insert identifiable landmarks along the way, such as local parks, fire stations, odd houses — anything that can confirm that people are on the right track, as shown in Figure 4.27.

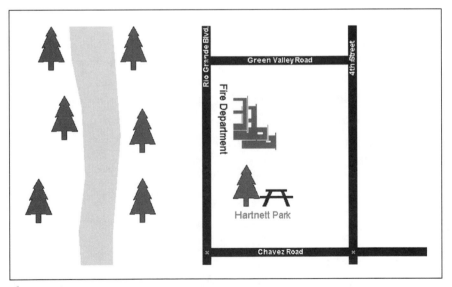

Figure 4.27 *Made with Visio Home, from Visio Corporation.*

4. Highlight your own building or house and include the address.

You might want to show where to park, if that's a problem. Make your house big, as shown in Figure 4.28; who cares if it is out of scale? Your house is the target for these people coming from all over!

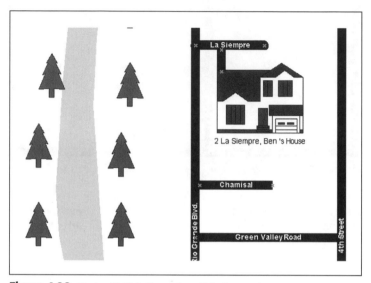

Figure 4.28 *Made with Visio Home, from Visio Corporation.*

5. Add directions for finding your place from key locations, as shown in Figure 4.29.

Some people understand verbal directions better than maps.

6. Add a giant invitation anywhere you can fit it in.

7. Print in color and distribute.

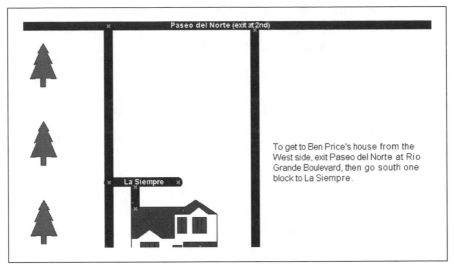

Figure 4.29 *Made with Visio Home, from Visio Corporation.*

Waving hello

Some invitations come via e-mail. They're not very pretty, but at least you got invited. To make sure your invitations get noticed, you can make them wiggle and move. One way to do that is to add a welcoming hello.

1. Take a picture of your front door, as shown in Figure 4.30.

   Take picture from the angle that a guest would see the door. You're trying to help them find their way to your front door, as well as make them laugh.

Figure 4.30 *Image taken with HP PhotoSmart Digital Camera.*

2. Find a picture of a hand, and make it at least as wide as the image of your entrance area.

   A photo or brightly colored graphic will do.

3. Print both.

4. Cut out the hand.

5. Fold a strip of paper about an inch wide and five or six inches long.

6. Glue one end of the strip to the center of the entryway, and the other to the hand, so the hand appears to spring out of the door, as shown in Figure 4.31.

Figure 4.31 *Original image of hand from Print Artist, from Sierra Home; modified in Microsoft Paint.*

7. (Optional) If possible with your picture of the door, cut a small slice through the paper so you can tuck just a little edge of the hand in there.

   That will keep the hand down until the recipient touches it, at which point the hand will leap up and wave a welcoming hello.

You could also make a rose spring out of your door, for a somewhat more sophisticated invitation, as shown in Figure 4.32. Feeling really inspired? Spray a little perfume on the paper.

Figure 4.32 *Images from HP PhotoSmart Digital Camera, manipulated in PaintShop Pro from Jasc.*

Leading the way to the party — with signs galore

When giving barbecues in our backyard, we find that latecomers sometimes end up at the wrong door, or wander around in front of the house where we can't hear them. Signs can point the way — and for kids, raise the anticipation of a party.

1. Find some clip art arrows, or make a half dozen from scratch. (Make each arrow big enough to go across the bottom third of the page).

   If you are making them, use bright greens, reds, and blues. Think of the arrow as one very thick line, with a triangle on the end, as shown in Figures 4.33 and 4.34. Or just draw the stem of the arrow, using two slashes to suggest the edges of the point, as in Figure 4.35.

Figure 4.33 *Arrow from ClickArt, from Broderbund.*

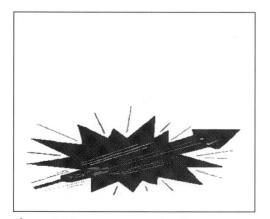

Figure 4.34 *Arrow from ClickArt, from Broderbund.*

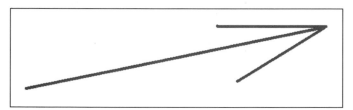

Figure 4.35

2. Add giant graphics celebrating cake, balloons, and whatever activities you expect to be going on — from dress-up to pin-the-tail-on-the-donkey games. Examples are shown in Figures 4.36 through 4.38.

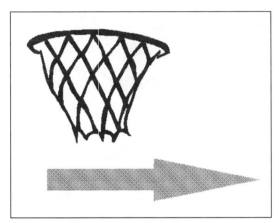

Figure 4.36 *Arrow from ClickArt, from Broderbund.*

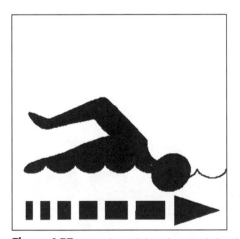

Figure 4.37 *Arrow from ClickArt, from Broderbund.*

Figure 4.38 *Arrow from ClickArt, from Broderbund.*

3. Add a little text, like "This way to Noah's Party!"

   Squeeze it above the graphic, or on the side, as shown in Figure 4.39. The text is the least important element. It is there just in case someone wonders whether they are headed for the right party.

Figure 4.39

Tip

Kids like the challenge of following the arrows, so you might use more arrows than you really think necessary.

Web Partying

Party Friends at http://www.makingfriends.com http://www.makingfriends.com/f_party.htm offers craft projects for parties, many of which take off from designs you can download and print as a starting point. They have lots of bead projects and other imaginative activities for many holiday events.

Decorating the door with banners

Years ago we made a Happy Birthday banner on the computer. We've hung it over the door to the living room for every birthday celebration since then, folding it up carefully between events and storing it in a big box. We reuse it in part because we are lazy, but also because we've gotten attached to having that same banner up, as a kind of tradition. You might, too!

In the old days, when computer paper always came in one continuous folded strip, people had to struggle with making giant characters out of hundreds, even thousands, of little characters, because there were no graphic programs. Then a program called PrintShop provided a way for you to just type words, leaving the giant letters to the software. Now that most of us have printers that use cut sheets of paper, we have to make our banners in pieces and tape them together. But with many of the current programs, making the text—and graphics—is fairly easy. The hitch? Reprinting various sheets until they come out right, as part of the banner.

If you have a program with which you can make a banner, just follow the steps as they take you through picking graphics, fonts, sizes, and frames. If your software doesn't advertise banners, here is how to make them from scratch:

1. In whatever program you are going to use, set the page to landscape orientation (that is, wider than it is high).

   The command for this is often Page Setup or Print Setup on the File menu. You may have to poke around on various tabs of the dialog box to find the options for orientation (Portrait or Landscape) (see Figure 4.40).

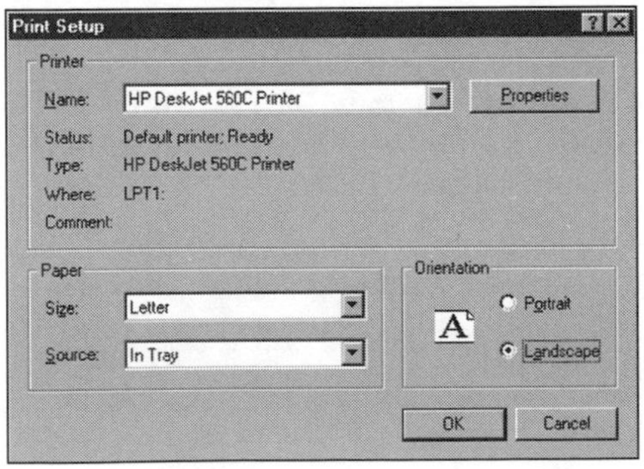

Figure 4.40

2. Set the margins to the smallest size your printer can handle.

Most printers refuse to print to the edge of the page. Their "print area" is less than the full width of the sheet of paper. When you are making a banner, that means you will face an unsightly gap between words if you just tape the papers together edge to edge. You're going to make the sheets overlap to reduce this gap, but the smaller your left and right margins are, the better.

3. Set your font size to about 288 points (four inches high).

You won't find this number on the drop-down list of sizes ordinarily offered. Pick Other, if available, or choose Font from the menu system (it may occur under Format), and then type this high number into the dialog box to get big letters. (Some programs only go to 255 points, which is good enough).

Tip

If your program can't handle such big numbers, switch to one that can. Painting and drawing programs can usually handle large sizes, as can programs designed for signs, banners, or posters.

4. Pick a font you like.

Consider one that looks handwritten, or like an ad for a circus.

5. Type **Happy** and print.

You want to see if a word like this can fit on a single page, as it does in Figure 4.41, and if you can read it at a distance.

6. Adjust font and size so the word fits on a single sheet, edging to the right side.

7. Type **Birthday** and print!

This word will probably span two pages. In some programs, you may have to type *Birth* on one page and *day* on another. If so, make sure the first text is shifted as close to the right margin as possible.

8. Add pictures at both ends, on separate sheets.

We favor cakes and balloons, but if you feel they would be false advertising, given the party you have in mind, try stars and fireworks — or pizza, as shown in Figure 4.42.

You could center these pictures on the sheet, or slide the beginning one to the right, and the ending one to the left, so they come closer to your text.

Figure 4.41 *ClarisWorks displays BrushScript font up to 255 points.*

Figure 4.42 *ClarisWorks shows the picture reduced to 33⅓% of normal, so you can look at two pages at once.*

9. Tape your banner together and get ready to make a few little changes.

Check that the banner, as a whole, looks balanced—not too much at one end, or all crunched into the middle. Is there enough air between words and art? Can you see what it says at the distance from which guests will first notice the banner? Don't be discouraged: Revising is part of the banner-making process.

Wrapping up a gift with homemade papers

Have you ever run out of birthday paper at the last moment? Maybe you still have several Christmas, Kwanzaa, or Hanukkah papers, or an elaborate nineteenth-century floral pattern you got to wrap that glass vase for your grandmother. But is it the right paper for the person you're giving the present to now?

Well, time to turn on the computer and make it yourself.

Starting with clip art

1. In any program that lets you add graphics and adjust their size, adjust the margins of a new document to the absolute minimum.

   You're going to fill up the page with pictures and then trim off the white edges for your wrapping paper.

2. Bring in a piece of clip art that has strong simple lines and an easily recognizable image. Put the image in the top left corner of the document.

   Obviously, a birthday theme would be nice, too. But use anything that interests the person you are giving this present to—and remember, the present itself may give you an idea for a picture.

3. Shrink the picture down so it is still easy to recognize, but small enough to fit in a square about two inches by two inches, as shown in Figure 4.43.

Figure 4.43 *Image from ClickArt, from Broderbund; manipulated in ClarisWorks.*

4. If the image seems a little Spartan, enclose it in a rectangle (see Figure 4.44), and pour in a bright background color.

Figure 4.44 *Image from ClickArt, from Broderbund; manipulated in ClarisWorks.*

5. Copy the rectangle containing the image and paste it in rows covering the whole page, as shown in Figure 4.45.

Tip

Make a row across the page, copy the whole row, and paste it down. Be careful not to copy a lot of white space, or you will be forced to leave all that white space between images; you don't want to overpaint an earlier image with new white space.

Figure 4.45 *Image from ClickArt, from Broderbund; manipulated in ClarisWorks.*

It's OK to have little white lines between the images, but if you want to add more color, use the paint bucket tool to pour another color into the gaps. Just make sure you are changing the color of the white space between images, not the background of a particular image.

6. Print at least six copies and paste together. (It's up to you whether you trim away the margins or leave them).

Making wrapping paper with "scribble-scrabble"

When our son was four, he called drawing "scribble-scrabble." And, as long as you don't try too hard to make a picture that looks like something real, you can make wonderfully vibrant wrapping paper just by scribble-scrabbling a giant abstract painting, printing it multiple times, and taping the pages together. Here are some hints for the artist in you:

■ Work in a paint program, because you don't need the exactness of a drawing program.

■ Play with the various brush tips available, because these make your lines more interesting, as shown in Figure 4.46.

Figure 4.46 *Drawn in ClarisWorks.*

- Drop in filled ovals, rectangles and, holding down the Shift key, circles and squares — wherever you feel the impulse.

- Erase quickly, but not heavily.

- Use the spray paint in quick bursts, and then long swirls.

- Use the Freehand Selection tool to cut out a segment, lift it up, and move it a little, for a nicely disorienting effect, as shown in Figure 4.47.

- Finish up as inspiration dictates, using any tools you haven't tried, plus a few of the ones you've gotten to like.

Figure 4.47 *Drawn in ClarisWorks.*

- Stand back and admire your new paper (see Figure 4.48). Now print a lot of sheets.

- Staple two sheets together to make a bag — and fold up another one as a handle.

Figure 4.48 *Drawn in ClarisWorks.*

Creating special bags to hold party favors

Kids pick up more loot at a party than they do in a week visiting with their grand-parents. To carry it all, they need a bag, or a shopping cart. You can make bags the way you make wrapping paper, stapling the sheets together and taping the sides so little fingers don't get cut on the staples. Or you can buy a brand-new stack of real paper bags and print on those. If you go this route, here are a few ideas:

■ Do a test run to make sure these bags will really go through your printer.

Keep the bags as flat as they come from the store, and feed them in bottom first so they don't accidentally jam open on their way through the printer.

■ Start with the kids' names, one per bag, so they each have their own.

■ Add a different graphic for each child, large enough to take up most of the side of the bag.

Odd faces are good. Use trucks and tools for kids who dig in the sand, hats and fashion models (Figure 4.49) for kids who like to dress up. Black-and-white drawings look great on brown bags. Beware, though, of yellows, oranges, and browns in your drawing, because they get lost on the paper.

Figure 4.49 *Image from ClickArt, from Broderbund.*

■ Seal with a lot of staples so nothing falls through, and cover the seams with thick tape, so no one gets cut on the staples.

Creating a lightweight box for a little gift

With clever fingers and a pot of glue, you can fit together a small box, decorated with designs you make on the computer, for a tiny present. The resulting box is fragile, so you won't want to entrust it with anything that might break easily; but for small, tough items, this box is a present in itself.

1. Start with a row of four squares, as shown in Figure 4.50.

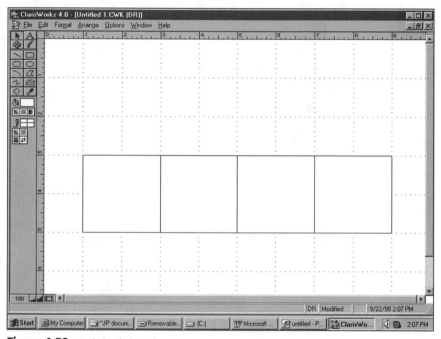

Figure 4.50 *Made in ClarisWorks.*

2. Add a bottom to the second square, and a top to the fourth square, as shown in Figure 4.51.

3. Extend the top and bottom with an extra little rectangle that can be folded up inside the box, and glued in place (later), as shown in Figure 4.52.

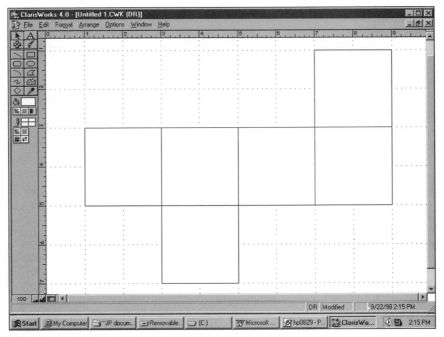

Figure 4.51 *Made in ClarisWorks.*

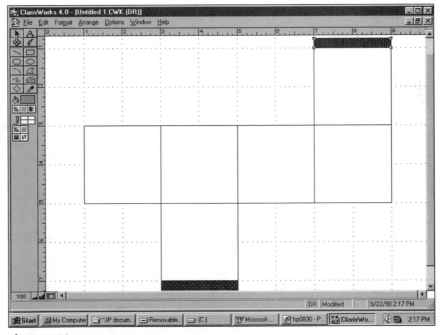

Figure 4.52 *Made in ClarisWorks.*

4. Add art to the four sides and top.

To suggest the contents, or purpose, of the present, you can put a different piece of art on each side, or the same one, following some common theme such as Bon Voyage, as shown in Figure 4.53.

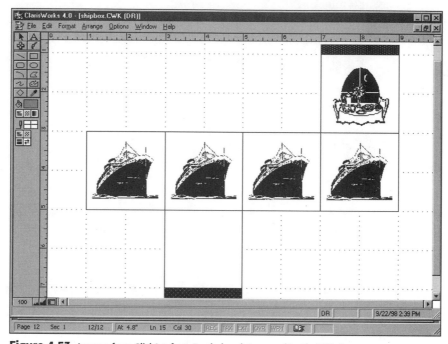

Figure 4.53 *Images from ClickArt, from Broderbund. Arranged in ClarisWorks.*

5. Add flaps that you can tuck in place and, if necessary, glue down, to the sides that do not have a top or bottom extension, as shown in Figure 4.54. These extra flaps will help you connect the sides to the top and bottom, strengthening the box. For easy folding, make the flaps slant in from the sides.

6. Print on the thickest paper you have.

7. Cut around the edges.

8. Crease all the folds (including those little ones attached to the top and bottom) and then assemble.

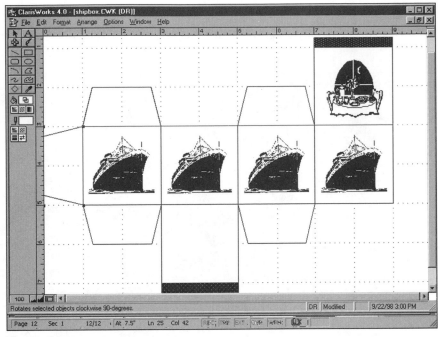

Figure 4.54 *Made in ClarisWorks.*

You can use tape for a quick hold, or glue for a more permanent fix. Oh, and remember not to glue the top shut before you put the present inside!

Envisioning Your Garden and Yard

If you can't afford to redo your garden or yard, but you know you want to — sometime — you can use your camera to capture ideas as you walk around a neighborhood you like or take a garden tour. Without a record, you retain an overall impression, but that's hard to follow when you actually get down to laying out flowers or setting a border. Having photos to go through lets you figure out exactly how someone else achieved the effect you admired and now want to emulate.

■ Take some shots of gates, fences, and gazebos you like, so you can answer questions like, "How did they support that crossbar, anyway?" Circle the feature you want to study later to highlight it (see Figure 4.55).

Figure 4.55

■ Snap flowers, bushes, and trees you like, as shown in Figure 4.56, so you can remember what they look like in a real person's garden, rather than in the surreal world of the seed catalogs. (Type a note or two right into the picture so you can remember the details later. In the winter, photos will help you remember how big and bushy sunflowers can get, so you leave room for them in your plan.)

Figure 4.56

■ Get some pictures of key trees, bushes, and plants at different times of the day, so you can plan areas for morning, noon, and twilight (see Figure 4.57).

■ Take pictures of the open area you are designing for, as shown in Figure 4.58. If possible, take these shots from each location in which you hope to have a place to sit or stroll, so you can sketch in the new view from there.

Figure 4.57

Figure 4.58

■ Combine your images, without trying to be realistic, to envision crudely what the effect of a hedge might be, or a barrier of flowers (see Figure 4.59), or a tree where there is nothing now.

Figure 4.59

Getting picky about your flowers or veggies

As you plan a vegetable garden or a flower bed, you have to make a lot of choices. But you don't have full-grown plants right in front of you from which to choose. What to do?

From your own collection of images, you can pull together images such as six-foot-high sunflowers and some ground covers. If there are some plants you've never been able to capture with your camera, you might want to grab some images from Web sites for gardeners. Or use a gardener's encyclopedia to set up criteria you want the plants to meet, to find out what will work in sun or shade, with blooms in certain colors, growing in your kind of soil, and so on, as shown in Figure 4.60.

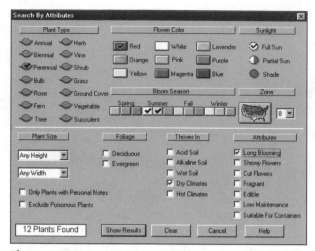

Figure 4.60 *Search mechanism from Garden Encylopedia by Sierra.*

The results of a search typically offer names and photos of several plants that just might work for you, as shown in Figure 4.61.

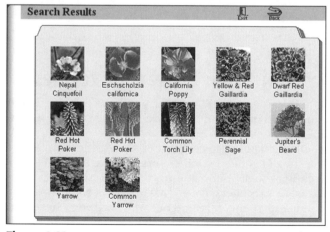

Figure 4.61 *Result of search in Garden Encyclopedia by Sierra.*

Usually, you can then look up more info about the plant (see Figure 4.62).

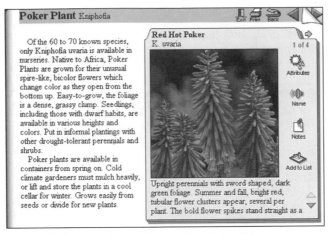

Figure 4.62 *Results from Garden Encylcopedia by Sierra.*

Because all these images are electronic, you can grab them to make your own list of finalists.

1. Capture the whole screen, including the image of the flower.

   On a Windows keyboard, press Print Screen; that puts an image of the screen onto the Clipboard. On a Macintosh, press Command-Shift-3; that puts the screen shot in a file called Picture 1 (through Picture 9) at the top level of whatever disk holds your system files.

2. Use a paint program to open the image of the screen.

3. Select the image of the flower and copy it.

4. Open a new document and paste the flower in, as shown in Figure 4.63.

Figure 4.63 *Image from Garden Encyclopedia by Sierra.*

5. Save that document.

6. Find other flowers, grab their images, and then paste them into your comparison document, as shown in Figure 4.64.

Figure 4.64 *Images from Garden Encyclopedia by Sierra.*

Mapping out the land

When we moved in to our house a few years ago, we found an old chile patch that had become a dumping ground for the previous owners — old bottles, rose clippings, boards with nails in them, broken tiles. We spent months clearing the debris. Then it rained for a few weeks, and we got our first crop — a whole field of tumbleweeds.

We didn't figure we could transform this half-acre in a summer, but we decided to draw up a plan, even if it might take us three or four years to complete. If you face a similar stretch of untamed turf, you might want to sketch out some ideas, walk outside and check your drawing against reality, and then sketch again as you perfect your ideas.

1. Measure the plot and make a rough sketch of the outside perimeter of your space, using a drawing program.

   We had no idea what the dimensions were until we put up a new fence around the old chile patch: 100' × 100'. Drawing programs let you place an individual object and then remove it without disturbing other objects — that's why we used Visio rather than Paint.

2. Divide the area into a simple grid with each cell big enough to hold a few bushes or a tree, as shown in Figure 4.65.

   We used a 10' × 10' grid so we could visualize the shed and cement area for basketball, and lay out our fish pond and little pool, without knowing exactly how big they would all be.

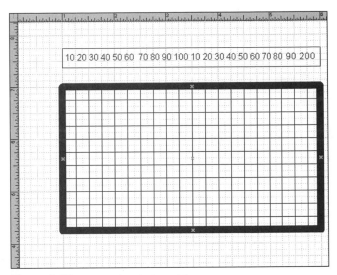

Figure 4.65 *Made with Visio, from Visio.*

3. Drop in some of the trees, ponds, and bridges you dream of, as shown in Figure 4.66. Imagine you are looking down from above.

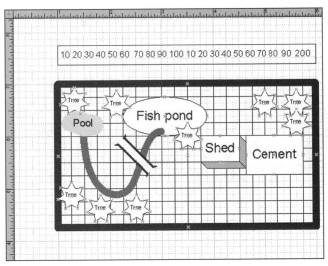

Figure 4.66 *Made in Visio, from Visio.*

4. Print your plan, take it outside, and start noting adjustments.

Here's where having a decent grid can help, especially in areas where you don't have many landmarks. You can pace off ten feet, or five, and say, "OK, so this is where the shed will be!"

Look around and imagine how the shed, pond, or flowers will look in that spot. You'll probably adjust your map half a dozen times, but each version takes you closer to a working plan.

Using photos to sharpen your vision of the yard to come

When you've got a rough idea where the largest elements will go — a few trees, a gazebo, or a winding path — you may want to visualize more clearly what your yard or garden will look like. It's time to bring together all your pictures and make some photo-montages, pasting pictures of trees on top of pictures of the overall space.

1. Start with a view from one corner or side of your yard, as shown in Figure 4.67. Begin with your unpopulated front lawn or the space you plan to dig up for your garden.

Figure 4.67 *Image from Photo LandDesigner™ by Sierra.*

2. Open files containing pictures of the large objects, such as big trees, and use the Freehand Selection tool to select the objects and then copy them.

3. Paste those objects into the scene, more or less where you want them, as shown in Figure 4.68.

Figure 4.68 *Images from Photo LandDesigner™ by Sierra.*

4. Fill in with pictures of smaller bushes, flowers, or grass (see Figure 4.69).

You will probably need to resize these images a bit to fit, making them a bit fuzzy. But you might as well be an impressionist. You want an overall look, nothing too precise. Nature won't let you plan your plantings the way an architect can lay out a bathroom.

Figure 4.69 *Images from Photo LandDesigner™ by Sierra.*

Using Landscape Design Software

To make the following pictures, we used Photo LandDesigner™ from Sierra, one of several great tools for imagining your lawn, backyard, or garden. Basically, you start with a backdrop such as a house or a row of trees, lay in some ground cover, pick trees and resize them to fit, and then add flowers (all of which are in bloom at the same time). Yes, the effect is a bit hyper, like a real estate photo, but you can play with design ideas, trying out one plant or another, clustering flowers here and there, until you begin to evolve some general guidelines—what will work where, and what won't.

If you are considering a big, complex job, you should probably check out some three-dimensional design software such as 3D Landscape from Sierra. You are walked through laying out the dimensions, putting up fences, power lines, telephone poles, driveways, raised beds, borders, you name it. You can be incredibly precise about the planting, even building sheds, houses, or arbors. You usually work in a view looking down from above, and then switch to a 3D view to see what it would look like from various angles.

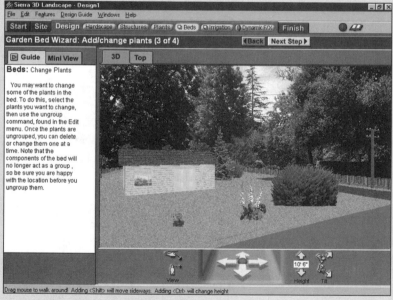

Made in 3D Landscape, from Sierra.

In several programs of this kind, you can preview the way shadows will move across the scene.

You can even get the program to show you what the trees and shrubs might look like in a year, two years, or fifteen, so that you don't end up planting them too close together.

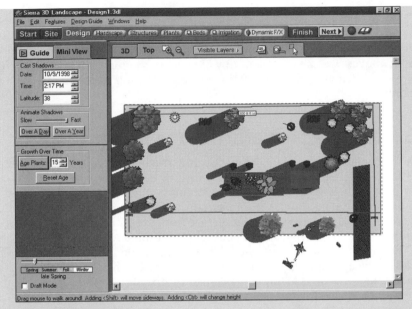

Made in 3D Landscape, from Sierra.

Made in 3D Landscape, from Sierra.

Hobby-Rama

People seem to love collecting. Whether it's stamps or shells, maps or matchboxes, we can make a hobby of almost any collectible. Here are a few ways you can make your collection more visible, fun, and perhaps even more efficient.

Beating the post office at the stamp game

When Jonathan was young, he discovered a sun-bleached, once-red album in the attic, full of stamps from fifty years before. The old ships and faces surrounded with ornately filigreed ovals seemed strangely pinched and pale compared with brand-new stamps. But he saw images from countries he didn't know; stamps were steamed off letters from India, torn from urgent correspondence from Russia under the tsars, and peeled off packages from some Austrian empire.

Stamps present us with a world in miniature, complete with kings, queens, and landscapes long gone. And now that the post office has gotten into marketing, we can get stamps designed just to sell, by celebrating the already famous. Elvis led the roll, with cartoon characters and Hollywood stars following close behind. The Alfred Hitchcock stamp comes with an actual cutout showing his famous profile. You can even get mousepads of famous stamps in history.

If You Really Love a Stamp

Sometimes you just love a particular stamp. It's special because it's rare, beautiful, or expensive. Or perhaps it just came from someone you're fond of.

You might want to try scanning the stamp. If you are using the kind of scanner that requires you to feed the image in through various wheels and grinders, and the stamp is not attached to an envelope, put the stamp inside a clear plastic envelope.

You can grab part of a series of stamps, such as the following image of a bear dance at the top of a set of U.S. stamps celebrating Native American dances.

Or capture a single stamp and blow that up, like the following picture of a hoop dancer.

You can take the single stamp and blow it up so it fills an 8" × 11" sheet of paper. Now you can look closely at every pixel in the hoop, and post the image on a far wall to admire.

Time to make your own! Not, of course, to fool the post office. Just for fun, you can put your friend—or your favorite image—on a giant stamp.

1. To make the scalloped edges of your stamp, zoom in so you can see every little pixel, and then make a short straight line; next to that, create a circle with a diameter equal to the straight line, as shown in Figure 4.70.

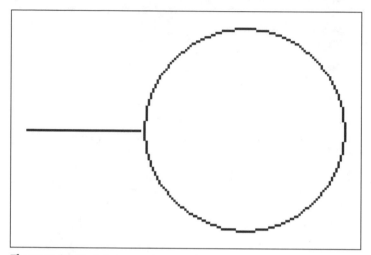

Figure 4.70 *Made in Canvas, from Deneba.*

2. In a paint program, erase the part of the circle that drops below the line. If you are using a drawing program, set the line to no color, set the fill color to white, and then draw a rectangle that will blot out the bottom half of the circle, leaving only the top part visible, making sure the line touches the half circle (see Figure 4.71).

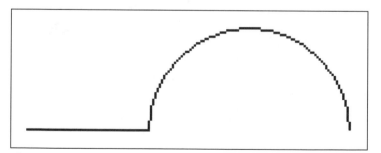

Figure 4.71 *Made in Canvas, from Deneba.*

3. Group your line and circle together, copy the combo, and paste the copies in a row, as shown in Figure 4.72.

Make your stamp as large as your piece of paper if you like. No need to fit it on a tiny little envelope. Your stamp can go up on the wall, like a poster, or it can be folded and put *inside* an envelope, as a surprise. It can even become a party invitation. So big is better.

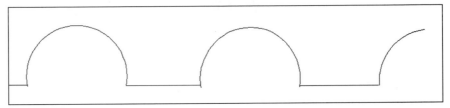

Figure 4.72 *Made in Canvas, from Deneba.*

4. Zoom out so you can see your whole page and use the rows to form the border of your stamp, as shown in Figure 4.73. (Don't worry if some of the corners come out a little odd — you won't have to tear these stamps apart).

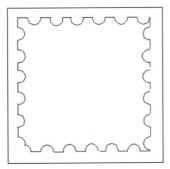

Figure 4.73 *Made in Canvas, from Deneba.*

5. Grab an image you think should be the focus of your stamp, shrink it to fit, and drop it inside the borders, as shown in Figures 4.74 and 4.75.

Figure 4.74 *Made in Canvas, from Deneba. Santa Claus from Print Artist, from Sierra Home.*

Figure 4.75 *Made in Canvas, from Deneba. Santa Claus from Print Artist, from Sierra Home.*

6. Add some text advertising the occasion being celebrated, or the person you are spotlighting, as shown in Figures 4.76 and 4.77.

Figure 4.76 *Made in Canvas, from Deneba.*

Figure 4.77 *Made in Canvas, from Deneba.*

7. Print on thick paper.

Tip

If you like the results, buy the special paper available for making T-shirt transfers, and put the stamp onto a shirt or handkerchief.

Tracking your triumphs

Some hobbies, like cake baking and gardening, yield wonderful results that don't outlast the week. Others turn out models that can break, or tables that get tarnished. If you create fragile things, perhaps you should make an album of your successes, so you can look back in triumph.

1. Start by taking or scanning a picture of your latest creation, such as the cake shown in Figure 4.78.

Figure 4.78

2. Insert the picture at the top of the page, leaving some room at the bottom for a description or recipe, as shown in Figure 4.79.

Figure 4.79

3. Add a brief description of what you did, and why, as shown in Figure 4.80.

We made a frame out of a coat hanger and newspaper, then smoothed papier mache all over it; the fins are just cut out of cardboard. We used white, brown, and black tempera over red, and glued the fish to a shingle.

Figure 4.80 *Assembled in Canvas, from Deneba.*

4. Print the image for your album. (And maybe make another copy to send to someone who'd be pleased to see what you've made).

Tip

Get a binder with a clear cover and slip your best image in the front. Or, if you like glue and cloth, use a T-shirt transfer sheet to put the image onto cloth, and then wrap the cover with that, including some cotton wadding to make a padded album.

Scanning Rocks, Shells, and Coins

If you have a flatbed scanner—the kind that has a lid that lifts up so you can put something right on the glass—you can scan your favorite crystal, razorback clam, or gold double-eagle. You can then enlarge the image, and attach it to the box in which you store these treasures.

Just be careful not to scratch the scanner's glass, or you'll have an unwanted dark spot on every picture from then on.

Blowing up the image of a three-dimensional object can reveal details and patterns you don't notice at the object's normal size. Yes, up close the picture becomes fuzzy. But across the room, you see the object in a new perspective. Like Claes Oldenburg's sculptures of gigantic ice-cream cones and two-story-high lipsticks, the change in scale may be intriguing. And, hey, if you don't like the giant blowup, you can always wad it up and toss it.

Labeling your collection with images

If you have boxes, bins, or even cartons full of little things, you may have to open a few before you find the seashells from your last trip to Florida, or the matchboxes you picked up in Japan. Labels help, but images work faster—and look a lot more interesting.

1. Size up all those containers and figure out one label size that will fit on each of them.

   To help you spot the difference between the individual labels, they should all be about the same size. Comparing pictures goes much faster when they are all the same size and scale.

2. Decide what kind of images to use to represent the contents—photos of real objects in your collection, or clip art pictures that more or less stand for what you have.

   If you take snapshots of one gizmo per box, you know you'll have an accurate picture on every box. If you must turn to clip art, though, make sure that the collection offers enough different images to label every container—and consider whether the images will still mean something to you in a few months.

3. Grab the image and fit it into the label space, as shown in Figure 4.81.

4. If necessary, add a text explanation (see Figure 4.82).

5. Consider making a whole sheet of labels, as shown in Figure 4.83.

Figure 4.81 *Assembled in Canvas, from Deneba.*

Figure 4.82 *Assembled in Canvas, from Deneba.*

Figure 4.83 *Assembled in Canvas, from Deneba.*

6. Print those labels, separate them, and slap them on those boxes.

If you are using special label sheets, print a few test sheets on regular paper and hold them up to the label sheets to see if your images are positioned correctly. You can also just get a sheet of label paper that is as big as a whole page and cut the labels out of that later. And as the great video artist Nam June Paik reminds us, one of the great inventions of the twentieth century is transparent tape.

Imagining a Scene

If you sometimes fantasize about your creations landing from outer space, or showing up in a familiar landscape, start with a photo of a landscape. If possible, find a photo in which you can easily recognize the scenery around the edges of the shot, because you are about to cover up the central area.

Then use a Freehand Selection tool to cut your creation out of its background. Don't worry if you can't trace it exactly—you aren't trying to fool the FBI. In many programs, a series of short clicks all around the edge will get a pretty good silhouette of your object.

Copy the object and paste it on top of your landscape. Just make sure that you leave enough of the landscape showing, so a casual viewer can see that your cake, fish, or whatever was just landing at Big Sur, or wherever.

Watching the skies

If you turn your telescope to the stars on clear nights, or study weather maps and the barometer, you may want to build up a book of your observations, using images to show what you can't easily describe.

1. Start with a picture of whatever constellation or weather condition you are exploring, such as the one shown in Figure 4.84.

   If you can't take a picture through your telescope, you may be able to get a picture from NASA over the Web.

Figure 4.84 *Image from ClickArt, from Broderbund.*

2. If the picture's big, print it on its own page. If it's small, put it at the top of the page.

3. Add a little table for your observations, as shown in Figure 4.85.

   You might find it easiest to create this on a separate page in a spread-sheet or word processor.

4. Use another image for the cover of your binder, as shown in Figure 4.86, adding text to it if your program allows.

Figure 4.85 *Image from ClickArt, from Broderbund.*

Figure 4.86 *Image from ClickArt, from Broderbund.*

 Tip

You might want to take pictures of the weather you're studying, as shown in Figure 4.87; then add your comments underneath, as shown in Figure 4.88, to put together a set of observations.

Figure 4.87

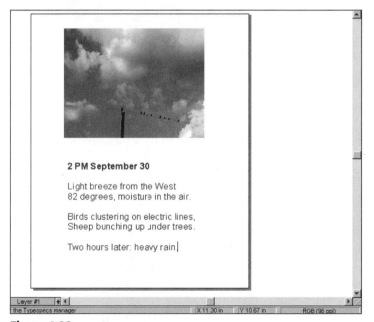

Figure 4.88

Ironing your life into a quilt

T-shirt transfer sheets pick up the colors and lines of your image, and when you place them on absorbent cloth like cotton and iron over the back, the colors and lines are transferred to the cloth. You don't actually feed a T-shirt through your printer (though some people have managed to slip a paper bag or two through the feeder mechanism). So if you are willing to use some squares cut from white jerseys or sheets, you can assemble a quilt with images stitched into a pattern on one side.

1. Decide on a standard size for all your squares.

   Six or eight inches square is large enough to show most images, without forcing you to enlarge the picture beyond recognition. Remember that you can have plenty of space between images — they don't have to line up one right after another to march across the quilt.

2. Figure out how many pictures you need.

3. Collect pictures on a certain theme — pictures of you as a child, tourist spots you've enjoyed, dolls you've collected, or planets you've studied through your telescope.

4. In each photograph, crop out any extraneous background.

5. Select a square central area, copy it, and paste it into a new document.

   You may want to just copy this to the Clipboard, and then paste it into a simple paint program such as Microsoft Paint or MacPaint.

6. Drag a corner to enlarge (or shrink) the image to reach your standard size.

7. With the image still selected, decide whether to flip it horizontally or mirror it.

   This flip is most important if you want to be able to read text or numbers, or recall a scene exactly the way you saw it. You need a mirror image on the transfer sheet in order to get the original on the cloth. With many images, though, you may not need to do the flip.

8. Print on the T-shirt transfer paper.

   Which side is up? It depends on your printer. You want to end up with the image on the blank side of the sheet. (The wrong side has two blue bars on it). The correct side has a gummy substance that absorbs the ink and then transfers it to the cloth, a little like a plastic appliqué.

9. Cut away any areas that are blank — that is, without anything you want to reproduce, but leave at least a quarter-inch border. (You'll use that to start peeling the paper off after you iron it).

10. Fold a clean pillowcase double on a Formica tabletop.

11. Place the cloth on top of the pillowcase and arrange the transfer paper on top, with the ink facing the cloth.

12. Fold back a quarter-inch corner of the transfer paper so you can peel it back later.

13. Preheat the iron at the highest setting for eight minutes. (Don't set the iron to steam, though!)

14. Iron the long edge for forty seconds; then the other edge for another 40 seconds, and go over the whole surface for another 40 seconds. Make sure you have heated it all evenly.

    If your iron sticks to the paper and seems to be getting covered with gunk, you may have printed on the wrong side. It's also possible that your iron is giving off steam, which dampens the paper and makes it gummy.

15. Hold the cloth down and peel the transfer sheet off while it is still hot.

    If it sticks, iron that section again and peel quickly.

Tip

This process tends to wash out colors a bit, so don't count on the brilliance of T-shirts that have been silk-screened or tie-dyed. Also, you may end up with a few spots that didn't get fully heated, so these areas will have less color than surrounding areas, or none. The only solution is to do it all over again on a new cloth.

16. Wash the cloth in cold water without detergent, and then wash again in cold water with a detergent that offers color protection. (Don't wash with anything else). Dry under a normal setting.

Cooking Up Images in the Kitchen

The kitchen is where we leave messages for each other (on the refrigerator), indulge or stick to our diet, and put up preserves. We don't recommend moving your computer into the kitchen, but we have found the graphics and text from a computer a big help in bringing the whole family together, around the dining room table.

Drawing up a little shopping list

A few months ago, after we came home from the supermarket, unloaded every bag, and stuffed the last frozen pizza into the freezer, our youngest said, "But where's the orange juice?"

We hadn't realized we were out. So after a moment of exasperation, we went into our office and turned on the computer to make up a form. When we were done, we printed that out and stuck it to the refrigerator with dolphin magnets. After a few days, the kids got into writing items on the list. In fact, they began writing requests for stuff they'd had at friends' houses — a new kind of microwave pocket with very orange superglue inside, candy that looks like the rocks at the bottom of our fish tank, frozen potstickers. Strangely, the kids rarely put up any requests for vegetables. But along with the excitement foods, they did get used to mentioning when they used up the last of the mayonnaise, OJ, or margarine. Our grocery success rate went up.

We tried various designs for our list and found that novelty and brightness worked best—a new design every month or so caught the kids' eyes and amused us. Here's how you can make up a list that attracts attention:

1. In any program that can use clip art, bring in an image of a list.

   If the image offers real lines, drag its corner handles diagonally to make it large enough to write on.

   If the image looks like it would be hard to write on, use the corner handles to shrink it, so it becomes an icon—a symbol in the corner or at the top announcing, "This is something for you to write on." Then add a dozen or so lines, to invite scribbling.

2. Insert some graphics that remind you and the kids of the supermarket. Ideas include the following:

   - Shopping carts. We've used these, adding shampoo bottles, detergent boxes and, yes, even fruits. The trick, as shown in Figures 4.89 and 4.90, is to select the extra item and choose Send to Back, so it appears to be inside the cart.

   - Staples like bread, milk, or orange juice—or, for the kids, frozen pizza, candy, and doughnuts.

   - Stuff in bottles, boxes, or bags.

   - Check-out clerks. Or store owners proudly standing in front of a fruit stand or meat on ice.

Figure 4.89 *Images from Print Artist, from Sierra Home.*

Figure 4.90 *Images from Print Artist, from Sierra Home.*

Tip

Make a series, running your image along the bottom of your list, as shown in Figure 4.91.

Figure 4.91 *Images from Print Artist, from Sierra Home.*

Sticking to your diet

You're on the third day of your new diet when you hear a little voice from inside the freezer calling you, saying, "A scoop of ice cream wouldn't hurt. You've been so good. You deserve a break."

If this scenario has ever happened to you, then you know that planning ahead can help. Some folks like to put up warnings on the refrigerator, just in case. Here's how:

1. Find a graphic that looks like a stop sign — eight-sided and red.

2. Invent text that will really stop you.

   "Stop" is good, but perhaps there's another, more personal, phrase that will really make you pause.

3. If you find another graphic to reinforce the stop sign, such as a hand commanding "Halt," as shown in Figure 4.92, or an ice-cream cone with a slash through it, add that.

Figure 4.92 *Images from Print Artist, from Sierra Home.*

Labeling your best preserves

If you can, pickle or preserve, you need labels. And those labels might as well be packed with color so they really stand out in the pantry or refrigerator.

For yourself

In September and October throughout New Mexico, we smell the peculiarly exciting smoke of green chiles being roasted in huge black barrels that turn continually over the flame of propane burners. Crowds wait nearby, breathing in the odors. And when the roasting of one barrel is done, some lucky person gets to carry away a burlap bag full of peppers whose skins have been so charred that they are ready to peel off. After our family prepares a batch, we freeze the chiles in plastic bags. But because Jonathan doesn't go for the super hots, we have to label them, indicating just how hot that particular batch is: Super Fiery, Very Hot, Medium Hot, and Mild. Words would do, but what fun is that? We like to use multiples of peppers as a warning. You can jazz up your food labels to suit your tastes too.

1. Place an image of the food in your document.

2. Copy and paste it as many times as you want.

3. Add your caution — or just the name of the food you're preserving (see Figure 4.93).

What's nice about labeling your own food is that you don't have to explain yourself to anyone else or develop a corporate image. You just have to include enough information to understand three months from now what the heck you meant.

4. Select the whole label, copy it, and paste it as many times as you can fit on the page.

5. Print the labels and attach to each container.

Tip

For any items you are going to store in plastic bags, put the food in one bag, and then attach the label. Seal the label and baggy inside another baggy. That way you will be able to read the label later, but the food won't damage it.

Figure 4.93 *Images from Print Artist, from Sierra Home.*

Just for friends

Our garden isn't very big, but with drip irrigation and weekly weeding, we have managed to get a continuous harvest of carrots, chile peppers, cucumbers, and, occasionally, cantaloupes. But the tomatoes come in waves. For two weeks, nothing. Then two or three dozen red spots show up deep underneath the green leaves.

Too many tomatoes means lots of spaghetti sauce. We freeze the sauce in plastic tubs that hold enough for one family dinner and give away half of them. To help our friends identify this foreign frozen object one week or month later, we put labels on the tubs. When you make them just for friends, the labels can be casual.

1. Get a box of the largest gummed labels you can find.

   If you can't find printable labels at your office supply store, get the sheets that are 8.5" × 11" peel-off labels — you can cut them into smaller labels yourself.

2. Find a graphic that has something — anything — to do with the food.

3. Add just enough text to let your friends know what's inside, as shown in Figure 4.94.

Figure 4.94 *Images from Print Artist, from Sierra Home.*

4. Print on the gummed label stock

5. Paste on the tubs or jars. If you think there might be rough handling in their future, use clear packing tape to completely encircle the label and the tub or jar.

For sale

Our neighbor has a backyard covered with strawberry creepers and makes enough jam to sell at the local farmer's market; she needs labels too, but more formal ones for her display. She makes sure that she has sheets of large round or oval labels, and then includes the following:

■ Her slogan, in just the right font, as shown in Figure 4.95

Figure 4.95 *Image from Print Artist, from Sierra Home.*

■ An image of what's inside, more or less

■ A date, so if people keep the jam too long, they will know to throw it out

And when she makes carrot cake for the bake sales at her church, she needs even bigger labels to include ingredients, because so many people are allergic to certain foods and disapprove of others (see Figure 4.96). If you enlarge your label and put it on foam-core boards (the kind kids use for school projects), you can have a sign advertising your wares too.

Figure 4.96 *Image from Print Artist, from Sierra Home.*

Concocting very special calendars

One mom we know toted up the number of different trips she had to make weekly taking her three kids to soccer, dance, band, and so on. Forty-five distinct trips in one week—and her ex-husband made fifteen more. She calls herself "the taxi." To keep each kid's life straight, she decided to use a personal information manager, making a calendar for each child one month in advance; she keeps one complete set of the calendars by her kitchen phone and another in the car so she can scribble in updates at the last moment.

Creating a personal calendar

If your life is like Mrs. Taxi's, you may already be printing out a calendar every week. And if you have teenagers, you know they can *understand* a calendar with their chores and meetings—they just don't seem to look at it very often, especially if it is just black and white. To get their attention, consider taking the time—a half hour, max—to make a colorful personal calendar for each child—one week at a time.

1. In whatever program you are going to use, set the document to Landscape orientation so it is wider than it is tall.

   For instance, if you are going to use Microsoft Word, choose File ⇨ Page Setup; and on the Paper Size tab, pick Landscape.

2. Type your child's name in big letters at the top.

   Another way to identify this calendar as belonging to a particular child is to get a favorite picture of the child, or clip art that represents a favorite activity, and put that at the top.

3. Enter the days of the week at the top of imaginary columns.

   You don't need a grid as you do in a traditional calendar, because you are only doing a week at a time, and you can stack things up under the days. But if you want something very neat, with a real grid, use a word processor or spreadsheet: Create a table with seven columns for the days of the week; and two rows, one for the days of the week, and one for the events of the week.

4. Use graphics to suggest unusual or special events for each day, as shown in Figure 4.97.

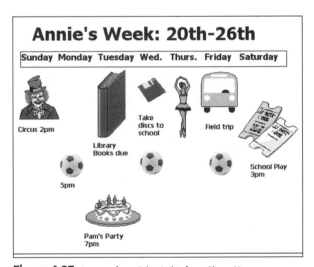

Figure 4.97 *Images from Print Artist, from Sierra Home.*

You'll probably need to shrink the art to fit, or cut it a bit. Make sure that the art from one day doesn't spill over into the next day's column.

5. If necessary, type in the event and time.

   If you feel you need to identify the events with text, you can use a distinct color for each type of appointment (red for the orthodontist, green for 4-H Club, and so on).

6. Print the calendar.

7. Mount prominently on the refrigerator.

Tip

You can make a multiweekly or multimonthly calendar using special paper that accepts images on both sides, such as HP's Glossy Calendar paper for the PhotoSmart printer. You print the image on one side, the calendar on the other, and then tape the pages together.

Advertising those chores, day by day

If you just want to remind your child of each day's routine chores during a regular week, you can create a visual checklist, one day at a time. At night, post the next day's chore sheet on the refrigerator, or laminate it and place it next to the cornflakes for breakfast.

1. In a paint program, type the day of the week at the top of the page.

2. Find an icon for each chore you want to remind your child of, as shown in Figure 4.98.

   For instance, a giant tooth for brushing A.M. and P.M.; a trash bin for taking the garbage out to the street; a hose for watering the roses.

Figure 4.98 *Images from Paint Artist, from Sierra Home.*

3. Print and post.

4. Provide a pencil or pen on a string, so the child can check off each chore each day. That gives a feeling of accomplishment.

Creating every-single-day lists

If you just want to remind your children to do the same chores every day, like cleaning up makeup, practicing the harp, and feeding the fish — decorate a chore list with the child's picture at the top, as shown in Figure 4.99.

Figure 4.99 *Images from Print Artist, from Sierra Home.*

Providing recipes even a new cook can follow

If you dread handwriting recipes for well-meaning friends and family who have enjoyed something you've made, putting them on the computer We find that a lot of folks ask for Lisa's recipes for stuffed cabbages, eggplant parmesan, and cheese enchiladas. At first she'd write down the ingredients, hit or miss, and talk people through the preparation. But now she has those recipes on the computer, and doesn't forget a step. Adding pictures helps liven up recipes and ensures you don't forget a step. It also shows what the end result ought to look like.

Get Cooking with Software

If you enjoy exploring new recipes, or want help finding just what you can make with the leftovers you have in the refrigerator, you may want to try cooking software. The first programs in this area got started more than 15 years ago, so the current versions are well-polished. They show plenty of pictures to tempt you, and some offer nutritional information, step-by-step instructions, and even videos of cooking techniques.

The very popular MasterCook from Sierra allows you to add your own recipes to the ones in its database. People can also post their own MasterCook-format recipes on the Web, so you can pick up literally thousands of extra ideas to expand your database. To figure out what to cook, you can identify the ingredients you have on hand and let the program suggest what you might prepare; or you can specify some nutritional guidelines, and get recipes that fit the criteria. Or you can just browse through the gorgeous pictures, pick one, and make that dish. If you need to shop for ingredients, get grocery lists tailored to a particular supermarket chain's standard layout, aisle by aisle. When you're ready to prepare the recipe, you can print it out, put it on the counter, and not care if it gets greasy because you can always print out another one. MasterCook has a variety of editions, including one on cooking light. (Windows and Mac CD-ROMs).

Another good cooking package is the Williams-Sonoma Guide to Good Cooking from Broderbund, with a thousand recipes, 50 complete meal plans, videos explaining how to perform various kitchen tasks, and the ability to prepare your shopping list for you. (Windows and Mac CD-ROMs).

1. Type up the ingredients and steps.

   You may want to use a word processor to do this, because we find it takes a fair amount of editing. Yes, you know what you do. But that isn't the same as making it clear to someone else how to do it. That's where the tinkering comes in.

2. Photograph the result, and place an electronic version of it at the beginning of your recipe, as a goal to be aimed at, as shown in Figure 4.100.

Figure 4.100 *From Print Artist, from Sierra Home.*

Sometimes inexperienced cooks and children can benefit from a visual aid for a particular part of the process. Inserting pictures into the recipe can show them how to perform a standard chore, such as chopping up the vegetables for stir fry.

3. Write your instructions, step by step.

4. When you come to an instruction you suspect a new cook might not understand, illustrate it with a photo, such as that in Figure 4.101.

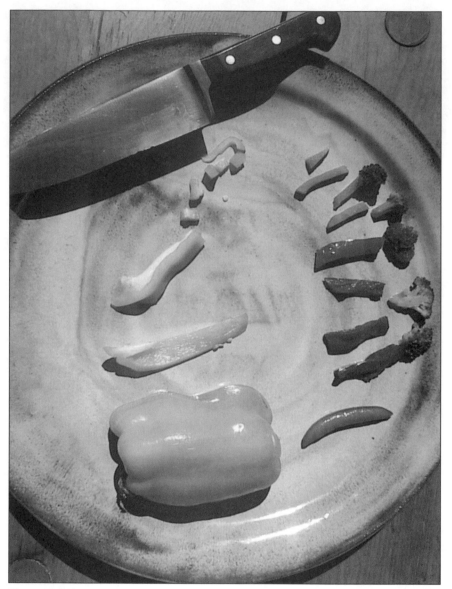

Figure 4.101

5. Continue instructions to the end.

6. Put in a photo of the result they should be aiming for, like the one shown in Figure 4.102.

Figure 4.102

Creating personalized aprons

We've found that when our kids help out in the kitchen, they like to put on the uniform—an apron. No, they aren't protecting their clothes from flour and grease, they just like looking the part of a chef. If we had a chef's hat, they would put that on too.

You can make a special apron for that special cook, putting a unique image on a plain white cotton apron. Before you start, get the special transfer sheets from an office supply store—and a new apron.

1. Find just the right picture, something the apron-wearer will really like. For our son Jonathan, for instance, that would be a pie!

   If possible, locate a picture that will look OK in its mirror image—no text, no cues as to which side is right or left. Look for something symmetrical, like the pie shown in Figure 4.103.

   If you have software that lets you flip an image completely so you are looking at the mirror image, then you can add a slogan or the person's name, and then flip the image. Or use Hanes T-Shirt Maker.

2. Get special paper for T-shirt transfers, such as HP Iron-On T-Shirt Transfer sheets.

3. Print onto the transfer sheet.

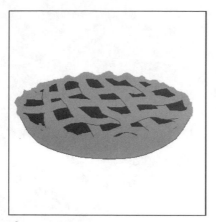

Figure 4.103 *Image from Print Artist, from Sierra Home.*

4. Put the transfer sheet on the apron and iron it thoroughly so the image comes off on the apron.

5. Peel off the transfer sheet, waiting ten or fifteen minutes before disturbing the apron.

Pet Pals

Some of us like to trade stories about our pets. Other folks think we're, well, a little too indulgent. If you, too, are indulgent with your pets, here are some ways to amuse yourself and your friends with graphics celebrating your pet's adventures.

Putting together pet memorabilia

Here's how to make an album that brings together your pet's great moments.

1. Collect as many old photos of your pet as you can find.

2. Scan them, if you have a scanner.

3. Size the electronic picture so it fits at the top of the page, as shown in Figure 4.104, to leave room for pet history below

Figure 4.104 *Created in Canvas from Deneba.*

If you are using paper photos, determine how much room they are going to take if you put one per page.

4. Underneath each picture, add a little description of the occasion, as shown in Figure 4.105.

Toby says, "Why are you resting by that bench, when you could be chasing me around the yard?"

Figure 4.105 *Created in Canvas, from Deneba.*

5. If you feel like adding a border, lay one in, as shown in Figure 4.106.

Figure 4.106 *Created in Picture It!, from Microsoft.*

6. Add speech balloons if you feel like it, as shown in Figure 4.107.

Figure 4.107 *Created in Canvas, from Deneba.*

7. End on a restful note (see Figure 4.108).

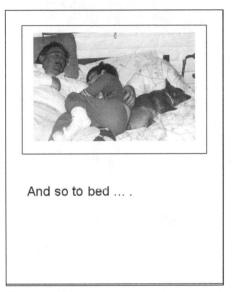

And so to bed ... .

Figure 4.108 *Created in Canvas, from Deneba.*

Taking your pet on an imaginary flight

What if your cat, pig, or dog were able to fly? You've seen toasters in midair, flapping their chrome wings, Peter Pan, and Superman. Why not Fido?

1. Start with a fairly close-up picture of your pet.

A pet who's lying stretched out on a rug can look like a flying squirrel when you get through with photo magic. Of course, it helps if your pet's eyes are open, as they are in Figure 4.109. Toby's a Welsh Corgi and uses his big ears so much we figure they could help him lift off the airstrip.

Figure 4.109

2. Find a nice, big picture of a panorama with plenty of sky for your pet to sail through, like the one shown in Figure 4.110.

    Views from a high place work well, because you'll end up at eye level with your pet, looking down at the scenery below.

3. Use the Freehand Selection tool to cut the image of your pet out of the background, and then choose Copy from the Edit menu.

4. Switch to your panorama and paste your pet in.

Figure 4.110

5. Move your pet around so that you can still see the sky and ground, and your pet appears to be hang gliding above it all, as shown in Figure 4.111.

Figure 4.111   *Created in MGI PhotoSuite, from MGI Software.*

6. Take another scene and paste your pet again to continue the flight, as shown in Figure 4.112.

Figure 4.112 *Created in MGI PhotoSuite.*

7. Browse other pictures for sky vistas that might appeal to your pet, like the balloon in the shape of a hot dog shown in Figure 4.113.

Tip

To make your photo-montage more convincing, you may want to edit out any annoying traces of the original scene—like those green patches of grass around your cat's tail that show up so oddly when superimposed on a light blue sky. Tools that can help include the Zoom, because you can tinker better when you work on a few pixels at a time. (You're less likely to cut off a tongue or tail). Also try the Eyedropper tool, which picks up a nearby color, so you can spray paint or pencil it in, replacing the bits of stray background that came with the cutout of your pet. For stray pixels, use the Eraser tool—but be careful it doesn't leave a huge white hole in your picture. (Some erasers replace what they remove with white, others with the current background color, so test it before using it extensively).

Figure 4.113 *Created in MGI PhotoSuite.*

Boasting about your goat

If you show your goat, heifer, sheep, or pig at the county fair or a science or 4-H competition, you can put up a poster showing what you've done and showing off your prize-winning animal. You may also want to provide vital statistics (age, weight, height), and list caretaking tasks (grooming, watering, walking, and feeding). Learning these odd facts about your sow will win over many visitors, some of whom may even toss popcorn to your star.

1. Get a foam-core board from the office supply store.

2. Center the star at the top of your first sheet of paper, as shown in Figure 4.114.

Figure 4.114   *Created in Canvas from Deneba.*

3. Use your word processing program to write up the key facts, in large fonts (24–48 points) so visitors can read them from a distance, as shown in Figure 4.115.

I feed my horse carrots, apples, water, hay, and #1 MegaHorse Vitamin-Fortified Bulk Feed. He likes Sprite and Pepsi, too.

Figure 4.115   *Created in Canvas from Deneba.*

If you have a lot to say, you can do this on a separate sheet.

4. If you have a lot to say about feeding or grooming, start another sheet with a different image and add your text, as shown in Figure 4.116.

Figure 4.116 *Created in Canvas, from Deneba. Image from ClickArt from Broderbund.*

Consider photographing a day's worth of food, in one picture per item, and then displaying the entire set.

Finding that lost pet

The saddest flyers are those announcing a lost pet. We hope you never have to make one. But if you do, here are a few suggestions to encourage people to be alert for your pet and call you if they've seen your darling:

■ Make the picture as big as you can while leaving room for the text, because the photo is the best way people can recognize your pet.

■ Say how much you miss your pet. People see a lot of these posters, but they may act if they realize how upset you and your family are.

■ Add your phone number in tear-off strips to make it easy for someone to take one and call you, as shown in Figure 4.117.

Figure 4.117 *Image from ClickArt, from Broderbund.*

■ Hand the flyers out door to door, in all nearby blocks, so you can personalize your plea, ensuring people will call if they do happen to see your pet.

Putting your pet on a pedestal

At Mount Rushmore, you can view the carved heads of Washington, Jefferson, Roosevelt, and Lincoln. Isn't it time you put your pet up there, too?

Of course, you might want to celebrate your pet by putting its picture next to the Statue of Liberty, as her pet, or on top of your state capitol building, or atop a local ski slope. When in doubt, go to your local souvenir store and get the biggest, most outrageously glamorous postcard showing some neighborhood tourist spot.

1. Start with a close-up of your pet looking suitably noble.

2. Zoom in, and use the Freehand Selection tool to outline your pet, as shown in Figure 4.118, and then choose Copy from the Edit menu.

3. Find a picture of Mount Rushmore, as shown in Figure 4.119, or whatever international monument you want to deface by adding your pet's picture.

4. Paste your pet into the picture of the tourist site.

Figure 4.118

Figure 4.119

5. Resize your pet's head to match the rest of the setting, and move the head around to take a position of prominence, as shown in Figure 4.120.

Figure 4.120

6. Print on postcard-size paper, or 4" × 6" paper, to pretend you are issuing a new souvenir card.

   If you have a PhotoSmart printer, you could use HP Glossy Photographic Paper in the 4" × 6" size. Several vendors offer postcard-size paper.

7. Send to your relatives with a bland message, such as "Wish you were here!" Or post on your bulletin board at work or the refrigerator at home.

Just to prove you're not alone, take a look at the Web site called The Tomb of the Chihuahua Pharaohs, at `http://members.aol.com/crakkrjack/index.html`, where you can get graphics for Egyptian projects in school, hieroglyphics, weird postcards, and a picture of Neferchichi (see Figure 4.121).

Figure 4.121 *The Tomb of the Chihuahua Pharaohs, at*
`http://member.aol.com/crakkrjack/index.html`.

Making Genealogy Graphic

In Lisa's family, genealogy meant collecting bits of information over Hungarian dinners in New York's East Side and at the farm of her father's parents in upstate New York. No one had ever organized all the connections and she had to puzzle out the family tree by fitting together anecdotes, odd pictures, and the people telling the tales.

Jonathan's family had shoeboxes full of pictures of people he did not know, charts drawn in the backs of albums seventy years ago, horrifying oil portraits from the nineteenth century, typewritten lists from a relative who had developed a database of Prices, and a family Bible with various births and marriages recorded inside the front cover.

It isn't always easy to reconstruct a family tree in unbroken lines. If you are looking for help, software programs and the Internet offer wonderful resources for genealogy. Instead of having to travel to the old country to look in the church and town registers, you can get much of that information over the Web. And the software helps you keep track of relationships and display charts. Scanning in the pictures you discover, and adding those to the documentation you develop, helps your children "get a picture" of your shared ancestors.

Whether you use genealogical software or not, you'll find that images — whether portraits or landscapes, pictures of prize bulls or awards won in 1885 — make the past believable and imaginable, whereas names, dates, and words often leave people cold. A good first step is simply recording what you've heard from relatives — and adding any snapshots they have around.

Documenting what it was like

Oral history — recording what people say about events they've lived through — preserves the kind of detail we all wonder about. If you can interview older relatives, their stories can provide a way for youngsters to understand where they came from — the influences on their ancestors and eventually on their own parents. These stories illuminate the dreams, ambitions, and disappointments of the family, and the day-to-day experiences, whether out on the ranch or in the tenements of New York's Lower East Side. Here are some tips on building the family history.

■ Find or buy a small portable tape recorder.

Don't count on being able to take good notes. Even a professional reporter has trouble getting every word down. Most of us end up with a few names and dates — and all the life has seeped out of the story. To get the real flavor of the person who is talking, tape recording is great. You don't have to be distracted with taking notes. You can listen carefully and elicit rich responses. Meanwhile, the tape recorder is taking the notes for you.

■ Transcribe word-for-word what was said.

If you can see that the person started in one direction and then changed the sentence midstream, go ahead and clean that up. But try, as best you can, to preserve the exact words spoken. Do not "improve" the transcript. Leave yourself plenty of time for this process: We find it takes about four hours to transcribe one hour of speech.

■ Ask for any pictures that might illustrate the story and scan those so you have electronic versions.

Best are faces, close up. But grab group portraits, pictures of the old homestead, even vacation shots. If you can find an old magazine, look for ads that show a product your relative talks about, such as an early telephone (as shown in Figure 4.122), a "grinder" washing machine from the 1930s, or a flapper's hairdo from the 1920s (as shown in Figure 4.123). "Grandma wore her hair like that???!"

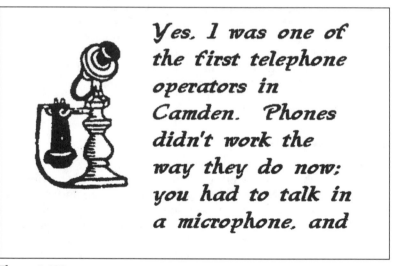

Figure 4.122 *Art from ClickArt, from Broderbund.*

■ Combine the text and pictures, so readers can see what your narrator is talking about.

Keep the margins wide, so the text is easy to read; use double spacing and plenty of short paragraphs, putting the pictures between paragraphs as shown in Figure 4.124. Or drop the pictures in on the side of the text as shown in Figure 4.125. Choose a font that reflects the period or suggests personal handwriting, as shown in Figure 4.126.

Figure 4.123 *Art from ClickArt, from Broderbund.*

Figure 4.124 *Art from ClickArt, from Broderbund.*

My little puppy's name was Vanessa, and I remember taking her to the artist's studio to have our picture painted. My mother was so upset because the bow would not stay in my hair, and the puppy kept moving, and every time the puppy moved, the painter would get mad, and we had to start all over again. It was a very dark place. I am glad my Mummy was with me. Vanessa grew up and had five litters of puppies. They ran around

Figure 4.125 *Art from ClickArt, from Broderbund.*

Your great aunt Em took over the math classes at the State Normal School back in the 1890's, and she became head of the place, I don't know, around the beginning of World War I, 1914 I think. She was independent and earned her own living all her life. She turned that place into a state college in 1925, and when she

Emma Thistle
1870-1935

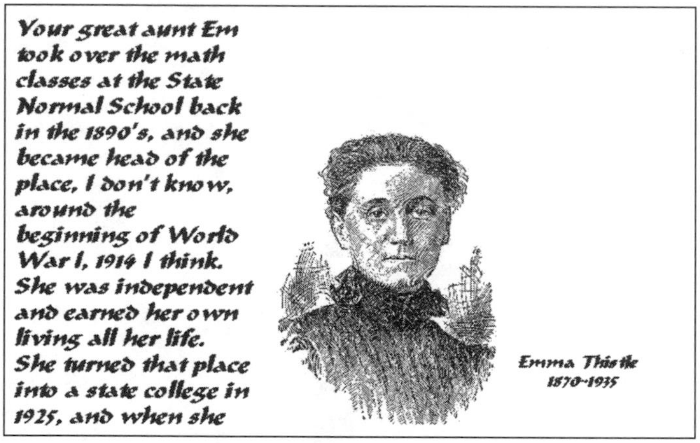

Figure 4.126 *Art from ClickArt, from Broderbund.*

Making a map of the old sod

Children love maps. We showed our kids where Hungary is and the town in Wales where our branch of the Price line lived from the eleventh through the eighteenth centuries, according to the old wives' tales, church records, and tombstones. Creating your own map will arouse your children's interest and make your family history come alive.

■ Start with the big picture, showing a whole continent before zooming in to the city or province your relatives came from, as shown in Figure 4.127.

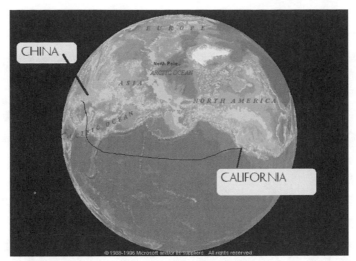

Figure 4.127 *Art from Microsoft Encarta World Atlas 97.*

■ Zoom in a little closer, to show the surrounding countries, as in Figure 4.128.

Figure 4.128 *From Microsoft Encarta World Atlas 97.*

■ Pinpoint or annotate the home town, if you know it, as shown in Figure 4.129.

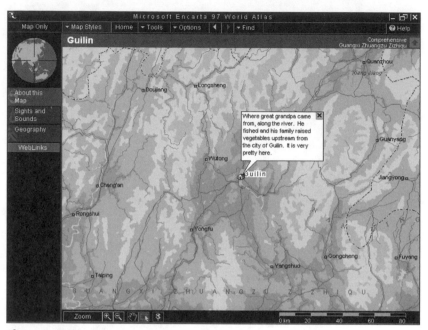

Figure 4.129 *Microsoft Encarta World Atlas 97.*

■ Add pictures of the local scenery, such as the one from Microsoft Encarta's Atlas 97 shown in Figure 4.130.

■ For older kids and for adults who want some historical perspective, add some historical background, like the Heritage materials available in the Rand McNally New Millennium World Atlas, shown in Figure 4.131.

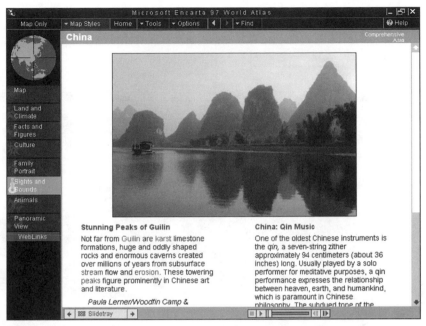

Figure 4.130 *Microsoft Encarta World Atlas 97, with image by Paul Lerner/Woodfin Camp & Associates.*

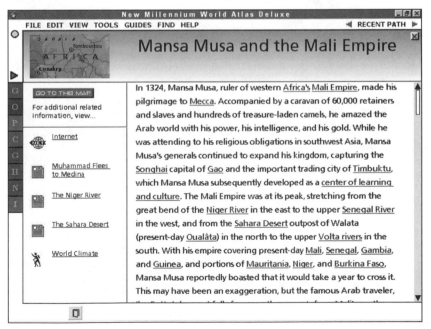

Figure 4.131 *From Rand McNally New Millennium World Atlas Deluxe.*

- If the area your relatives came from is geographically distinct from where you live now, consider including some natural or geological background, such as the material on the volcanic origin of the Hawaiian islands shown in Figure 4.132.

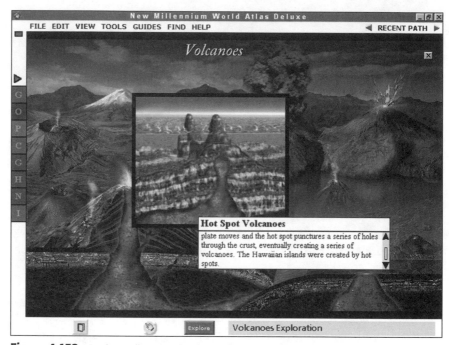

Figure 4.132 *Rand McNally New Millennium World Atlas Deluxe.*

Using software to dramatize your genealogy

If you're facing a pile of notes, photos, and lists, you may be wondering how to bring the family story together in one place. Software can help. If you haven't already committed yourself to a particular product, consider the following possibilities, most of which cost less than $90.

- **Family Tree Maker Deluxe** from Broderbund (now a division of The Learning Company, recently bought by Mattel). A best-seller, with good navigation, lots of features, ten CDs of data, and another few hundred CDs for sale with individual family trees and census records. Their index includes over 170 million names from seventeenth through twentieth century records in the U.S. If you spot a relative, you can order another CD with more information. The software lets you make up books chronicling the family history, including a family tree, tales, images, table of contents, and index. A timeline helps you correlate family and world events. The Web site lets you post your own research on a home page, offers classes on genealogical research, and links you to more than 50,000 home pages made by people who want to share their own family information. (Mac and Windows).

■ **Ultimate Family Tree Deluxe** from Palladium Interactive (also acquired by The Learning Company and then Mattel). This is another excellent program, with a good interface, 1,800 photos, flags and maps, photo-editing software, and the capability to send photos with e-mail; there's also plenty of room for notes and stories. Comes with a 90-day guarantee. The Web site offers more images to download (Mac and Windows).

■ **Family Tree Maker** from Mindscape (another affiliate of The Learning Company). Pick the deluxe version, which includes Corel PhotoHouse for editing photos, and software, so you can send the genealogy to someone else to view on their computer, without all the original software you used to create it. The index has 200,000 surnames and coats of arms, and there's a good calendar. Visit their great Web site, shown in Figure 4.133 (Windows).

Figure 4.133 *Family Tree Maker website from Mindscape.*

■ **Generations Deluxe Family Tree Software** from Sierra. Designed from the ground up to let you put pictures into charts, with three extra CDs with name databases, and a read-only version so you can circulate your work. Lets you import data developed on other genealogy software so you don't have to retype material. Stores your current family mailing addresses, so you can send them updates. A calendar reminds you of birthdays and anniversaries. (Windows).

All of these programs connect to the Internet, so you can fetch information from the many Web sites devoted to genealogical information, including images. The last two—Family Heritage and Generations—are best equipped to incorporate almost any kind of picture into your growing database. The Generations software lets you build wonderful charts with lots of images, as shown in Figure 4.134.

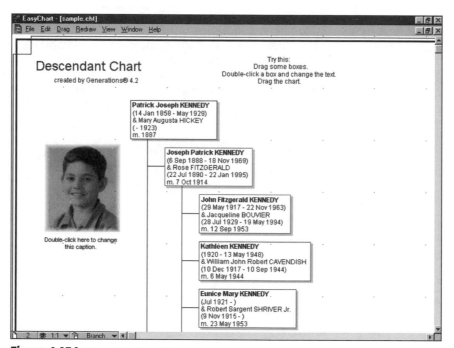

Figure 4.134 *Generations from Sierra.*

In each of these programs, you are building a database—a set of records that show relationships. The Family Heritage and Generations software make it easy to add images to the records, as shown in Figure 4.135.

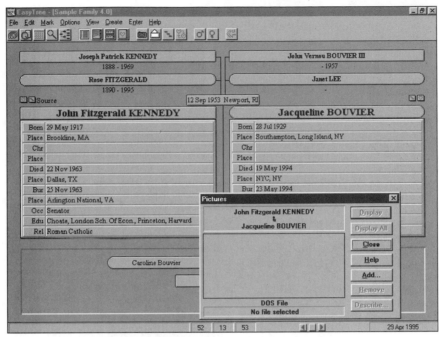

Figure 4.135 *Generations from Sierra.*

Surfing for information and images

In other eras, people remembered who begat whom and passed this family history down from one generation to the next, in front of the fire. In today's high-tech world, in which so many of us have lost touch with our relatives, we may have to look this information up on the Web.

For example, wondering about the route Jonathan's Welsh ancestors took to the United States, we used Web resources to piece together evidence from the electronic versions of birth lists, marriage announcements, cemetery records, ship manifests, military enlistment data, real estate deeds, and various family histories posted by other Prices (the name is about as common as you can get in Wales). It's odd, but fun and exciting, to find some nineteenth-century great-great-great-grandfather in the census — not quite the same as meeting him, but still a window into the family back then.

Your e-mail and Web browser programs turn out to be critical aids to your genealogical research, and both can help you collect images as well as names, dates, and details about your ancestors.

- Start with the Web site for your software — you'll find tons of links there.

- Check out Cyndi Howell's list of genealogical sites at http://www.cyndislist.com/. She has 40,000 links arranged in helpful categories, including photos, photo restoration, and maps.

■ For period images going back to the 1840s, visit the Library of Congress's American Memory site, at http://lcweb2.loc.gov/ammem. These images are gorgeous, and you can order a paper version if you want. Figure 4.136, for instance, shows Lincoln and the capitol in nineteenth-century daguerreotypes and Figure 4.137 is from a collection of images prepared in Detroit around the turn of the twentieth century.

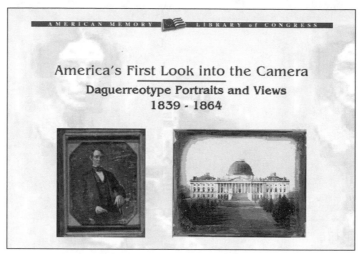

Figure 4.136 *American Memory from Library of Congress.*

Figure 4.137 *American Memory from Library of Congress.*

■ If you like looking for pictures at auctions and flea markets, a number of sites offer to sell you "lost" or "unidentified" photos that might be pictures of your ancestors. For example, check out `http://www.rootsweb.com/ ~neresour/ancestors/index.html` or `http://users.erinet.com/ 31363/photos.htm`.

If you happen to participate in America Online, it has a major section devoted to genealogy. Here's how to get the most out of it.

1. Choose Interests on the Channels window.

2. Choose Hobbies, and then double-click Genealogy on the scrolling list.

   You see the Genealogy window shown in Figure 4.138.

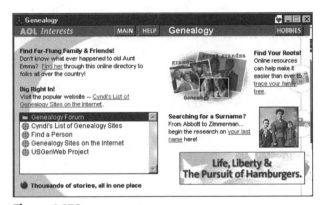

Figure 4.138 *America Online.*

3. In the list on the left, double-click Genealogy Forum.

   This takes you to the Genealogy Forum window, which offers a guide to beginners, plus access to tons of data about your relatives.

4. Click the Beginners button to get a quick-start guide.

At the Surnames Center, you can join forums devoted to discussing and posting information about the 100 most common surnames (that's the genealogical term for last names), the descendants of the people who took the Mayflower to Plymouth Rock, and, well, the rest of us. You'll find news about ancestors and living relatives, Web sites with full family trees and individuals' pedigrees, and, often, historical data stored in a format called GEDCOM, which can be read by any genealogical software.

1. On the Genealogy window, click Searching for a Surname or in the Genealogy Forum, click Surnames.

   This takes you to the Surnames Center.

2. Click Surname areas and then double-click the list that begins with the same letter your last name starts with.

   You see a list of forums.

3. Double-click the one that has your name on it.

   If no forum has your name, back out of this to the Surname center, and post a message on the Message Board Center, to start a forum for your family.

4. Type in a last name and a place, or a first name, and click List Articles.

   If there are any articles relating to those names, a list appears.

5. Double-click the article you want to read.

Just beginning? Take online classes about how to get started in genealogical research. These classes show you how to navigate gigantic lists like the Social Security Death List (55 million and growing), the research done by the Church of Jesus Christ of Latter-day Saints (the Mormons), and an amazing number of parish and vital records that have been entered into computer form (databases, word processing documents, and genealogical software records).

Also, every year dozens of local and national organizations meet to update one another on their discoveries in libraries, churches, and town and county seats around the world. These conferences will inspire (and can overwhelm) you, if you really want to wade in deep.

■ Look in the list on the Genealogical Forum for classes and conferences.

Wonder how your great-great-grandfather died in that guerrilla raid on Kansas during the Civil War? Or what happened to the gliders who flew in support of the invasion of Normany on D-Day? Post a message on the History message board. The Genealogy Forum offers a great way to learn from other folks who may already have investigated the same topics you're interested in — ethnic backgrounds, countries, states, or surnames.

You'll find stories of weddings, rescues, accidents, and coincidences. You'll see relatives meeting for the first time, and total strangers helping one another out with key facts. If you have a question, you'll find sympathetic ears here, and maybe an answer.

■ On the Genealogy Forum, click Messages.

The Genealogy Forum hosts dozens of genealogical chat sessions every day—though most seem to start late at night, after people have finished their chores. You may find a family reunion, off-topic schmoozing about last night's storm, or useful research advice for beginners. Many localities have their own chat sessions, as participants swap yarns and sources on the history of the town, county, province, or state—or the tale of a particular ethnic group.

■ On the Genealogy Forum, click Chats. Then check out schedules for the day, or click a session such as Family Tree House, which is open all day.

Creating a family newsletter

If you have some relatives who would really like to know what you find, you can publish more than that newsy letter at the holidays by sending out a newsletter about your discoveries. Here are a few ideas that have worked for others:

■ Take your camera for a visit to places from which your family came and do a story on your visit, as shown in Figure 4.139.

Figure 4.139 *Newsletter template in Complete Publisher, from Sierra.*

■ Tell one person's story per issue.

People love stories, not facts. And sometimes your digging turns up a diary, or a newspaper story about a relative—or maybe a great-uncle wrote up a booklet you found in the basement of the library. When you have enough information to tell a real story, devote the whole issue to that, as shown in Figure 4.140.

Spring 2001

the van Daam family newsletter

**Medieval Duchess Sat for Portrait—
Administered Castle and Market Town**

Marguerite de Aragon van Daam married
Henri, Duke of Navarre, in 1605, and the
couple celebrated by posing for matching
portraits, one of which we display here.
We have just discovered a small biography
of Marguerite in the Amsterdam archives,

Figure 4.140 *Image from ClickArt, from Broderbund.*

- If you have been chatting online with someone who has traced a whole branch of your line, grab all those archived chats and the resulting e-mails, and turn them into a story—with any art you can beg, whine, or cajole out of the other genealogist.

- If you begin to suspect that some part of the family story is, well, a myth, go ahead and try to debunk the tale, but brace yourself—most people would rather have the glamour than the truth.

- Keep the questions and requests to a minimum.

Unfortunately, although most of your relatives will enjoy getting news about the family, few have the interest—and therefore the time—to go to the local church or city hall and ask for the records from another century, much less to travel to do so. Try to limit requests for information to direct e-mails; any newsletter that becomes a list of questions is quickly tossed.

Posting a family Web page

Yes, every family ought to have its own Web page.

If you just want to post pictures of your pets, that's great. But don't figure you can publish your genealogical research on that kind of site. No one else will get past your cat.

There are so many ways to make hash out of a Web site, check out a few dozen sites to note what you *hate*. Here are some tips from the pros:

Sampler

Here are examples of the incredible range of documents you can brighten up with digital imagery, using scanned or digital photographs, clipart, and color printers to catch people's eye, show off your message, and get beyond the black-and-white world of text, to share the fun and beauty of color images. Pick a project and flip to that section to get tips on how to make it.

Projects at Home

Create a card for Mother's Day, or almost any other event, in Celebrating with Cards.

Made with Microsoft Picture It! and Jasc's Paint Shop Pro.

Show people how to get to the party by making up an invitation that waves hello, in Party Time.

Image of hand from Print Artist from Sierra, modified in Microsoft Paint; the house belongs to Lisa and Jonathan.

Envisioning Your Garden and Yard

Use your digital camera to snap images of your yard before you start redesigning it, so you can drop pictures of flowers and trees into it, to envision the future.

Plan your new garden or backyard with digital photos of your own trees or plants supplied by gardening or landscaping software, and ideas from Envisioning Your Garden and Yard.

Images from PhotoLandDesigner from Sierra.

Hobby-rama

Make up your own stamps, track and label your collections, stargaze, make your life into a quilt, all in Hobby-rama.

Made in Canvas, from Deneba.

Use the zoom feature in your software to study the stamps you love — up close.

Stamp from U.S. Postal Service.

Pet Pals

Play with your photos, so your pet can fly over Big Sur, as in Pet Pals.

Created in MGI Photo Suite from MGI Software.

Promote your pets to the pedestals they deserve.

Neferchichi from The Tomb of the Chihuahua Pharoahs, at http://members.aol.com/crakkrjack/index.html.

Bringing Genealogy to Life

A newsletter can bring the whole family together.

Newsletter template from Complete Publisher from Sierra.

Use images to brighten up your family Web page.

Made in WebStudio from Sierra.

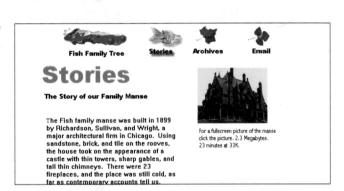

Love and Romance

Starting with clipart like this, you can make a gigantic poster for Valentine's Day in your imaging software.

Made in PrintArtist from Sierra.

Make a colorful announcement of your love in a giant poster, like this one in Love and Romance.

Image from Print Artist from Sierra.

I love you!

Kisses for the Kissable

Decorate your Valentine's Day gifts, or make romance all year long, with suggestions from Love and Romance.

Image from PrintArtist from Sierra.

In the Kitchen

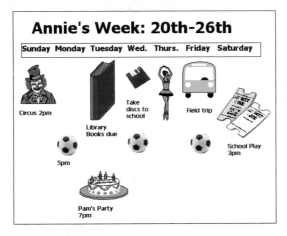

To remind yourself, or your kids, of their schedules, make the weekly calendar into a graphic—then post it on the refrigerator.

Images from PrintArtist from Sierra.

For chores you want kids to do every day, put their pictures up among images of the chores.

Images from PrintArtist from Sierra.

Make up your own labels for chiles, jam, and bakesale items in Cooking Up an Image in the Kitchen.

Images from Print Artist from Sierra.

Projects at Work and School

Make up your own postcards to advertise
your services, as in Showing Off Your Home Business.

Image from PrintArtist from Sierra.

Dreaming of the open seas?

Cruise on by, and see us.

Use digital images on do-it-yourself
postcards to get quick notice to your best
customers.

Created in Print Artist from Sierra.

The Greek isles have been the target of cruises since Odysseus set sail for Troy, and once again many

Several new cruises made their appearance last summer, and we loved the way they

The rugged rocks, and the deep blue sea. Many of the islands seem to have fallen apart, with rocks tumbling into the warm Mediterranean. The white and gray rocks stand sentinel against the sun, jagged and rough, while kelp divers swim below, and pearl divers go even farther down, to capture the few remaining oysters in these waters. Most of the boats offer at least three

The lemon crop has been downright spectacular this year in southern Mexico, and we should see

Several wholesalers and importers have already announced price cuts on bulk shipments of

The Mexican lemon has a little more tang to it, experts say. Most shoppers will not complain, though, because new fertilizing and watering has made these fruits swell up so they give California and Florida citrus a run for their money. Big may not be best, but as you know, customers always pick the big lemon over the little one, and these stand up to that

High-contrast pictures saturated with bright colors help your newsletters come alive.

Image from PrintArtist from Sierra.

Polishing Health Care

Reward your patients and encourage their behavior with graphic celebrations, as in Polishing Health Care.

Created in Print Artist Craft Factory from Knowledge Adventure. Proprietary format only; screenshot was all we could get.

Use cartoon drawings and real pictures of your clients to encourage them to take your medical advice.

Created in Print Artist Craft Factory from Knowledge Adventure.

Brightening the Classroom

Insert a student's name and photo into a paper pocket with a chore displayed graphically as a reminder.

Image from ClickArt from Broderbund.

Make up very personal awards for students who do well on their assignments, like Davy, in Brightening Your Classroom.

Background image from ClickArt from Broderbund.

Marketing Your Organization

WE BUILD 'EM.
DO YOU WANT TO HELP?

BRIDGES TO DIGITAL
COMMUNITY

56 HENRY STREET, BROOKLYN HTS, NY 37891 212 333 4456

WE BUILD 'EM.
DO YOU WANT TO HELP?

BRIDGES TO DIGITAL
COMMUNITY

56 HENRY STREET, BROOKLYN HTS, NY 37891 212 333 4456

WE BUILD 'EM.
DO YOU WANT TO HELP?

BRIDGES TO DIGITAL
COMMUNITY

56 HENRY STREET, BROOKLYN HTS, NY 37891 212 333 4456

Use pictures to extend your slogan in a series of posters.

Images from PrintMaster Gold from Mindscape.

Using graphics can help you set your sights on your market, in Marketing Your Organization.

Made in PrintMaster Gold from Mindscape.

Snake Collectors!
We Have Our Eye On You!   --Reptilia

3100 Santa Monica Boulevard, Half Moon Bay, CA 87107 (505)

Community Activities

Make a strong but simple poster for your fundraising drive, or a community organization, in Volunteering.

Made in PrintMaster Gold Publishing Suite, from Mindscape.

Sports and Games

Make up trading cards for your own sports stars in Sports and Games, in Chapter 6.

Made in AppleWorks from Apple.

Around the Neighborhood

Make up a series of posters asking DO YOU BRAKE FOR GARAGE SALES?, leading customers right to your yard, in Around Your Neighborhood.

Lisa and Jonathan Price.

Use instant images to make a map of your neighborhood,
as you and your kids learn your way around.

Lisa and Jonathan Price.

■ Choose a background that is simple, such as white.

Complex backgrounds like the one shown in Figure 4.141 make it almost impossible to read any text you put on top of them.

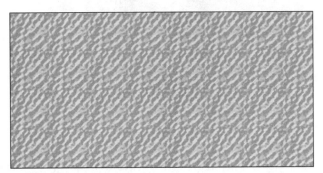

Figure 4.141 *Web Studio from Sierra.*

■ Put your site's name at the top. It is not cute to hide your name at the bottom.

■ Skip the text saying that you welcome people to your site. Of course you do.

■ Put a menu at the top, right above your Web site name, as shown in Figure 4.142, so people can immediately go to the main sections. And put this menu at the top of every page so people can jump from one page to another without coming back to the home page.

Figure 4.142 *Created in Web Studio, from Sierra.*

■ Never, never, never put a big picture on a page, like the one shown in Figure 4.143. Particularly avoid this on your first page.

Figure 4.143 *Web Studio from Sierra.*

Big pictures take too long to download. Most people will hit the Stop sign before they finish downloading that wonderful picture of the trees in front of your house or the view up your driveway. In general, banish any pictures bigger than a thumbnail from the first page, and before you take someone to a page that does have a large picture, warn them by indicating how long it will take to download with 33K or 56K modems—the kinds most people have at home.

■ When you get to a section, if you have several topics, start right off with a submenu so viewers can pick one and get on with it.

■ When someone clicks one of your buttons and goes to a new page, that page should show that the button was selected—it should be darker, shadowed, or boxed, as shown in Figure 4.144.

■ If you insist on making a big version of a picture available, put a caption below a thumbnail (see Figure 4.144), warning people how long the large version will take to download, so no one clicks it by accident and gets stuck with an interminable download.

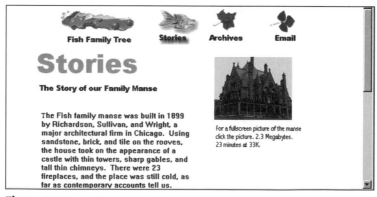

Figure 4.144 *WebStudio from Sierra.*

■ Break up your text into short paragraphs.

Three lines per paragraph is good; four is a lot; five is too much. Do not dump big files onto a Web page. Edit them for the Web.

■ If you have genealogical database files or big text files that someone else might want, make them available on special pages, but warn everyone: "This is a long download, so don't come here unless you really, really want the material." Spare the innocent.

■ Keep alert to what you like at other sites. Imitate the good stuff.

Expressing Love

Romance blossoms with images, tokens, glances, and gifts. And now the computer—that cold, hard calculator, that heap of metal and plastic—can help you surprise your honey with warm notes, intriguing cards, and intimate gifts for the holidays, anniversaries, or that special weekend. All you have to do is add the kisses.

Flowers can astonish with their softness, color, and aroma, and pictures of flowers remind us of their beauty. So, if you don't have the time or money to strip a dozen roses and toss the petals on the bed, try images instead.

We like the ease with which you can pick a flower from The Floral Collection, a set of two dozen photos and drawings of flowers in the Printable Expressions line, grab a suggested sentiment, and print—adding your own creative 32 characters, if you wish. The mix-and-match approach, shown in Figure 4.145, results in a beautifully designed card almost every time, thanks to the hard work of all those designers. (We particularly enjoy the fuzzy "felt" paper they provide, because it gives a soft feel to both images and text).

Figure 4.145 *From The Floral Collection, from Hewlett-Packard.*

Remembering that cruise

Maybe it wasn't a cruise, but just a quick vacation. You both remember that trip fondly, so when the busy spell sets in and you never seem to have enough time for each other, remind your loved one of those moments together.

1. Seize an image from your album or scan one from the magazines or brochures.

2. Adjust the image so it will fill up the bottom half of the page in portrait orientation.

Portrait orientation just means the paper is taller than it is wide, as for a painting of a person. Arranging the size of the image this way means you can fold the paper in half, if you need to, to make a card, or just deliver it as a flat sheet.

3. Add your personal joke, wish, or whatever across the top, as shown in Figure 4.146.

Figure 4.146 *Image from Hawaii, a collection of images from Corel.*

4. If you have some greeting-card paper, put that in the printer.

   Papers like the Hewlett-Packard Glossy Photo Greeting Cards offer a glossy surface for photos; and a crease, so you can fold the paper over. Put the glossy side up.

5. Print the image.

6. If you feel like adding a message "inside" the card, write the text on the bottom half of a page, and print that on the reverse side.

   Put the picture in so it is nearest to you, but upside-down.

You can also take up the whole page with an image and text if you like, as shown in Figure 4.147, if your love has the heat of a lava flow; or move the image to the top, adding your text like a slogan at the bottom, as shown in Figure 4.148, to make a poster.

Figure 4.147 *Image from Hawaii, a collection of photographs from Corel.*

Figure 4.148 *Image from Hawaii, a collection of photographs from Corel.*

Starting with a poem

If you particularly like some poetic lines, take them as an inspiration for a card. For instance, if you like John Donne's complaint against the sunrise, you might put a modernized version of his first few lines under an image of the sun coming up, as shown in Figure 4.149:

```
Busy old fool, unruly Sun,
Why do you thus,
Through windows, and through curtains call on us?
Must to your motions lovers' seasons run?
```

Figure 4.149 *Created in Print Artist, from Sierra.*

Or, if your tastes run to Robert Burns, find an image like the one shown in Figure 4.150 to match the following lines:

```
My love is like a red red rose
That's newly sprung in June:
My love is like the melody
That's sweetly played in tune.
```

Figure 4.150 *Made in Print Artist, from Sierra.*

Dreaming of you

Pucker up and blow your lover a kiss. Now capture that picture and iron it right onto a pillowcase so your kiss will be right at their ear, all night long. You need a perfectly smooth pillowcase, so even if you buy a new one, iron it first.

1. Get out your camera, digital or otherwise, and have a friend snap you blowing a kiss.

    Ask the friend to get as close as possible while still keeping you in focus. The more you fill the frame, the better.

    If you don't have the time or the wish to use your own picture, grab a piece of clip art, like the giant lips shown in Figure 4.151.

Figure 4.151 *Made in Print Artist, from Sierra.*

2. Edit the image so that your head is emphasized.

    Cut out the background. You don't have to be super precise, but by enlarging the image (zooming in with the magnifying glass) you can delete the distracting background by using the Pencil or the Spraypaint tool with white as the paint color. You want the background around your head to be white.

3. Print a test run of the picture on regular paper to make sure it looks OK.

4. Put T-shirt transfer paper into your printer.

   For example, HP Iron-On T-Shirt Transfers will work. In an HP printer, you put the unprinted side down on top of a stack of plain paper. Flatten the sheet. (Don't try using a sheet that has begun to curl; it will probably jam.)

5. On the File menu choose Printer Setup, find Paper Type, and choose HP Premium Inkjet Paper or Special Paper; then find Print Quality and choose Presentation or Best. Click OK.

6. Print the image on the transfer paper.

7. Preheat the iron for eight minutes at its highest temperature.

8. Trim closely around the image, leaving a little corner so you can peel the image off the cloth later. Fold that corner up, so it won't get ironed to the cloth later.

9. Lay the pillowcase out flat on a table or ironing board.

   Make sure that the cloth has no wrinkles, moth holes, tears, or seams where you are going to put the image.

10. Place the transfer sheet on the pillowcase, image side down, and iron very, very slowly from one end to the other, along the sides, and then make circles over the entire transfer for another minute or so.

    When you start, make sure that you are completely covering the edges of the transfer. Take about a minute for each lengthwise pass, and another minute to cover the whole transfer again. Make sure that you do not accidentally seal down your folded corner.

11. While the transfer is still hot, peel it off, using the folded corner to start. If the transfer won't come off, reheat that section to loosen it.

12. Let the pillowcase cool off for several minutes before doing anything with it.

Now you may want to put a pillow in the pillowcase, or just wrap the pillowcase up as a surprise. But from now on, your kiss will live in your lover's dreams.

Edible love

If your sweetie is so scrumptious you could just eat her up, or lick him all over, surprise him or her with a decorated container of a favorite food. The special wrapper makes a thoughtful gift into an expression of love.

1. Buy the chocolates, cookies, ice cream, raspberries, baklava, or whatever, and preserve the container the food comes in.

   You're going to put a wrapper around the real container. You can't make reheatable cartons in your printer, so just start with the one you get at the store and add to it.

2. Figure out about how many inches of wrapper you need to go around the original container. You don't have to be super-exact on this, because you'll probably want to have some overlap.

3. Figure out how high the wrapper needs to be.

   Don't worry about the top yet—just the height of a piece of paper you put around the container's sides. Of course, with some containers you may decide your wrapper should go over the top too, and that is OK.

4. Now that you have an idea of the dimensions of your wrapper, locate some art that will appeal to your honey or advertise the contents and arrange it within that space.

   It's fine to repeat the same picture over and over around the whole wrapper, as shown in Figure 4.152, where the lovers turn over and over, kissing. If the box is big, you can surround it with a lacy heart, as shown in Figure 4.153. Or you can zip around the outside with high-speed hearts, as shown in Figure 4.154. Or you can use pictures from your last vacation, as in Figure 4.155, just as a reminder of good times.

Figure 4.152 *Made in Print Artist, from Sierra.*

Figure 4.153 *Made in Print Artist, from Sierra.*

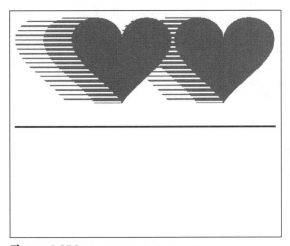

Figure 4.154 *Made in Print Artist, from Sierra.*

5. If your container has a top you haven't overwhelmed with wrapping paper, draw its shape on the screen and fill in with a gift tag, as shown in Figure 4.156.

6. Fold up a narrow strip of paper, tape one end to the food container, and tape the other to the cutout of your gift tag, so it jumps up.

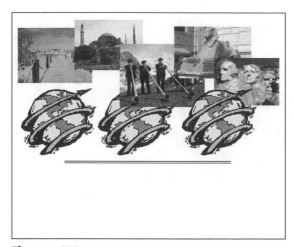

Figure 4.155 *Made in Print Artist, from Sierra.*

Figure 4.156 *Made in Print Artist, from Sierra.*

Remember that you don't need to seal this container perfectly, because you are just decorating it, not making a Tupperware™ container to hold the food itself. Let the top wiggle a little, if you like.

Appealing scents

If your love has a sensitive nose, or a sore back, consider a present like massage oil, incense, essential oils, or a coupon for a session of massage or aromatherapy. Then add a drop of the scent to your card before slipping it in the envelope.

1. Find an image that expresses the mood you hope the present will elicit. (You don't need to get a picture of a massage or a giant nose).

2. Invent your own "coupon" beneath the image or on top of it.

   You can attach a real gift certificate on the back so all you have to do is set the mood of relaxation, as shown in Figure 4.157, or give a hint of the experience, as shown in Figure 4.158.

Figure 4.157 *Made in Print Artist, from Sierra.*

Figure 4.158 *Made in Print Artist, from Sierra.*

Invitation to a special dinner for two

If you're both too busy to take time to chat until late at night, and you haven't had an adult conversation for weeks, it's time to go out. To make the evening even more special, prepare a real invitation, like the one shown in Figure 4.159. The invitation doesn't have to be fancy to be enjoyed.

Figure 4.159 *Made in Print Artist, from Sierra.*

Valentine's Day

Here's the big event of the year for romance. You can show you care more than a card company. How? Make your own banner (as in Figure 4.160), card (as in Figure 4.161), or poster (as in Figure 4.162)—or all three!

■   A banner shows you've actually thought ahead, so artistic or not, it's going to please your sweetie pie. Soft pastel colors will work best; after all, you're not advertising a sale. And this is one time in the year when you can indulge in drippy sentimental art, unapologetically.

Figure 4.160 *Made in Print Artist, from Sierra.*

■ For a card, put the official greetings on the front, and then slip the sentimental stuff inside.

Figure 4.161 *Made in Print Artist, from Sierra.*

■ Use a giant color printer at a copy store or blueprint service to make your poster on shiny paper, at about $15 a square foot. The best printer is the HP Design Jet, which can handle widths up to 54 inches, and any length, because it prints on a roll of paper.

Figure 4.162 *Made in Print Artist, from Sierra.*

Projects at Work and School

IN THIS CHAPTER

- Showing off your home business
- Improving health care
- Brightening the classroom
- Marketing your organization

Showing Off Your Home Business

We run a home business. Heck, we run half a dozen home businesses. Most are long-distance, like writing this book for folks all over the world, but some are local, like when we give speeches or workshops on writing for Webzines right here in the towns along the Rio Grande. We've found digital photography, scanning, and color printing to be a great help in inventing what big business would call "a corporate identity" for our various enterprises. The key ingredient, we think, is color — it catches the eye, emphasizes your message, and, if you pick the right color, makes a strong statement all on its own.

Saying who you are with your letter paper

Whether you're writing to buyers, potential customers, suppliers, or the Chamber of Commerce, you probably want to look as if you are a big, established firm, the kind that has its own preprinted stationery delivered on a forklift. Even if you are already making lots of money, turning out first-rate products, and satisfying customers everywhere, you may not have had time to design your own stationery.

Now that you have your color printer, though, you can print your own stationery at the same time you write a letter. You can create a template in your word-processing program, so that every time you dash off a letter to a banker, it looks good. You'll be able to print on whatever paper you usually use, and although the richness of color depends on your printer, any colors you can manage will make your letter paper stand out.

Starting with a logo or an emblem

If you already have a logo for your business, you'll probably want to use that on your stationery, to reinforce its impact and maintain your company identity. For instance, for our mom-and-pop consulting business, the Communication Circle, we use a big sunburst on all our labels and stationery. The color (bright yellow) and the shape (a circle) are simple enough to stand out, and if anyone thinks about it, the logo echoes our dba name — the name we are "doing business as."

If you don't already have some kind of a logo, ransack clip art collections for a graphic that catches the tone of your enterprise. You'll probably need to browse one or two giant collections, because as soon as you start looking for a graphic to represent yourself and your business, you need to get tough, asking questions like the following:

- Will my typical customers enjoy this graphic?

- Will they respect it?

- Does it express the tone of my business?

- Does it print well?

- If I want to use it on small items such as business cards, and big items such as posters, will it be readable at those different sizes?

- Does this graphic really make my business stand out from that of my competitors?

If your printer does a better job printing graphics with big solid colors than it does with subtle photographs, steer clear of photos for your stationery. Whatever you print has to look good each time you print it. So avoid any images that emerge a bit washed-out or bleached. If photos are not your printer's strong point, move toward graphics that have simple lines and solid (not subtly mixed) colors.

You should create the stationery in whatever program you usually use for word processing, so that you can easily use the template over and over. Generally, making stationery in an art program limits what kind of text you can write. Also, you should probably avoid printing a bunch of sheets and then running them through the printer a second time, when you write your letters — the heating that the paper gets on its first pass through the printer tends to warp and wrinkle the paper just enough for it to jam on the second pass. Also, if you are like us, you may have trouble remembering how to place the paper in the tray upside down and backward, or whatever way you have to put it so that the text comes out on the correct side of the paper. That's why we recommend printing the "stationery" at the same time as your letter. Following are some ideas that we have found work well for us and our clients:

- Place the emblem or logo in the top left corner, as shown in Figure 5.1, to leave room for your name and address on the right.

  In a clip art or graphics program, copy the image you like; then go to your word processor and paste it into your word processing file, telling the program to save the image with the text. Another method is to insert the art from a file. The problem with this second approach is that in the future, your word processing program may expect to find the art file in the same location as it was when you first created it and stored it on your hard disk, so if you move the art file, your logo may not print.

Figure 5.1 *Image from PrintArtist from Sierra.*

- If your letters are almost always short, sign off with your emblem, dropping it to the bottom, as a farewell, as shown in Figure 5.2.

- If you've just discovered a graphic that doesn't already have a life of its own as a logo, repeat it a few times to form a tasty border, as shown in Figure 5.3.

Tip

If you are using Word, you can best use this art on the left if you divide your page into two columns, place the border art into the left-hand column, and then expand the right-hand column as much as you can, to create the area for your actual letter. Recipients won't know you are working in two columns; they will just see dancing graphics on the left, and your text on the right.

Figure 5.2 *Image from PrintArtist from Sierra.*   **Figure 5.3** *Image from PrintArtist from Sierra.*

- You can also shrink the graphic, to make a series across the top (see Figure 5.4).

Figure 5.4 *Image from PrintArtist from Sierra.*

■ Make a border by highlighting a rectangle at the center of the page, with a very light wash of color (so you can read black type on top of it), and then apply your emblem on top, matching the background color if possible, as shown in Figure 5.5.

To do this in Word, click the Drawing tools, and when the tools appear below your document, draw a rectangle and pour in a fill color using the Paint Bucket icon. Then select the rectangle, and from the Draw menu, choose Order ⇨ Send Behind Text. In this way, you can type on top of your colored rectangle.

■ If you don't find any graphics to suit your image, try using simple blocks of color to create an abstract painting; and drop your homemade piece of art in as a header (at the top) or footer (at the bottom), as shown in Figure 5.6.

Figure 5.5 *Image from PrintArtist from Sierra.*

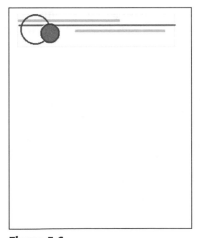

Figure 5.6

- If you have a program with lots of borders, print out a few to see which look best on your printer; then select the top or bottom part of the border, copy it, and paste it into your word processing document, as shown in Figure 5.7.

Tip

Use a white oval with white lines to blot out part of the border if it seems too heavy.

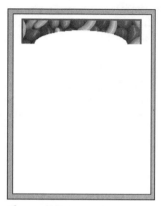

Figure 5.7 *Image from PictureIt! from Microsoft.*

Unfortunately, Word and WordPerfect have trouble enabling you to write "inside" of a piece of clip art that you have pasted in or next to the art. Yes, you can do it. But, no, you will not be happy trying. Paragraphs fly up and down, art disappears, pages go and come. So place your art at the top or bottom, to be sure it won't drive you crazy. There is one exception: If you have a tall and thin piece of art, you can make it the first column of a two-column arrangement, as suggested earlier, expanding the second column so it is much wider than the first one, to accommodate a real letter.

Adding your name and address

Your graphic element sets the tone for your letter. Following up on and strengthening that impression will be the font you choose for your company name and address. Your choice of a font is very important, because it works nonverbally, but powerfully, to suggest your company's level of professionalism, sense of humor, self confidence, and reliability. The same company name in a different font becomes, well, a different company.

Bringing Art to the Edge with Preprinted Papers

One of the few things your personal printer can't do is print to the edge of the paper; in fact, as you can see in the figure, many programs won't even let you run art out to the edges of the screen. Unfortunately, that constraint means you can't run art out to the edge of the page, where it would stay out of the way of any running text. But preprinted papers offer you artwork that extends to the edge or top of the paper, along with similar looking envelopes, business cards, and brochures. From vendors such as Paper Direct (1-800-A-Papers), you can get nicely laid-out, colorful letter paper ready for you to drop in your address and go. These papers make economic sense if you want to experiment a little before settling on a design, if your business itself changes its emphasis from quarter to quarter, or if you rarely send out more than 20 or 30 letters per month. You pay a little more than $20 for a box of one hundred sheets, $15 for 50 envelopes, and about $25 for 500 blank business cards, all with the same design. You feed these through your inkjet or laser printer, adding your own slogan and return address; and for a fraction of the price, you have designer stationery. Of course, if you begin to do more frequent or larger mailings, you should consider having your own design preprinted on reams of paper, just as bigger companies do. A stationery supply house or large local printer will let you finger various papers and pick a texture and color that are appropriate—something you can't easily do with mail-order vendors or do-it-yourself techniques.

Made in PrintArtist from Sierra.

You need to choose a font that speaks for you. Think of the corporate identities you know well, and then pick up any advertisement, brochure, or container those companies produce. The same font shows up everywhere — reinforcing their corporate pitch, their positioning, their vision of their relationship to you. FedEx trucks do not look like UPS trucks. Look carefully at your most intense competitors, and you may find they are already capitalizing on the "look" a certain font gives them. Those of you who use Macintoshes may not know the exact name of the font in the manuals, but Apple cared enough to commission a special Garamond font exclusively for use in those manuals, to give just the right "feeling." But which font is right for you? To decide, try some experimenting:

1. Select a font, type your company name in 48-point, and then space down a few paragraph returns, typing it in 36-point, as shown in Figure 5.8.

Figure 5.8 *Created in PrintArtist from Sierra.*

2. Select the text and copy it.

3. With the text still selected, transform it to the first font you are considering.

If you don't have many fonts, get more. Check any clip art collections you have, because they often come with dozens, or even hundreds, of new fonts. You can also browse the Web for fonts.

Tip

Microsoft gives away a few fonts on its Web site (http://microsoft.com/typography/default.htm), and lists hundreds of other sites offering free fonts, from Casa de Toad to more highfalutin places. Adobe (http://www.adobe.com), Bitstream (http://www.bitstream.com), and Monotype (http://www.monotype.com) all offer great fonts, but, alas, for serious money. The cheapest and most lurid fonts come from Expert software, at |about $10 a CD; they are worth every penny, but not a dime more.

4. Type the name of the font, way below the second name, just for reference.

5. Click below the name of the font and insert a page break.

6. Paste the text onto the next page. Apply another font, add its name at the bottom of the page, and so on.

7. Print all the pages and compare them, as shown in Figure 5.9.

Figure 5.9 *Created in PrintArtist from Sierra.*

As you look over the printed fonts, ask yourself questions such as:

■ How much would my typical customer enjoy this font? Respect it?

■ Is it thick enough, thin enough, tall enough, small enough?

■ What overtones does it give off? Are there any situations or organizations you associate with this font?

Once you settle on a font you like, you need to use it to display your company name and address. To you, your company name is key, so if you're like us, your first impulse may be to make your company name big enough to read at twenty paces. But to your readers, your name and address only need to be big enough to identify the letter ("Oh, this is from so and so!") and make it easy to read ("How do I contact these folks, anyway?"). In fact, the greater your involvement in high technology, the smaller some customers like your name (as if you had to prove the high quality of your printer by using 8-point type). Here are some suggestions for putting your name and address on your paper:

■ For your company name, use a color that is the same shade as your graphic, or a close variation.

- Align the company name and address flush right if you put them at the top, with a graphic on the left. Even if you decide to center some elements, you don't have to center everything, as you can see in Figure 5.10.

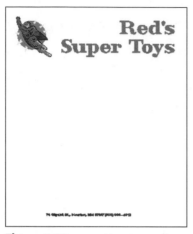

Figure 5.10 *Created in PrintArtist from Sierra.*

- Consider putting your address, phone number, and so on, in one line along the bottom of the page, as far down as your printer can handle. That way, people can get the information they need to reach you, but the details won't intrude on your graphics and name. (Yes, the name should still go at the top, as an announcement.)

- When you have your name and address where you like them, write an entire letter and see how it works with the new stationery layout, as shown in Figure 5.11. (You may want to adjust the size of the address, given the size of your regular text.)

Figure 5.11 *Image and text in header created in PrintArtist from Sierra.*

■ Save your file as a template, or stationery, so you can use it over and over without accidentally covering it with text.

Tip

You can borrow your design, font, and layout ideas from the stationery, and put them onto do-it-yourself business cards. Your office supply store (or a mail-order vendor such as Cheap Sheets or Paper Direct) can offer sheets on which you can first print the cards and then tear them apart afterward. If you don't use a lot of cards, and think you might change your mind about the look in a month or two, this approach works well—instead of stockpiling 500 cards you aren't going to use any time soon. You'll have to adjust your margins for the card stock (instructions come with the paper), and work in a tight space, so some aspects of your design or graphics may need to be changed, but hold onto your font as a constant!

Making a Dramatic Fax Sheet

You can extend your corporate identity by creating a fax cover sheet that echoes your stationery—its graphics, its font, and its overall message. If possible, start with the same stationery you created for letters, so it matches exactly. Then, using the same font you chose for your company address and the core text of your letters, add the word "Fax" in large type below your company name, and put the following on separate lines: To, Fax #, Phone #, Pages, Date, Subject, and From (followed by your name), as shown in the following figure. Make sure your address is legible even on a bad fax—if you made the address smaller than 12-point, enlarge its size to 14-point, to be sure. Leave room in the bottom third of the page for comments like "Urgent!" Save the file as a template with a name like MyFax.

Making postcards for announcements and thank-you's

Like us, you've probably gotten a postcard reminding you that you are due for a dental checkup. Our dogs get reminder cards from the vet. Would you like to use a colorful postcard to remind your customers, clients, or suppliers of your existence?

You may not have the kind of business that requires you to call people to make sure they are going to come in for their appointments, but you probably want to make sure they think about you, at least every once in a while. If you have a sale coming up, you can dramatize it for your best customers, sending a real postcard instead of the usual flyer. If you have just passed a milestone, won an award, or made big news, celebrate it with a postcard, rather than a press release. Use special postcard papers, or heavy paper if you are clever with scissors.

■ Award a prize to a customer, as shown in Figure 5.12. Give them your thanks for being a valued customer.

Figure 5.12 *Created in PrintArtist from Sierra.*

■ Let your graphics tell the story, issuing a general invitation to come in, even when you aren't having a sale, as shown in Figure 5.13.

■ Encourage daydreaming your way, as shown in Figure 5.14.

Recipients have to flip the card over to get your business name, but they just might tack a great-looking card up on their bulletin board, and think about you every time they look at it.

Figure 5.13 *Entire card from PrintArtist from Sierra.*

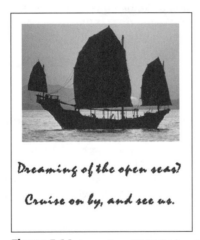

Figure 5.14 *Image from PrintArtist from Sierra.*

■ If you do have a sale, have the postcard offer a special discount for pre-ferred customers only, as shown in Figure 5.15.

Tip

Printing on glossy postcard paper costs money, so you probably aren't going to want to make up postcards for a mailing list of more than a few hundred. If you need more than 500 postcards, you can do the job more cheaply by sending your electronic file to a professional postcard maker. You can find the names of people who specialize in this kind of printing in the classified ads at the back of art magazines, because artists hire them to make announcements for their shows, with a photo of some artwork on the front.

Figure 5.15 *Created in PrintArtist from Sierra.*

■ Keep the back of your postcard simple, using the font you have established as yours in the stationery, and focusing on the basics — company name, phone number, address, and a one-sentence pitch; no more.

Letting folks know — with a newsletter

The best newsletters bring your ideas to the attention of your customers, offering them facts or insights they can use, so they begin to think of you as an expert. It's fine to include some promotion, announcing recent deals, awards, or favorable press. But in addition to boasting about your successes, you must offer something of real value to readers — insider information, tips, advice, recommendations, even your own perspective on the industry. Without that, you don't have a newsletter — you just have an annoying sales brochure.

Estimating size, length, and frequency

To many readers, the more issues you distribute, the more reliable your company seems. But how much do you have to say? And how often can you afford to take off a day or two to write it up, edit the few contributions that others make, lay it out, print it, and ship it out? The following guidelines may help you get started:

■ Start small, perhaps using two sides of a regular sheet of paper, as shown in Figure 5.16.

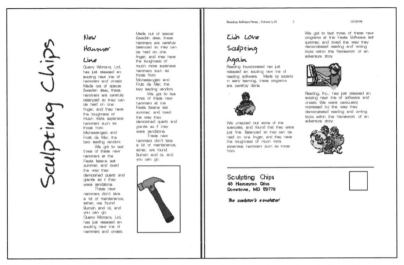

Figure 5.16 *Created in Word from Microsoft, with images from PrintArtist from Sierra.*

You can always expand later to an 11" × 17" sheet, folded to make four pages, or a stapled set of pages. But begin with a core idea and let that grow. A few paragraphs on this or that, a graphic, a few more paragraphs, and you're done. But what is this newsletter all about? And who is it really for?

- Make a list of topics you'd like to cover — and another list of the people who would likely form your ideal audience, the people you'd most like to get a response from when they read your newsletter.

- Guesstimate how often you could get around to writing the whole issue yourself.

People always politely agree to contribute, and then rarely do. Or if they do send in an article, it is in a file format you never heard of, or the authors take a thousand words to say that so-and-so got promoted, or the piece is completely unusable. To determine if you really have the stamina for this project, imagine doing it entirely by yourself, month after month. Still want to do it?

Naming your newsletter

Okay, so no amount of reasoning can stop you. You are going to put out a newsletter. But what should you call it?

- Make up a name that plays off the work you do.

Your newsletter name indicates who you are, what you represent, and how you view that subject. The name can be silly, homespun, or austere. It can be abstract or local. But don't just call it your company newsletter, which suggests photos of bosses shaking hands and ribbon-cutting ceremonies. Make the name of your newsletter embody the perspective you are trying to convey.

■ Pick an expressive font for your newsletter name, as shown in Figure 5.17.

Figure 5.17

This doesn't have to be the font you have identified as your organizational standard, because that font has to work at various sizes. Your newsletter name, usually, will only appear in one or two sizes, so you can look for a font that looks good at 36 to 72 points, without worrying about how it would work in running text.

■ If you're going to print the newsletter yourself, pick the same color to use for the name and all headings throughout the newsletter, as shown (alas, in black and white) in Figure 5.18.

Continuous use of a single color brightens the page and functions as a signal that says, "I am a heading!" (A big problem with a lot of newsletters is that you can't distinguish a heading from regular text.)

■ Put the name of your newsletter on the left or right if you want to avoid the boring balance of centering.

Figure 5.18

Most newsletters are too perfectly balanced. They use two columns to support a solid roof—the logo and name, plus volume number, date, and publisher, all in a big blob at the top, right in the center. Balance may provide the foundation for a strong building, but when we eyeball a design, symmetry is picked up very quickly and then easily ignored. Putting the title a little off-center creates a more interesting composition.

- If you make your newsletter name into a piece of art, you can stack it along the left-hand side of the newsletter as a vertical banner, to get it out of the way; and focus on your lead headline, as shown in Figure 5.19.

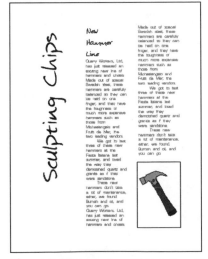

Figure 5.19 *Image from PrintArtist from Sierra.*

■ Don't use a lot of lines to separate the newsletter name from the rest of the newsletter.

Horizontal lines, often known as rules, split up the page and draw attention to themselves, leading readers to ignore your actual text. Not good. Overused, they act like prison bars, preventing readers from reaching the text.

■ Avoid graphics in the nameplate area, but if you must have a logo, keep it as simple as you can.

The details that make a corporate seal interesting on a stock certificate are as annoying as gnats when you shrink the seal down to an inch-and-a-half diameter. Those little lines do not reproduce well. People keep coming back to the fuzzy, jagged lines, trying to make sense out of them; after a while, the image acts like an itchy scab that one can't help picking at. Are they reading your newsletter at those times? No. So just boldface the name in text, and skip the art if you can.

■ In the nameplate area, include the name, volume number, issue number, date, and, if you really must, a motto or slogan.

The motto can reflect your main theme ("Campaigning for a clean environment") or your audience ("For shipping professionals"). Avoid putting your corporate name into the nameplate area, because its presence tends to conflict with, or overshadow, your newsletter's name. If you feel you must put your organization name into the nameplate area, keep it as small as the smallest nearby text, such as the slogan.

Slimming those columns down

Newspaper columns are among the most readable arrangements of text around. The narrow width makes skimming easy. If the font size of your running text is also large enough (say 10 to 14 points), and you accept standard line spacing in your word processor, these columns can offer a lot of information without straining the eye or causing misreadings. By contrast, paragraphs full of long low lines of text that creep across the entire page can undermine easy reading, as when the eye swings back to start a new line and accidentally rereads the same line again or skips a line, or one forgets the train of thought while the eye wanders.

■ For text, choose three columns with plenty of "air" between them.

■ Avoid vertical lines. Use space, not lines, to separate columns.

■ Make most art fit neatly into one, two, or three columns.

On the other hand, too large type in narrow columns produces ugly ragged margins, as shown in Figure 5.20.

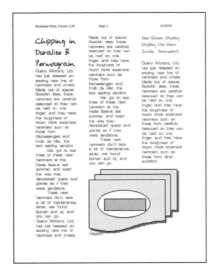

Figure 5.20

You can put a box around art, and as long as the box extends to the edges of columns, the art will look as if it belongs. Art that intrudes partway into a column poses a problem. You could just leave the rest of the space in that part of the column blank, which looks weird. Or you could wrap text around the art, which leaves you with a word, another word, part of a word, a syllable, and so on, next to the art — hard to read and embarrassing to look at.

Announcing your contents

Even in a two-page newsletter, a table of contents helps readers anticipate what you are going to cover. Once you go beyond a few pages, a table of contents encourages people to open the newsletter and continue reading.

- If your newsletter has fewer than six articles, consider advertising them on the mailing address box — the first thing a reader sees in many cases — as shown in Figure 5.21.

- For a lot of articles, grab the first column on the left on the first page, and consider putting a little shading behind the text, in the same hue you've chosen for the title and headings, but a lot lighter (so you can read the black text on top of it).

Don't demote your table of contents, or slip it in just anywhere. The table of contents advertises the value of your newsletter. Even though *you* know every article word for word, because you rewrote them so many times, the reader picks up your newsletter while going through the mail, wonders what is for lunch, skims the first page wondering, "Is this worth wasting my time on?" The table of contents says "Yes, this is interesting!"

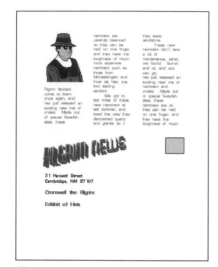

Figure 5.21 *Images from PrintArtist from Sierra.*

Choosing simple graphics, not fuzzy photos

You don't have to use photos. The most embarrassing parts of most newsletters are the photographs, many of which start life out of focus, a little blurred, and with the subject matter far, far away; the bad photo is then poorly reproduced, because the paper and the printer aren't good enough to show the details. This double curse makes the newsletter itself look amateurish. So do what your printer — and your paper — can do.

- If your printer can handle photos on the paper you intend to use for your newsletter, great: just get good pictures!

The worst in-house newsletters show photos of people pressed together behind a table, their faces bright from a flash, the rest of the room in darkness. Even when you know the people in the picture, you sometimes have to read the caption to figure out who is who. Skip these nightmarish, self-congratulatory photos.

Avoid complex backgrounds and foregrounds that might distract attention from the subject, as the wire fence gets in the way of the cat in Figure 5.22. Get plenty of light. Go for a lot of contrast between the bright areas and the dark areas, as shown in Figure 5.23. And move in close — very close, as shown in Figure 5.24, where we land right in the pile of lemons.

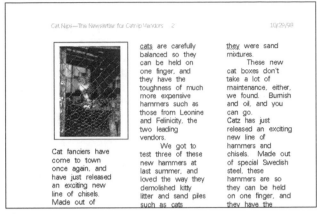

Figure 5.22 *Image from PrintArtist from Sierra.*

Figure 5.23 *Image from PrintArtist from Sierra.*

Figure 5.24 *Image from PrintArtist from Sierra.*

■ If your printer does best with clip art graphics, use those.

For any issue, try to select all your graphics from the same collection, so they have a uniform look, as shown in Figure 5.25. When graphics come from different sources, your newsletter may look as if it were assembled without much thought or taste; the clash between artistic styles jumps off the page for the reader, more dramatically than it does for you, because you are thinking theme, subject, and message, but the reader just opens the page, and sees the clash, right off. Loosen your grip on the idea the picture should illustrate, broaden your reach, so you can get a uniform series of images.

Figure 5.25 *Images from PrintArtist from Sierra.*

■ If your printer has trouble with the more subtle color combinations and thin lines of some clip art, consider pure line art (all you see are black lines on white backgrounds), as shown in Figure 5.26, or images with blocks of one color or another, not a range.

■ Put a caption under each picture if it really illustrates something. If your graphics are just for fun, more decorative than meaningful, you don't need to identify them with a caption.

■ A box often helps set off a picture.

You can put a box around art using borders or the drawing tools that come with your word processor. This might be better than doing so in a graphics program, because with the word processor you can cheat a little to adjust to the surroundings; for instance, if you see that the picture is a little smaller than the column, you can make the box exactly fit the column margins, neatening things up.

Figure 5.26 *Images from PrintArtist from Sierra.*

Creating a mailing area

The last page gets folded over to form an area in which you put the mailing label, postage, and return address — plus a teaser for a few articles, if you want. So the key question is: How are you going to fold your newsletter?

Easiest is to fold the newsletter in half. That gives you tons of room for your return address, and so on.

Trickier is a trifold, because no two people fold a newsletter in thirds the same way, and you very much want the fold to correspond to the division between running text and the mailing area. If the fold bends your text, your newsletter looks amateurish.

■ Leave plenty of room between the bottom of your running text and the beginning of the mailing area.

You might use a horizontal rule to put an end to the running text. That works. But make sure that you leave at least half an inch between that and the fold, so there's no possibility of overlap.

■ Keep your return address and article teasers well over on the left, and up, up, up, so they do not dribble down to the bottom of the page (see Figure 5.27).

The post office gets touchy about return addresses that spill over into the recipient's address area. In fact, if your text goes too far to the right, or too far down, you may get your newsletter back in your lap.

■ Leave plenty of white space for the mailing label.

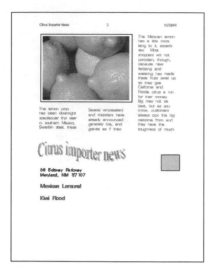

Figure 5.27 *Image from PrintArtist from Sierra.*

Don't put a rectangle in, showing where the label should go. Inevitably, someone will lay the label over the box, which looks sloppy.

Tip

If you do regular mailings of several hundred newsletters, consult with the post office about getting permission to print the postage on the newsletter. You have to sort the newsletters by ZIP code and fill out a form every time you do the mailing, but you don't have to individually stamp each one.

Creating certificates and awards

People love getting awards, even though they laugh them off. Most graphics packages come with some predesigned awards, and mail-order vendors such as Cheap Sheets and Paper Direct offer predesigned stiff cardboard forms with bright borders, for you to fill in. You can create your own awards, though, so they mirror your own business.

- Use a font that looks like handwriting, so it reminds people of a graduation certificate, as shown in Figure 5.28.

- Set your page in landscape orientation, so it is wider than it is tall.

- Put the first phrase (such as "Employee of the Month," or "Our Customers Thank You!") about a quarter of the way down the page, in text about 36–48 points.

- Put the winner's name in the biggest font you can use that will still fit on one line. (This *must* be the biggest item on the certificate).

- Add a date at the lower left, and your company name at the lower right.

- Put your name at the bottom left.
- Sign with a dramatic flourish, very large, with a colored pen.

Figure 5.28 *Created in PrintArtist from Sierra.*

Polishing Health Care

If you're a health-care professional, you know how different your clients are, and how important it is to give them individual attention. Pharmaceutical companies and other vendors offer spectacularly printed "information packets" to pass along to your patients, warning against gum disease, diabetes, and unwanted pregnancy. Occasionally, though, you need to supplement these generic handouts with your own instructions. And, in an increasingly competitive environment, you need to emphasize your own personal contribution, so to establish a closer bond with your patients — from toddler to senior citizen — you can strengthen that personal connection by making your own colorful reminders, office accents, instructions, and awards.

Creating personal reminders

You've seen it happen a thousand times. You tell patients what to do, they do it a few times, and then they forget, or get confused, or trail off whatever practice you've tried to get them to establish. Perhaps you should put them in the center of your reminder.

- Create a generic reminder, such as a mini-poster urging kids to brush their teeth (see Figure 5.29) — and then add a place for the patient's name, printing a new one for each patient to take home and tape up in the bathroom or bedroom.

You could print these out the night before the appointment, as part of patient preparation. The fact that the poster has the child's name on it makes this much more immediate and personal than a booklet from a toothpaste company. Children will probably think you made it just for them while they were in the chair.

You can add art or calendar graphics at the bottom, too, if you think the patient will like checking off a job well done each day. You can show them how to do this. This kind of activity always engages children — and less cynical adults.

Figure 5.29 *Created in PrintArtist Craft Factory from Knowledge Adventure.*

■ For grownups who need to "hear" your voice of authority , to remember to take their pill sets every day, put a picture of a doctor or nurse at the bottom of the page, as shown in Figure 5.30 — and then sign it in their presence, just as you would a prescription, giving it a very personal authority.

■ Create a template with your message. Then, take a digital picture of the patient, and while the patient is in the office, drop that picture into your reminder, as shown in Figure 5.31.

Adults often nod knowingly when you tell them to do something such as wear a hat when they go out in the sun, but few do so. A reminder with them in the picture will amuse them, and take the discussion a little beyond, "Well, I know I ought to, but..." Ask them to put this poster up wherever they will see it at the crucial moment — before going outside, or exercising, or whatever. For instance, you might remind asthmatics to use their inhaler before going to play football by showing the patient's face and an inhaler, along with the message in text.

Figure 5.30 *Created in PrintArtist Craft Factory from Knowledge Adventure.*

Figure 5.31 *Created in PrintArtist Craft Factory from Knowledge Adventure.*

■ Use images you create as part of your work, for a shocking reminder.

Our dentist uses a miniature TV camera to take pictures of our teeth. Projected on the screen, these images show exactly how ugly and vast a cavity can be. What if he were to drop one of these pictures into a reminder to floss? The revolting nature of the image would certainly prod us into flossing. Of course, our dentist is too kind to do this with our tooth shots, but less abrasive images might include an X-ray run through a scanner and dropped into a reminder to take anti-allergy pills every day. Similarly, a snapshot of a sprain taken while it is still red might help a teenage athlete remember to tape his or her ankle before school, if headed with the warning, "Don't let this happen again! Tape, tape, tape!"

Making instructions easy to follow

When you start to practice in your field, you assume that if you tell a patient to do something, the patient will do it. Gradually, you discover the many confusions, resistances, and habits that get in the way. You may conclude that the only way some patients will remember something is if you go to their house every day and remind them.

Well, instead of making the trip, you can send your personal instruction sheet, in which you talk to them face-to-face — photographically. By individualizing your reminders for particular patients, creating a direct statement from you, you offer them a personalized document, and you probably increase the chance that they will post it at home and follow it.

1. Put your own photograph at the bottom of the reminder, as a kind of signature, so the patient sees that these instructions are really coming from you, as shown in Figure 5.32.

Figure 5.32

2. Write the instructions simply, putting each action in a numbered step that is at least 16 points, so it can be read at arm's length, as shown in Figure 5.33.

1. Put foot up on pillows.

2. Put 8-10 ice cubes in plastic bag.

3. Put cotton cloth over foot.

4. Lay icebag on top of cloth for 10 minutes.

Figure 5.33

Numbering the steps makes them more efficient — people are about a third more likely to follow numbered steps than unnumbered steps. Making the text larger than normal helps the slow reader, the nervous reader — and anyone who may be reading the paper while it lies on a counter. Instructions are not always read like a novel. So you want the key elements to stand out. Put any explanations into separate paragraphs, in smaller text, and indented, so that the patient understands at a glance that these paragraphs are less important.

3. Leave a space at the top left.

4. Capture the patient's photo and put at the top left, adding names, and a title, as shown in Figure 5.34.

5. Print out your new, personalized instructions, and go over them step by step, getting agreement, and probing to make sure you are understood.

Now this is between the two of you. It is not a case of abstract ideas floating down from some faceless authority figure, or dimly recalled advice from last week. Because both of you have a face, the instructions take on the flavor of a conversation, albeit a bit one-sided.

If you anticipate some resistance on the patient's part, or sense a tendency to slack off after the worst symptoms go away, make this into a contract between you and the patient. Have the patient sign his or her name under the photo, and then, with some fanfare, sign your name under your own photo. Lending this kind of formality to the instructions helps ensure that the patient will follow them, perhaps as long as necessary.

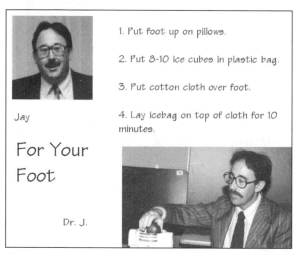

Figure 5.34

Tour of the OR

If you have a young patient coming in for surgery, the hospital probably offers some kind of tour, displaying hospital gowns and letting children put on surgical masks and gloves, to lessen the shock of unfamiliarity when they come in for the operation.

You might want to supplement this tour with your own booklet. Build the booklet in advance, and then put the child's face on the front, dressed up in a mask, with a title like "Billy has an operation."

Use pictures of yourself walking into the room where the child will get on the gurney, putting on a surgical gown, wearing a mask, washing up, and so on. Put a sentence or two underneath each picture.

Then, after you have printed the child's picture on the front of the booklet, go over it, event by event, with the child, answering questions that come up. The pictures make it easier for the child to understand what you are talking about, whether or not the family has taken a hospital tour.

Later, parents can go over the book several times with the child, who can play with a sample mask and gloves, if you can provide those. By making yourself part of the picture book, you provide a rehearsal of what is going to happen, making it less frightening, and assuring the child that, despite the weird outfit, there is a friendly face behind the mask.

Relaxing your patients

Dentists know where their patients are looking while the drill buzzes. So right above the dental chair you often find three or four posters showing dreamy land-scapes or calm vistas. Depending on your practice, you may want to imitate this effort to lower anxiety. Too many medical offices are decorated by interior deco-rators, which means that the prints on the wall are carefully color-coordinated, but meaningless to the patient. If you take pictures on vacation, or collect clip art images you like, consider making large prints of these and positioning them on the walls patients see most often.

■ Choose a landscape you like, such as the one in Figure 5.35, so you can chat about your visit there.

Figure 5.35

■ Or pick something fuzzy such as the clouds seen in Figure 5.36, or mist, or the ocean at dawn.

■ Include at least one picture in which you look silly, such as Figure 5.37.

Sacrificing your dignity a little humanizes you, and shows that you have a life outside of the office — always amazing to patients who are used to the bureau-cracies of big city or county hospitals, or HMOs.

■ To make these photos as large as posters, take your file to a quick-print store that has a printer that can generate images on glossy paper at sizes from two to four feet or more.

Figure 5.36

Figure 5.37

Many stores that service architects, engineers, and landscape designers have gigantic printers that can handle blueprints, and these companies often add printers that turn out full-color, glossy prints at these large sizes. Hewlett-Packard, for instance, offers a printer called a DesignJet, which can print posters on half a dozen different kinds of paper, ranging from heavy-weight paper for signs, through glossy and semi-glossy photographic papers to coated papers that will stay bright for 20 years indoors. These printers can even blow your image up so that, in strips, it can form a wall mural you could mount in your waiting room.

Activities for restless fingers

If you have a number of children waiting, you know that your collection of toys quickly gets boring for them. You might put together a few paper activities to keep the kids occupied; they'll be amused, and their parents will be grateful.

■ If you can stand flying objects in your airspace, draw a simple paper airplane like the one shown in Figure 5.38. It's not educational, but it keeps kids under 12 busy for ten or fifteen minutes, testing it out.

Figure 5.38 *Airplane made in PrintArtist Craft Factory from Knowledge Adventure.*

▪ Create a simple tic-tac-toe game like the one shown in Figure 5.39, laminate it and hand it out with washable-ink pens, so the sheet can be reused over and over.

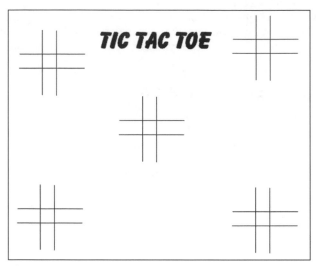

Figure 5.39

▪ If you make it a practice to take every patient's picture on the first visit, you can furnish small photos for finger puppets for the kids — as shown in Figure 5.40. Hand them out with scissors and tape, so children can make a puppet out of their own faces.

Figure 5.40

Rewarding good behavior

Yes, even grown-ups get a kick out of being recognized for success, whether it's for maintaining cholesterol levels, recovering from gum disease, or keeping the weight down. If you add a patient's photo, your award will probably go up on their refrigerator, reinforcing the desired behavior.

- Use your paint program to draw spotlights or open theater curtains, to highlight your star, as shown in Figure 5.41.

- Use a hand-written font, so the award reminds people of a graduation certificate.

- Put the person's photo in the center of the page, a little above the middle, in the place of honor.

- Add their name underneath.

- Toward the bottom, throw in the date and your name.

- Sign with a wide-tipped pen, with a flourish.

Figure 5.41 *Background created in Print Artist Craft Factory from Knowledge Adventure.*

Brightening the Classroom

Whether in preschool or high school, children and young adults enjoy a classroom that turns into a multimedia environment. Mobiles, artwork, bulletin boards, window decorations, and so on, all grab the students' wandering attention and refocuses it, filling their world with color and form, and letting them admire their own creations, hung from ceiling to floor. In the past, teachers have spent many hours in the copy room making up worksheets for kids to fill in; and they have spent, and continue to spend, their own money to buy posters, art-work, and books to follow various themes, such as Alaska or the rainforest; and teachers have done their best to make drawings children could use as the basis of their own work. Now, thanks to clip art and the Web, plus color printing, the computer can help teachers and students fill their environment with even more diverse objects, a lot more quickly and conveniently than before.

Identifying classroom chores with pictures

If you are teaching students to take responsibility for their classroom, you may be handing out assignments every Monday or, if you are brave, you may be switching around who does what chore every day. Many teachers use poster-boards with glued-on pockets of cardboard bearing names like Blackboard and Sink, slipping students' names into those pockets, as a reminder. You can make this kind of chore board a lot more vivid and appealing if you add images to reinforce the name of the task, and photos to identify who should be doing what. Here are some suggestions along those lines:

■ Use clip art of the tool for a chore, as shown in Figure 5.42.

Figure 5.42 *Image from ClickArt from Broderbund.*

■ Put the task next to the tool, as shown in Figure 5.43.

Figure 5.43 *Image from ClickArt from Broderbund.*

■ Show what has to be worked on, as shown in Figure 5.44.

Figure 5.44 *Image from ClickArt from Broderbund.*

■ Using text and images to make pockets for each chore, make up a laminated card for each student, with name and photo (as shown in Figure 5.45), to drop into the pocket, so they can see what they have to do this week.

Figure 5.45

■ Slip the student's card into the chore's pocket, as shown in Figure 5.46.

Figure 5.46 *Image from ClickArt from Broderbund.*

Advertising a book

Sometimes you may want your class or a reading group to go through one book over the course of a week or so; or you may have another book-related assignment that everyone in the class is supposed to accomplish in a given period of time. Here is a way to advertise that goal:

1. Scan the front cover and put that at the top of a piece of posterboard.

2. Scan a few illustrations and arrange those underneath.

3. Use huge type for the title.

4. Make another piece of text, "Book of the Week," cut it out, and place it diagonally across the posterboard.

5. Hang a class list underneath the posterboard, so students can place a giant checkmark on the list when they fulfill your requirements.

One fact a day

Learning comes gradually, and many teachers like to establish a routine for learning one new thing every day, or studying a person or place for a week, while the attendant facts sink in. Use color and image to reinforce the names, words, people, or events.

■ Put the word right into the picture, as shown in Figure 5.47 and Figure 5.48.

Figure 5.47 *Image from ClickArt from Broderbund.*

Figure 5.48 *Image from ClickArt from Broderbund.*

■ If the picture is dark, use white text so it stands out, as shown in Figure 5.49, the Person of the Week.

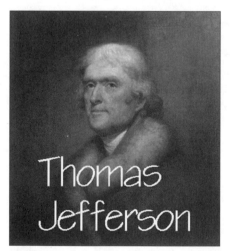

Figure 5.49 *Image from ClickArt from Broderbund.*

■ Look for line art that you can duplicate for students to color in, such as to learn the Plant of the Week, as shown in Figure 5.50.

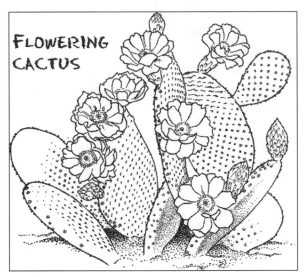

Figure 5.50 *Image from ClickArt from Broderbund.*

Covering the school's books to protect them

If your school insists that students cover their books, you can turn that chore into a fun way of exploring a theme through art.

1. Pick art that lets you talk about the theme as students color it in, as shown in Figure 5.51.

2. Look for several images, each quite distinct in shape, but related in subject matter.

   For instance, in Figure 5.52, we have one shape, a circular frame, showing the Victorian woman reading That shape stands out distinctly in contrast to the rectangle enclosing the woodcut of a Renaissance man reading an early book (refer to Figure 5.51). The bookcase in the background also gives you a chance to talk about the spread of a popular press.

Figure 5.51 *Image from ClickArt from Broderbund.*

Figure 5.52 *Image from ClickArt from Broderbund.*

3. Urge students to cut out several of these, color them in, and glue them on the front and back of large sheets, leaving enough paper to fold over and tape inside the book, as shown in Figure 5.53.

Figure 5.53 *Images from ClickArt from Broderbund.*

Such makeshift covers will disintegrate within a few months because they are not as tough as the covers available from office supply stores. But by then you can have a new set of images ready for students, on another theme.

Honoring diversity

Where did you come from? What ethnic strains do you take pride in, in your family? With the current emphasis on diversity and pride in difference, teachers are often called on to discuss ethnic backgrounds in a way that draws students together, rather than isolating them from each other. Some teachers like to have students diagram their family tree on the blackboard, in their best handwriting. But we suggest you offer cutouts of a series of similar images, such as leaves, that they can paste onto a gigantic tree, or squares they can put together into a quilt.

■ Look for a series of similar clip art subjects, such as the leaves shown in Figure 5.54.

Students can cut them out and color them, adding their ethnic origins; and then everyone gets to glue them on a giant tree.

■ For more variety and personal expression, offer a range of trees, bushes, ferns, and flowers, and let students color them in, creating an unnatural, but original, forest growing from their roots.

You can see a part of such a forest in Figure 5.55, where a South American fern grows next to a Hawaiian palm and a Norwegian spruce.

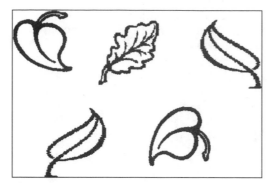

Figure 5.54 *Images from ClickArt from Broderbund.*

Figure 5.55 *Images from ClickArt from Broderbund.*

Creating number lines (1, 2, 3 kangaroos)

Number lines stretch around the classroom, going from one to over a hundred, so students can see the distance between 10, 20, 30, and so on. The regularity of the rhythm, the steady beat of numbers going on around the room, helps children understand that two units over here are the same as two units over there, and starts them on their way to understanding the interchangeability of units. One is one is one, whether it is on the left or the right.

To add a little spice to activities such as bean counting, consider making the number line a line of similar images — trees, kangaroos, or sports figures.

■ Under your number line, create a second line of pockets, made out of two strips of paper: a wide one on the bottom taped to the wall, and a thinner one taped to the wide paper at the bottom, but open at the top, to receive images. A good size for the pocket is the width of a little person's hand.

■ Ransack your clip art collection for a series of ten very similar images, such as those in Figure 5.56.

Figure 5.56 *Images from ClickArt from Broderbund.*

■ Put a border around each image, print ten copies, and have students cut them into individual cards, like the one shown in Figure 5.57.

■ Have the students drop the cards into the pockets following a pattern, such as surfer, ballerina, hockey player, and so on.

They've already worked on patterns by making trains of different-colored rods, beans, beads, and buttons. Explain that you want the same pattern repeated over and over. Then talk about who ended up as Number 1, 11, 21, and so on. To gauge the distance between two numbers, have students remove all the images in-between and count them. To show that the figures are interchangeable, shuffle them, and have students lay them out in a new pattern, so that they do not start thinking of the surfer as Number One. Like a unit, an image can fall anywhere on the line.

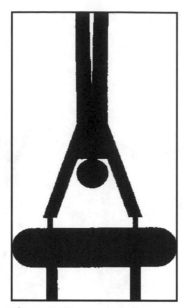

Figure 5.57 *Image from ClickArt from Broderbund.*

Repopulating the rain forest (animals in trees and bushes on murals)

Unless you live near a real forest, it's hard for children to imagine how it functions; and a rain forest, the center of so many elementary school modules, is even more alien than the typical North American national park, the model most of us have of an extensive forest. You've shown the videos, looked at the pictures in books, and talked and talked. Perhaps it's time for a mural, or a play with a virtual rain forest as the backdrop. Following are some suggestions for how to engage the whole class in constructing a new rain forest.

- Put the images of several very different leaves onto one page, or enlarge a clump of leaves to fill a page, as shown in Figure 5.58. Then print out half a dozen copies, and have the Leaf Team cut them out and decorate them with images of bugs.

- If you have a photo of a tree trunk or two, print some of those out for the background (see Figure 5.59).

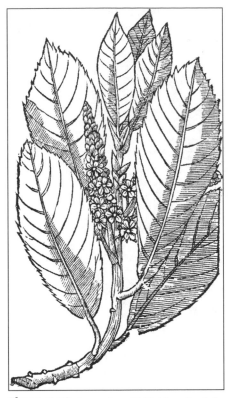

Figure 5.58 *Image from ClickArt from Broderbund.*

Figure 5.59 *Image from ClickArt from Broderbund.*

■ Grab images of bushes, ferns, and flowers (see Figure 5.60)—whatever plants might live on the forest floor—and enlarge them, providing lots of copies to the Forest Floor team.

Figure 5.60 *Image from ClickArt from Broderbund.*

■ Collect several images (such as the ones shown in Figures 5.61 and 5.62) showing animals, reptiles, and birds, some of whom might actually live in a rain forest, and enlarge them to fill up a single sheet each, printing several copies of each, for the Critters Team.

■ On the paper or wall you are going to use as a background, draw two barely visible lines to divide the forest floor from the middle range, and to show where the forest canopy begins, at the top.

■ Have the students paste their images up in waves. Start with the critters, then the forest floor, and then the leaves from the middle to the top, and (probably) a few more birds and animals on top of all that.

Figure 5.61 *Image from ClickArt from Broderbund.*

Have the animals and birds peek out of the undergrowth, even if they are mostly hidden.

■ Hang a few tree trunks from the ceiling, a few feet in front of your wall, and glue leaves all over them, to give some depth to the scene.

Figure 5.62 *Image from ClickArt from Broderbund.*

Giant flash cards for dinosaurs

Dinosaurs fascinate young children—real monsters with claws, and their own theme park. You may have one bright kid who can rattle off all those long names, but most kids have trouble learning anything other than the stars of Jurassic Park. If you're doing a module on dinosaurs, consider making flash cards like the one shown in Figure 5.63 on full-size sheets of paper, and then have students color them and use them for Dino Lotto. The rule is that, in order to pick up a pair of matching dinos, the child must correctly pronounce the name.

Figure 5.63 *Image from ClickArt from Broderbund.*

If you can find a photocopier to enlarge to poster size, make one copy of each card to put up on the wall. Let children color these on special occasions.

And keep the card trick in mind for any lessons in which you want students to learn a variety of unusual new names or terms, such as Figure 5.64, showing a Corgi, which is Welsh for "short dog."

Figure 5.64 *Image from ClickArt from Broderbund.*

Putting planets in orbit around the room

When your class hits the unit on astronomy, you may want to make stars and planets more tangible, more real, by having students build a set of the planets, and ring them around a sun, to make a solar system.

1. Find an image of each planet, plus the sun and the moon.

2. For each image, type the name of the celestial object, as shown in Figure 5.65. Remember: You can use white type if the image is dark.

Figure 5.65 *Image from ClickArt from Broderbund.*

3. Print out two color copies of each object.

4. Have the students cut out each of the two images and paste them on both sides of a circle of posterboard.

5. Use thread to hang each object from the ceiling grid, in the correct order, beginning with the sun.

Discuss how far apart these objects really are. Have students walk from the sun to Pluto, estimating how long it takes for a ray of sunlight to get there. And enjoy watching the planets spin around and around as a breeze hits them.

Documenting that science fair project

Yes, when it comes to science fair projects, we're always looking for a good hypothesis, scientific methods, and quantifiable results. But most science fairs seem to crescendo in a gym full of posterboards explaining how to test for the best laundry detergent, or why sugar is bad for your teeth.

Often we see the parents' hands at work, trying to make a banal experiment seem spectacular, while another child's good work gets little attention because of poor presentation: it is squiggly, illegible, or a little dirty. Once you've explained the rules and students have started on their projects, you might want to demonstrate some successful presentations, because most students rarely think about that aspect of their projects.

■ Start with three foam-core panels.

Foam-core boards are cardboard on the outside, sandwiching a very lightweight plastic foam, so they are quite stiff. You can get special sets of these boards already taped together, so the three boards stand up on their own as a unit, making a kind of cubicle for the project. Avoid traditional posterboard; it wilts, falls over, has to be laid flat, and therefore loses all oomph.

■ In a word processor, use page breaks to separate each section of the report, putting a large (72 points or so) and brightly colored heading on each page: Hypothesis, Purpose, Materials Used, Methods, Results, and Conclusion.

To make the display easier to follow, each of these headings should be the same height, font, and color, so viewers can quickly spot the sequence of topics.

■ Devote one sheet of paper to the hypothesis, in letters approximately 48 points high — a little smaller than the heading itself, but big enough so anyone can read the text.

For many projects, the hypothesis can be in the form of a question: Which human vitamin makes beans grow faster? If you are strict, the hypothesis should be one sentence: I hypothesize that Vitamin E makes beans grow faster than any other vitamin supplement. If you need to explain the reasoning behind the hypothesis, or the motivation for an unusual project, put that text in a separate paragraph, at least 36 points, so that casual viewers can read it across the table.

■ If you have a Purpose section, keep the background and context as short as possible.

■ Once you get to the section on Materials Used, use a series of close-up photos or clip art illustrations, such as the one shown in Figure 5.66, adding 24-point captions identifying each image.

■ For Methods, show photos of each major stage (see Figure 5.67 and Figure 5.68), adding a one- or two-sentence caption.

Figure 5.66

Figure 5.67

Figure 5.68

- In the section on Results, show the results with photos; concrete evidence plunked in the middle of your table; or numbers ranked in rows and columns, and then turned into a full-color graph, as shown in Figure 5.69.

The physical evidence makes a project convincing. When Noah tested which formula for play dough was eaten fastest by our dogs, he displayed four plastic jars with the remaining play dough, so kids could taste each flavor for themselves. When he tested which formula made the strongest adobe brick, he put the winner on the table, in front of his display, so people could see the straw in the mud.

- Make the type announcing the Conclusion just as big as the Hypothesis, to close off the project.

- Lay all these materials out from one panel to the next, trying to focus the Method on the center panel (even if you have to spill over onto the right-hand panel at the end, resolutely shoving the Results and Conclusion onto the right-hand panel).

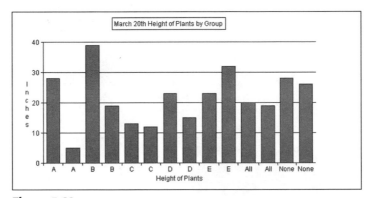

Figure 5.69

Point out to students that this sequence is chronological. First they had an idea, or hypothesis; then they refined their purpose, got their supplies together, did the experiment, came up with results, and finally drew one or more conclusions. So, as we read from left to right, and top to bottom, we go through the full exercise of a scientific experiment.

Rewarding success

From basic arithmetic through complex equations, math means solving a lot of problems, and, alas, for teachers, many tests to grade. To encourage students, many teachers set some kind of standard to meet, such as 50 multiplication problems in 5 minutes. Then, when a child actually gets 100 percent, the event is announced and the child is handed some tangible reward. But what kind of reward? You can make personalized rewards for students to take home and show to their families — if you plan ahead.

■ For each child, put a personal congratulations on top of a suitable image, as shown in Figure 5.70; or next to it, as shown in Figure 5.71; and then print it, so you are ready the moment that child succeeds in meeting your criterion.

Figure 5.70 *Image from ClickArt from Broderbund.*

Figure 5.71 *Image from ClickArt from Broderbund.*

■ Take a photograph of every child and slip it into a clip art image, to make the award even more personal, as shown in Figure 5.72.

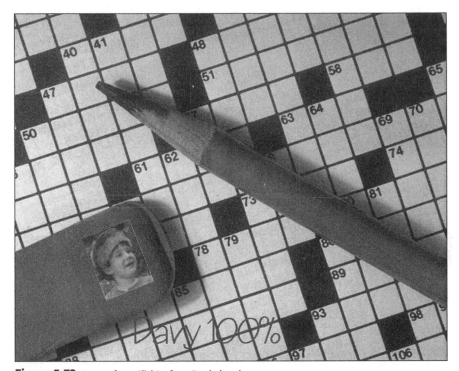

Figure 5.72 *Image from ClickArt from Broderbund.*

Inviting family and friends to the school play (flyers and posters)

The secret to making sure that your important newsletter is really read by parents is simple: include their kid's picture. Parents will forgive typos, misspellings, smarmy slogans, and other nonsense that principals like to put in their newsletters if pictures of the students are included. Better, though, is a series of individual shots, making each child a star.

■ Start the year off by taking each child's picture.

■ Plan several issues of your class newsletter for each semester, with the aim of getting each child's picture in at least once each term.

■ Invent reasons for mentioning the students, such as "The Blue Math Group," "Hall Monitors of the Month," and, if all else fails, "This Month's Bright Spots."

■ Put the student's name underneath the picture, in a font as big as you can manage, without competing with your headlines, as shown in Figure 5.73.

Figure 5.73 *Images from ClickArt from Broderbund.*

Tip

Want to encourage parents to help in the classroom? When a parent does participate, take a snapshot and include it with a big caption, "Thanks to Deirdre's Mom for Her Help on Our Field Trip." You'll soon get more volunteers.

Marketing Your Organization

Going digital can make marketing work for small businesses, volunteer organizations, nonprofits, and so on—the very groups who can't afford old-fashioned marketing, which focused on TV commercials, full-color magazine ads, and 20-page newspaper inserts at the holidays. Taking an electronic approach lets you reuse the same logo on letterheads, business cards, brochures, reports, invoices, and forms without having to pay a professional designer to create all those items separately. Going electronic means marketing based on your strengths — you know your clients and customers; you can customize your pitch so it really speaks to individuals.

At least, that's what we've found in our home business. When layout meant attaching pieces of art and text to cardboard using a wax stick, you had to create each communication from scratch, each time — the whole process was extremely labor-intensive, and cost a lot of time and money. And so everyone figured that they would use the same strategy for every customer, as with every marketing piece aimed at a mass audience, not individuals.

We've found, though, that the computer speeds up the design process, allows customization for particular people within our audience, and lowers the cost. Of course, no amount of software can give you the taste and experience of a professional designer, but if you keep your marketing simple, you can do your own design work. And remember, you already have an advantage over an outside designer. You know your own work, your industry, your competitors, and your clients, in a way that no one else can. You already have positioned yourself within that world.

■ You've spent a lot of energy coming up with a name for your organization. That name is your brand, your promise, your unique identity, as shown in Figure 5.74. Ad maestro Jerry della Femina used to boast that he once slipped a client's name into a 30-second commercial 19 times. Your name is the heart of your marketing.

Figure 5.74 *Image from PrintMaster Gold from Mindscape.*

■ You know who you're talking to. You've discarded certain markets, certain potential customers, certain arenas of competition. You've picked your world, positioning yourself already, as a reptile company does in Figure 5.75.

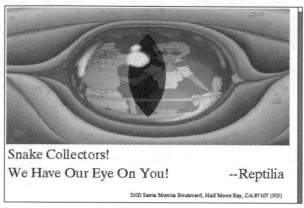

Figure 5.75 *Image from PrintMaster Gold from Mindscape.*

■ You know how your clients or customers measure quality. You understand that no amount of marketing can make up for sloppiness, inaccuracy, delay, lack of consideration, impoliteness, or poor work. You have worked furiously to make your product or service excellent. You aim high (see Figure 5.76).

Figure 5.76 *Image from PrintMaster Gold from Mindscape.*

What you may not have is a marketing plan. A marketing plan doesn't have to be an elaborate production like the hundred-page business plan you formulate when you are looking for a bank loan. Your do-it-yourself marketing plan simply answers questions like the following:

- What concrete, measurable result do you want to achieve with your marketing? Of course, number one should be increasing profit or return on investment.

- Whom exactly do you have to talk to in order to achieve that result (beyond customers, consider clients, vendors, suppliers, middlemen, the community)?

- What benefits do you offer people? What do they get out of working with you, buying from you?

- What is your USP (Unique Selling Proposition) — the way you differentiate yourselves from competitors? Have you put this into a theme song? A phrase you repeat over and over, on all your literature?

- What kind of person do you want to portray yourself as? Or what kind of people are you as a group? What characteristics do you want to emphasize? What tone do you want to take?

- How much money are you going to spend on marketing, as a percent of your gross revenue? Yes, you need a budget, but using your computer and your own experience, you can probably keep this to 5 to 15 percent of gross, depending on what market you're in.

Notice that this plan doesn't specify what form your marketing will take. You have to experiment to find out. You've probably already been doing some things that work, and are wondering about others. In the following sections we'll give you some ideas for sprucing up the kind of vehicles you've been using, and trying out a few more, following your bare-bones marketing plan.

Picking your colors, font, and symbol

Color gets our attention. Adding color to a brochure expands its likely readership by as much as 40 percent. Used to distinguish the important from the unimportant, to group text and pictures by purpose, and to lead the eye from one highlight to another, color can improve readers' understanding of your points by as much as 75 percent. When you use color deliberately, people learn better, retain what they have learned, and recall it better.

So pick one color, or a simple color combination (no more than three colors), to embed in your logo, use in headings and running text, slap into the background, and generally make into your motif. What color is Coca-Cola? What does the Apple logo look like? IBM made its reputation as Big Blue from the color on its machines, boxes, and annual reports. Your color choice reflects and expresses your identity.

■ Experiment with the colors offered in your word processor. Write your organization name down several times, applying a different color to each one, as shown (alas, in black and white) in Figure 5.77. Which disappear into the white page? Which look garish, weird, ugly?

Figure 5.77 *Image from PrintMaster Gold from Mindscape.*

■ Try your favorite colors out at various sizes and with various backgrounds, as shown in Figures 5.78 and 5.79, which compare two colors against a photo. For instance, try them on your company name at 72 points, 36 points, 18 points, and 10 points. At all these sizes, does the name look okay in that color, on the white page? Or do you need to back it up with a contrasting color, to get the full impact? (That's okay for title pages, logos, report covers, and so on.)

Figure 5.78 *Image from PrintMaster Gold from Mindscape.*

Figure 5.79 *Image from PrintMaster Gold from Mindscape.*

Do you have a logo—an emblem or symbol that represents you? Just putting your name on a poster is good, but even better is having an icon next to it. On your computer screen, there's a reason for all those icons representing different tools and commands. At first they seem like hieroglyphics. But after you find out what one does, you begin to reach for it automatically. The concentrated visual metaphor—the icon—takes on meaning the more often you use it. Similarly, if you put your logo on every bit of material you distribute, it will gradually sink in for your customers, triggering a way of remembering you—a shorthand, or mnemonic, for you.

■ If you don't have a logo, one way to start is to doodle with the letters of your name, joining them together like initials in embroidery, to form an interesting shape, like the logo for a toy company shown in Figure 5.80.

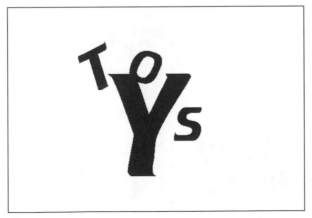

Figure 5.80 *Image made in PrintMaster Gold from Mindscape.*

■ You can put your entire name in a distinctive font, using that as a logo. For instance, a company that sells doors, cornices, railings, and other elements recovered from urban buildings being torn down came up with the font shown in Figure 5.81.

■ Skim through clip art showing various geometric shapes, to see if you can fit your name inside or around one, like the cabinet makers did in the example shown in Figure 5.82.

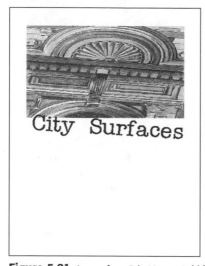

Figure 5.81 *Image from PrintMaster Gold from Mindscape.*

Figure 5.82 *Image from PrintMaster Gold from Mindscape.*

■ Look for clip art that relates to the tools you use or the services or products you provide, like the image shown in Figure 5.83 chosen by designers of special window treatments.

Figure 5.83 *Image from PrintMaster Gold from Mindscape.*

■ Try your draft logo out at sizes ranging from half an inch (for business cards, as shown in Figure 5.84), to headers on your Web pages, to full pages (to get an idea of how the logo would look on large posters such as the one shown in Figure 5.85, or on billboards)

Less dramatic, but equally important, are the font or fonts you are going to use for headings and running text. One or two fonts, used in bold, italic, big and little sizes, give you plenty of ways to emphasize or de-emphasize text, showing readers what is most important or should be read first, and demoting the less critical, or supplementary, material. The consistent use of one or two fonts reinforces your image. Their overtones, their look, their ease or difficulty — all work in a nonverbal way to indicate what you are like, and how you see your relationship with your reader.

Figure 5.84 *Image from PrintMaster Gold from Mindscape.*

Figure 5.85 *Image from PrintMaster Gold from Mindscape.*

Creating posters

Today you can take an electronic image to a service bureau to print on large pieces of paper, cloth, or Tyvek (that funny hybrid paper that is so hard to tear, when you get it as a wrapper for FedEx packages). You can make your own billboard on your computer if you want. More often, though, you need posters that measure three or four feet on a side. These work well in trade show booths, as backdrops for lectures, as decorations on your office walls, and as co-op ads with friendly resellers, clients, and suppliers.

- Distill your basic message into a single phrase or sentence—no more. The best posters use a variety of visuals to hammer home a single idea, and the idea is summarized by the slogan, as shown in Figure 5.86.

Figure 5.86 *Image from PrintMaster Gold from Mindscape.*

- Decide how many posters you want if you are creating a series, and then find that many images, all from the same artist (to ensure they are the same style), all in the same medium (photo, line art, oil painting), and all with a similar palette of colors, as shown in Figures 5.87, 5.88, and 5.89.

Figure 5.87 *Image from PrintMaster Gold from Mindscape.*

Figure 5.88 *Image from PrintMaster Gold from Mindscape.*

Figure 5.89 *Image from PrintMaster Gold from Mindscape.*

If you have beautiful images, you don't want to ruin them by stretching your text across the middle; that just makes your text an annoyance. On the other hand, if you have a large swath of unimportant darkness or brightness, like a deep shadow or a bland sky, try floating your words there, in a contrasting color (black on white, white on black, or, if you have corporate colors, something like yellow on a dark area, or blue on a light area).

- ■ If you decide that your text should not be superimposed on the image, then scout out part of the image to cut off, so you can have a blank background for your text, as shown in Figure 5.90.

If possible, slice at an angle, to make the overlay more interesting and more interconnected with the image than a simple band across the bottom or top. Adjust the size of your blank space to leave plenty of room for your text; you don't want to shove it into a corner.

- ■ Consider surrounding all of your posters with the same border, in your chosen colors, as in the series of posters shown in Figure 5.91.

Figure 5.90 *Image from PrintMaster Gold from Mindscape.*

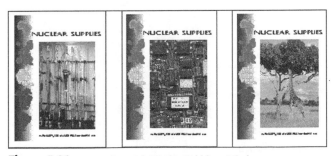

Figure 5.91 *Images from PrintMaster Gold from Mindscape.*

Remember that when you have a service bureau or copy center print your posters, the images can extend to the edge. They can also "bleed," that is, spill off the edge into space. That can be a nice effect if the picture—and your text—seem to work together, fitting together like pieces of a puzzle, or somehow sticking together. On the other hand, if your artwork and text seem to fly apart, you may want to impose a border, to keep everything together.

■ Apply your logo, usually in the corner, like a signature.

Report and proposal covers

If you make your money by writing reports or making proposals, you know how impressed clients can be by a dramatic cover. Often that's the only place you can get away with a little theatrics. But even a cover has work to do—announcing the subject, the request that resulted in the proposal or report, the date, the people or groups you are addressing, and, just as important, reflecting your own organization's identity. Each of these jobs gets its own area and treatment, so one message doesn't get blurred with another.

■ Divide the page into functional areas, such as title, Request for Proposal numbers, dates, the group you are addressing, and your organization, as shown in Figure 5.92.

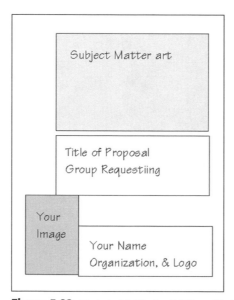

Figure 5.92 *Made in PrintMaster Gold from Mindscape.*

The traditional approach just stacks these elements from top to bottom, making each line a little smaller than the one above it, but having all of them centered. This approach results in an extremely boring, text-heavy cover, one that only a Pentagon staffer would love.

Of course, your title deserves the spotlight. That's the key job of the cover, after all — to tell people what is inside. And if you have a subtitle, that needs to live right next to or under the title. A natural location for this information is the top third, where the eye starts down the page.

But you can get more room for play if you devote the middle of the page to the title, using it to separate all the information about the receiving organization (and its referral number, invoice number, or whatever) from all the information about you.

- Choose two pieces of art — one reflecting the subject matter, the other showing you or your organization.

Both images need to be the same medium — both photographs, for example, or both line art. And both need to look as if they came from the same hand; in other words, a stunning photo of a shining white rocket with orange flames leaping from the nozzles won't work well with a grayed-out black-and-white photo of you on a bad day.

- Keep the subject matter art big, but off center, so it leads the eye toward the title, which can live above it, around it, or on top of it.

- Bend the text of the title to respond to the shape of the art representing the subject of the report or proposal.

- Put your own image at the start or end of the information about your company, as shown in Figure 5.93.

Figure 5.93 *Image from PrintMaster Gold from Mindscape.*

You can think of the picture of yourself as the speaker, the person who is announcing the subject, in which case you might put the image before the text about you. Or you can think of the picture of yourself as your visual signature, in which case you might put it at the bottom of the page, on the right or left.

■ Use your logo discreetly, without overpowering the report.

Sure, you prepared the report or proposal. But it ultimately belongs to the receiving organization, or at least they may think so. So try to incorporate your logo as if it were just an identifying mark, not a boast.

■ Use your own color combinations for the text — the boldest of colors for the title, and the least dramatic for your own organization name (as long as you can read that color on the background).

If your colors clash with those of the images you have chosen, settle for the most appealing colors within the images, so that the cover looks coherent.

■ Print in full color and cover with clear plastic.

If you are using photographs, pick a paper that has a glossy finish, such as HP Premium Photo Paper or one of the HP PhotoSmart photographic papers. For full-color graphics other than photos, use the HP Premium Inkjet Glossy Paper. A hard but clear plastic cover lets readers see your work, but protects it from scuffing.

Catalogs

A catalog may display rows and columns of data such as specs, product numbers, and dimensions, but a catalog comes alive with images of your products or services and descriptions that appeal to your customers. If you offer hundreds of products, for example, you probably keep track of them in a database, and some of your pages may just be reports generated from the database. If you have enough computer storage, your database may also include artwork and marketing descriptions for each product. Otherwise, you may want to use a word processor such as Word; a simple layout program such as PageMaker; or an industrial-strength document publishing program such as FrameMaker to ensure that the beauty pages come out neat, gorgeous, and consistent.

In general, you'll take your electronic files to a real printing company, because for quantities above a few hundred copies, they can do the job faster and cheaper than you can. Printing companies can also trim the paper, so you can create a design in which your cover images flow right out to the edge of the page (something you can't manage on most home printers), and you can choose a size other than 8.5" × 11" if you want. You also get a wider range of papers than you can find at an office supply store, which means you can work out your design on regular size paper on your own printer, and then ask the printing company to re-duce it in size, to fit on pages of a smaller trim size (the outer dimensions of the actual paper of the catalog). Their papers can also handle printing full-color photos on both sides, something not always possible at home. Generally, with professional printing you can achieve a reduction of 10–20 percent in the overall size of the text and photos, because thanks to better paper and hardware, the resolution is higher than you can manage at home. In other words, use your home printer to generate proof pages, at a slightly larger size than you will ultimately use for the catalog itself.

- ■ Decide trim size first. That's the actual size of the paper, after it's cut or trimmed.

8.5" × 11" is always convenient, because the printing company can use 17" × 11" sheets and fold them to be stapled together. Similarly, 4.25" × 5.5" is a low-cost, efficient trim size, because the company can just start with standard letter-size sheets. Sizes such as 7" × 8" or 7" × 9" require some trimming, but they are standard sizes and printing companies know how to deal with them. If you want any other dimensions, you should call three or four printing companies, and ask how much extra they charge for the size you want.

If you choose any size other than 8.5" × 11" decide beforehand if you want to work at that size in your software, and just imagine shrinking it all onto better paper than you have at home. Also consider if you want to shrink the margins on your document, so that what you print out is the same size as it will finally be. Remember, though, that if you shrink your margins and print on ordinary paper, you will be seeing a lot more white space around the edges of your pages than a user would; to get the right impression, cut the edges off along those margins.

- ■ Whatever software you use, think grid: How many columns are best for you?

One column works best for leisurely reads, like a rambling catalog of features for balloonists, as shown in Figure 5.94. One bookseller, for instance, writes four or five paragraphs about every book he remainders; as you move through the catalog, you get a sense of his taste, his interests, his love of these books. That's appropriate for selling small numbers of highly differentiated products. But what if you sell electronics, or pots and pans, or chili products? You need some standard organization, a routine way of presenting each item, so that readers can tell what text goes with what picture, where one product ends and the next begins, to allow the comparison of items without confusion. (Confusion closes catalogs.)

A two- or three-column grid (see Figures 5.95 and 5.96) works best for catalogs offering anywhere from a few dozen products to a thousand products. You can bounce art from left to right or make some art two columns wide. As long as you have white space between one product and the next, readers can still skim through without confusion.

- ■ Develop a standard page—the most routine page you can imagine—by deciding where art will be anchored and where text will appear, as shown in Figure 5.97.

Figure 5.94 *Made in PrintMaster Gold from Mindscape 6.3.*

Figure 5.95 *Made in PrintMaster Gold from Mindscape 6.3.*

Figure 5.96 *Made in PrintMaster Gold from Mindscape 6.3.*

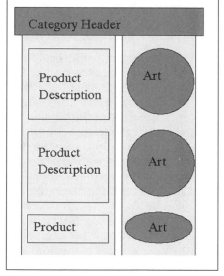

Figure 5.97 *Made in PrintMaster Gold from Mindscape 6.3.*

In design, art hangs from an anchor spot. That is, you figure out where it starts and how far it can expand before you cut it off. Often art starts at the top left corner of the space available, and extends to the right; it might be allowed to span one, two, or three columns.

In fine, highly refined designs, text lives in its own space, never ventures out of that area, and never or rarely allows art to intrude; the text may be limited to captions under the art, or constrained to the right-hand column — but wherever it is assigned, it stays put. In pedestrian designs, art frequently overrides the text, taking over its space for a while; and text sometimes pops up in an unexpected column. In lowbrow design, text pours around the art like mosquitoes around campers at twilight, resulting in an itchy page, and one that's hard to make out.

■ Put your order form in the middle, so it can easily be found and torn out.

Make the order form a self-mailer, like the one we describe a little later in this chapter, so people can fill it out and send it in without complicated folding, bending, tearing, or stuffing.

■ Make your cover echo the contents.

The best covers pick a single product to feature, one that illustrates the quality and desirability of all the others. Most covers toss up a handful of items. The worst covers jam a dozen bargains on the cover. Think of the catalogs you get every holiday season. Which one do you want to imitate?

Creating a portfolio of successes

If you need to demonstrate the quality of your work, but don't sell products you can put in a catalog, consider a portfolio of successful projects. A portfolio works well for people who offer complex services that must be customized or localized for a particular client, in a specific set of circumstances. So you don't have a standard gizmo for sale — you have talent, taste, and expertise, and the only way a potential client can see those is through examples of your work. Therefore, the guts of your portfolio should consist of three sections for each project: a description of the context and challenge, an illustration of the situation before, and one or more illustrations of the situation after you worked your magic. Portfolios work well for a great number of professionals, including artists, architects, interior designers, contractors, gardeners, creative folks in advertising, book designers, interface designers, editors, and writers. (When your work is verbal rather than visual, your "illustrations" are simply examples of the text before and after.)

- Create a header and footer that will identify every page as yours, and provide the name of each project, as shown in Figure 5.98.

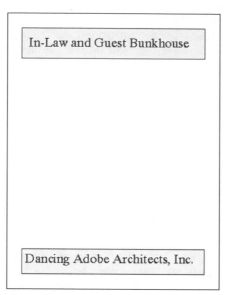

Figure 5.98 *Made in PrintMaster Gold from Mindscape.*

Tie together all these disparate pages, using the header — the text that appears at the top of every page, and the footer — the text at the bottom of every page. Put your company name and logo into a generous footer. On each project, put a descriptive title into the header.

- Create a single page describing the situation you faced, in three distinct sections: the challenge, the constraints, and the solution.

This page explains to your client the ways in which you had to overcome local problems. You hope the client can then understand that you do not think this project is a perfect match for their situation, but, rather, shows your adaptability, and inspiration, in dealing with a client's needs.

- The **challenge** should describe the client, the client's request, and the client's circumstances, motivations, and background. (Consider putting in what filmmakers call an establishing shot — an image that shows the customer's logo, building, or face).

- The **constraints** you know all too well — the limitations in budget, personnel, time, and materials.

- The **solution** shows your brilliance; make a bulleted list of the bright ideas you had, successes we will see when you show us the After pictures.

Separate these elements into distinct sections so that readers can skim them quickly, without getting lost in a complex description, or overly long paragraph.

■ Create a Before picture using a photograph or photocopy of the original, or the raw materials you had to work with. Title this "Before," as shown in Figure 5.99, in which an architectural team shows the condition of a street and surrounding buildings before they went to work to improve them.

Usually, one awful picture will do. If you have a sequence of Before images, you need to provide a corresponding sequence of After images, which correct each problem.

■ Create a series of After images showing the wonderful results of your work, as shown in Figure 5.100, which shows what a transformation the architectural firm has made to the street shown earlier in Figure 5.100.

You're allowed to gloat. Put in three to seven images here. Close-ups and long-distance shots. Just make sure they are all well-lit and glamorous. You cannot afford poor production quality here.

■ Create dividers, so you can separate one project from another.

If you are concerned that your pages will get dirty, buy plastic sleeves to protect them. These reduce the clarity of your images, but may be necessary if you use the same portfolio over and over, or if you put it out in a public place.

■ Find a nice binder to pull all these pages together.

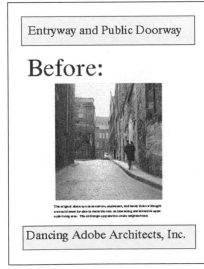

Figure 5.99 *Image from PrintMaster Gold from Mindscape.*

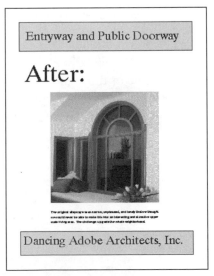

Figure 5.100 *Image from PrintMaster Gold from Mindscape.*

Three-ring binders with clear covers let you slip your company name (and perhaps a glossy photo) into the front and back cover and along the spine — identifying the portfolio as yours. If your material can be handled in sets, like a collection of photographic prints, consider a box. If your images are outsize, go to an art store and buy the fanciest art portfolio you can afford. Don't skimp on the binder; as the cover of your portfolio, it creates a strong first impression.

■ Create a table of contents and drop that in front of all the projects.

Tip

Create several different sets of project portfolios, to hold in reserve. When you go to talk to clients, select the projects that seem most relevant to their needs. Put their names on the cover, phrased something like "Portfolio of our work for Mrs. Janie Sanchez." The more personal you make the portfolio, the more the client feels you understand their situation.

Succeeding at direct mail

We all get too much mail. When we skim through the pile, we tend to toss out anything we suspect is irrelevant, boring, too expensive, or just plain junk. What we do tend to look at is the mail we know brings checks, family news, or something relevant to us personally. So if you are going to succeed at direct mail, you need to make your pitch as personal — and appealing — as possible. With Avery's Self-Seal Mailer paper, you can print on two sides, fold the sheet up along the creased lines, and seal the mailer with its own gummed band. Paper like this makes it easier to prepare these mailers at home.

■ On the "inside" page, design your pitch as a whole page, making sure that you do not put headings on top of the folds (see Figure 5.101).

Two or three columns of text will make this page easy to read. Big colorful graphics work well — photos will only succeed if your printer does them well.

■ On the "outside" page, create a special box for the panel that will end up as the "back" of the mailer.

Don't let this spill over to the fold. Keep plenty of white space between this box and the panel that gets folded under.

■ On or near the address panel, put your name and address, small, in the top-left corner. Then, as large as possible, add a photo of the person you are writing to if available. Failing that, add your own picture, waving hello, as shown in Figure 5.102.

Figure 5.101 *Image from PrintMaster Gold from Mindscape.*

Figure 5.102 *Image from PrintMaster Gold from Mindscape.*

One tool that can make your mailings much more personal is a database that can accept photos of your clients. If you have this kind of personal Rolodex system, or a database such as FileMaker, which accepts images in its records, you can start snapping pictures of every client, dropping those into the database, printing the address side of the mailer as a report from your database. No one can resist opening something that has their picture on it. (For clients you haven't yet photographed, use your own photo, so they recognize that this is coming directly from you).

■ In the final third of your "outside" page, put another boxed section, making sure it has plenty of room between its border and the address area, as shown in Figure 5.103.

Figure 5.103 *Image from PrintMaster Gold from Mindscape.*

Community Activities

IN THIS CHAPTER

- Bringing new life to community activities
- Helping your favorite teams
- Getting involved in your neigborhood

Volunteering

You may not think of what you do as volunteering. You're helping out. You're doing what you can to support your local school, hospital, nonprofit organization, or community center. What these organizations have in common, of course, is that almost everyone involved does the work for free. That changes the rules from regular jobs, because you can't order anyone around. In fact, in our experience, what people want most is not pay, but appreciation — and the satisfaction of accomplishing something worthwhile.

You can offer a big hand to any nonprofit by taking charge of the agenda, the announcements, the ads, and the posters. Using your digital images and your printer, you can draw attention to the group's goals, keep the work on track, and reach out to new members.

Making sure meetings are attended

Lots of people complain that they don't know when the meetings are, even when you send them notices. Most notices get tossed in the trash. Or people read them, make a half-hearted decision to attend, and then, funny thing, forget when the meeting is, or where, or whatever.

Getting people to attend may hinge on appealing to their heart and their work ethic. Remind them why the group exists — for their children, their patients, their church. And, to make the meeting stick in their mind, identify the topics you will discuss. If people know in advance what you are going to talk about, they are more likely to come, because they have something to say on one or another topic — or all of them.

Of course, some participants see any meeting as, first of all, a chance to schmooze. Chatting is great, and makes everyone feel at ease, but without a real agenda, and someone to keep people on track, meetings often disintegrate into gossip sessions, and real decisions get postponed or waffled to death.

You can do your small bit for order by offering to create the agenda for the next meeting, sending that out ahead of time as a kind of vision of what the group hopes to accomplish. No, you don't have to be as formal as "Old Business" and "New Business." But you can list decisions that have to be made.

1. In the meeting before you intend to create your agenda, make a list of every topic that people want to talk about next time.

2. Rephrase these topics as open questions.

   For instance, if one person wants to buy the school a new copier, but other folks think the group should just repair the old one, you might pose that debate as "School copier: Should we buy a new one or repair the old one?" By raising the topic as a question, you focus the debate help people think through their position ahead of time.

3. Get together with anyone who has kept notes, to make sure that you have not overlooked a topic or, by mistake, included a topic that should not be discussed at the next meeting.

4. Arrange the topics in whatever order you think makes sense and won't lead to chaos. Get the leader's OK.

   Some decisions have to be made before others. Some are so controversial they will take hours to debate, so perhaps you can dispense with the easier issues first.

5. When you get home, type up the topics on one sheet of paper in a large font, such as 18 or 24 points, so the text is hard to miss.

6. Add at least one graphic that relates to the group's purpose.

For instance, the local Parent Teacher Association would recognize their school (see Figure 6.1). Participants in the daycare center would relate to the safety pins in the border of Figure 6.2, even though most use disposable diapers. In both cases, enlarging the text and art transforms the agenda from a boring typewritten notice into a poster you can put up around the site, and a letter that's going to get noticed when it's delivered.

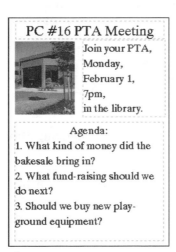

Figure 6.1 *Made in PrintMaster Gold Publishing Suite, from Mindscape.*

There's no reason why your agenda has to look like the boring ones from work. At work everyone must come to the meeting. With any volunteer organization, you may need to motivate folks to overcome the inertia they feel when they get home from work. It's easy to overlook an optional meeting. The more colorful your agenda, and the more it reminds them of the group's purpose, the more likely people will attend — and once at the meeting, stick to the topic.

Figure 6.2 *Made in PrintMaster Gold Publishing Suite, from Mindscape.*

Announcing events and work sessions

You know the experience: The day after a work session, in which only five people out of 50 showed up, everyone else you invited claims they weren't informed. Of course, you sent them all letters, announced it at every meeting for three months, and called everyone two weeks in advance. But when a project involves work or, worse, giving up a few hours on a weekend, many people get unaccountably forgetful.

You'll never persuade everyone. But you can make a deeper impression on the folks who waver, get busy, double-book, or invent an excuse. How? Make a series of posters to advertise any upcoming event, and then mail letter-size versions of those to your members; use graphics to catch their attention, and beat the date and purpose into their minds.

■ Round up volunteers by emphasizing the rewards of attending. Food is good. And dessert is best (see Figure 6.3).

Figure 6.3 *Made in PrintMaster Gold Publishing Suite, from Mindscape*

■ Don't be afraid to play on the emotion of the moment, or to use sentimental imagery, as shown in Figure 6.4.

Figure 6.4 *Made in PrintMaster Gold Publishing Suite, from Mindscape.*

■ Perhaps you can shame folks into doing some of the work. But do it with a sense of humor, as shown in Figure 6.5.

Figure 6.5 *Made in PrintMaster Gold Publishing Suite, from Mindscape.*

- If people share a real interest — no, obsession — put that front and center. If they drool over the picture, they won't forget the time and place (see Figure 6.6).

Figure 6.6 *Made in PrintMaster Gold Publishing Suite, from Mindscape.*

- In Roswell, New Mexico, the whole town makes money when tourists pour in to celebrate the alleged crash-landing of aliens half a century ago. Profit's a good motivator, particularly when it's mixed with community spirit, as shown in Figure 6.7.

Figure 6.7 *Made in PrintMaster Gold Publishing Suite, from Mindscape.*

Appeals to community spirit work best when bolstered by the reminder that everyone stands to make a profit, even if that reminder is indirect.

Fund-raising can be fun

It's always easier to raise funds for a winning team, and although everyone gives out of the goodness of their hearts, they appreciate a guarantee that they will receive some recognition. Small, local businesses want everyone to know who bought the pom-poms for the cheerleaders, and even large corporate businesses like to see a banner on the outfield wall in Little League stadiums. Making the thank-you part of the pitch increases your success rate. So build that promise into your fund-raising, and give the companies a big thank-you right away, including them on your team even before they donate.

1. Create an image that represents the team, charity, school, or organization as glamorously as possible.

2. Include the donor's name on the page so it can act as a poster to put in a window, as shown in Figure 6.8.

Figure 6.8 *Made in PrintMaster Gold Publishing Suite, from Mindscape.*

Make it easy for contributors to post your flyer or miniature poster right away; the more publicity you get, the more donors give.

Make one of these posters for each possible vendor, complete with their name, to show you are already willing to include them in the booster organization, and to show them how they can get credit for their donation.

3. In the cover letter, offer a 2' × 2' poster like the one shown in Figure 6.9 to dramatize their contribution, as a gesture of thanks for any contribution over $100 or so.

At $15 per square foot, your poster would cost $60, but you still make $40. The poster advertises your program and lets the business show that they are big contributors, so everyone who knows your program will appreciate their charity. Any donor who contributes this much should also get your business: Make sure everyone knows who gave a lot, and at every meeting, and in every letter, encourage people to go in and say, "I'm from the group, and I just want you to know how much we appreciate your support." This makes everyone feel good, and practically guarantees another donation the next time you ask.

Figure 6.9 *Made in PrintMaster Gold Publishing Suite, from Mindscape.*

In your thank-you posters to businesses, emphasize the appreciated partnership, mutual respect, and common support; donors will put up your poster and every customer will get your message.

4. Make up an honor roll of donors you especially want to thank, putting it in a prominent place where other folks in the community can see it, as shown in Figures 6.10 and 6.11.

Spend the money to do this right. Make a poster, laminate it or weather-seal it, and put it on an outside wall or in a big window where lots of people, including your donors, will see it. You have to make sure that donors feel they are really appreciated; when they sense that, they can't do enough for you.

A little color, and a prominent place, ensures that donors feel appreciated.

Focusing on a picture of what the donor lent or gave, and adding your thanks, makes a poster that the donor will cherish for a long time.

Figure 6.10 *Made in PrintMaster Gold Publishing Suite, from Mindscape.*

Figure 6.11 *Made in PrintMaster Gold Publishing Suite, from Mindscape.*

Campaigning

If you're looking for donations to the blood drive or contributions of food and clothing for the needy, you have to get the word out the way a political campaign does. One, two, or three basic posters will do, including one that's letter-sized so you can post hundreds everywhere, and two larger sizes for dropp-off spots or key locations.

■ Include a picture of the person or group you're trying to help, as shown in Figure 6.12.

Figure 6.12 *Made in PrintMaster Gold Publishing Suite, from Mindscape.*

■ If you need a lot of supplies, include the details on your poster, making it easier for people to give.

If you just say you need supplies, no one knows if they can provide what you are seeking, so few will think to offer any. But if you name the key things you need, as shown in Figure 6.13, you may get a higher response from the people who own or sell those items.

Figure 6.13 *Made in PrintMaster Gold Publishing Suite, from Mindscape.*

Showing your goal—in this case, a clean beach—helps focus your appeal, as does listing the actual supplies and work you need.

■ If you have a strong emotional appeal, keep the text and picture as simple as possible, as shown in Figure 6.14.

Figure 6.14 *Made in PrintMaster Gold Publishing Suite, from Mindscape.*

Babies upstage everything else, as actors will tell you, so give the emotional image the spotlight, and keep everything else simple.

Livening up a newsletter

Many organizations rely on newsletters to announce meetings, launch campaigns, or recruit new members. But most newsletters are heavy on text and light on graphics. Why not reverse the emphasis and make the newsletter a little more fun to look at?

■ Make the picture the story and reduce the text to an introduction or a caption, as shown in Figure 6.15.

You may have to write all the articles yourself this way to avoid the long pieces that the officers normally contribute. Instead of 1,000 words, write a single paragraph. Reduce a story to a caption under a picture.

Figure 6.15 *Made in PrintMaster Gold Publishing Suite, from Mindscape.*

■ For each issue, gather the art from the same source so that the images work together, as they do in Figure 6.16, rather than looking thrown together.

Figure 6.16 *Made in PrintMaster Gold Publishing Suite, from Mindscape.*

When pictures are the focus, make sure they look alike, so your newsletter has some consistency within each issue.

■ Make each page a picture, adding text on top of the image.

To announce a community meeting, use an image everyone will recognize, adding a little text on top, as shown in Figure 6.17.

The Community Association holds its winter meeting at the Town Hall on Wednesday, December 28th, beginning at 5pm. Everyone is invited. Cake and cookies from the Brotherhood Bakery will be served, along with punch made from Mayor Sanchez's favorite recipe.

Figure 6.17

Viewers will recognize the scene and then read your text in a newsletter in which every page is a giant picture.

Celebrating Sports

Digital imaging enables you to make up your own sports cards, a roster of the whole team (with their faces staring out at the proud relatives), transform a picture of your kid into a big-leaguer's picture, prepare for the big game with signs and bumper stickers, and make your own posters of sports images you like.

Making your own sports cards

Kids trade 'em, stack 'em, look up their prices, and speculate about their future value. Sports cards have evolved from bubble-gum inserts of baseball heroes to complete sets of football leagues, hockey players around the world, and so on. Some of the Little League, Pop Warner, Young American Football League, and Youth Soccer team photographers offer special deals, turning your child's official portrait into a trading card for only a few bucks extra.

If your child's team doesn't have a slick photographer like that, you can do just as well on your computer. You can experiment on your own little player, and if all goes well, offer to make the cards up for everyone on the team.

1. Start by resizing the electronic version of your photograph so that it is roughly 2"× 3" inches, or wallet size (see Figure 6.18).

Figure 6.18

2. If your software lets you pick different line widths, adjust the line tool to its largest width, or about 36 points, and choose a line color you like.

3. use the rectangle tool to surround the picture with a colored rectangle, as shown in Figure 6.19.

Figure 6.19

4. Add your child's name at the bottom or top of the frame.

   If you want, you could add your child's position or jersey number, too.

5. To make your child into a star, add an award or honor at the top, as shown in Figure 6.20.

Figure 6.20

6. Copy the image and paste it into your document as many times as it will fit, so it fills up a page.

7. Print on the thickest and glossiest paper you have.

   If you only have regular paper, you can cut out the images and glue them on cardboard strips.

8. Cut out each image.

9. If you have collected statistics on your athlete, make them into a little bio to put on the back, as in shown in Figure 6.21. Print, cut out, and glue on the back of each image.

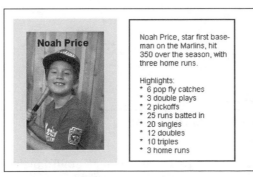

Figure 6.21

10. For a real trading-card look, laminate each card so the sandwich of papers is not too obvious.

Celebrating the whole team

Generally, when parents don't feel part of the team, they just root for their own child. Even under a football helmet and pads, parents can spot their kid. But the more the grown-ups get to know the other kids, the more likely they are to participate in all the extra activities that make a team successful—pep rallies, potlucks, beef jerky sales, and car washes.

One way you can build team spirit among the parents is by making up a visual roster of the entire team, including names and jersey numbers, so even a grandparent with bifocals can spot the family athlete. Hand the roster out at game after game and, gradually, parents of team members will recognize other players, besides their babies. It may not be team spirit, but it's a start.

- Make sure you have correctly spelled first and last names, and have the correct jersey numbers.

  If anything causes parental bitterness, it's a misspelled name.

- Put a graphic representing the team at the top of the sheet (see Figure 6.22).

Figure 6.22 *Image from ClickArt from Broderbund.*

- If you have enough time and patience, put each child's picture next to his or her name in the roster, as shown in Figure 6.23.

You'll need more pages for the pictures, so you're beginning to make a real program. Perhaps you could start selling the program as another fund-raiser!

22

Noah Price

Right Tackle,
Kick Return

"Let's go!"

25

Bennie Price

Tight End

Figure 6.23

Morphing into a big leaguer

Sometimes a child has a favorite major-league player, someone they'd love to be as fast as, and famous as. You can make that dream come true, sort of, by mounting your child's head on the star's torso. You're not likely to fool anyone, but that's not the point. It's more like a private joke between you and your child.

1. Get a picture of your child and use the freehand selection tool to carve out the head, as shown in Figure 6.24, and then copy the selection.

    Don't worry about the shakiness of your hand as you try to move around the ears and hair. You can do some mild editing later to get rid of any background you pick up by accident.

2. Paste your child's head into a new document.

3. Zoom in so you can see each pixel.

4. Set the fill color to white and then use the pencil tool or eraser tool to get rid of the unnecessary pixels (the ones that show the wall behind your child, or the sky).

5. Zoom back to normal size.

6. Bring in an image of the hero, next to the flying head.

7. Adjust the size of the hero so the two heads are more or less the same size, as shown in Figure 6.25.

8. Using the freehand selection tool, drag your child's head on top of the hero's neck.

9. Zoom out again and erase unwanted pixels left behind by the hero who just disappeared.

Figure 6.24

Figure 6.25 *Baseball player from ClickArt from Broderbund.*

10. Zoom back to normal to judge the effect, as shown in Figure 6.26.

Figure 6.26

11. Print.

Getting ready for the big game

When our son Ben's team made the play-offs, his game was scheduled for 8 A.M. The coaches asked that the players get to the field at 7 A.M. So the parents decided to meet in a supermarket parking lot at 6 A.M. to decorate our cars with shoe polish, crepe paper, balloons, and pom-poms so we could caravan to the game in style, honking as we went.

If any of this craziness sounds familiar, you might want to use your computer to simplify the task of decorating your car — and cleaning it up afterward:

■ Find a clip art graphic to represent your team, and use that on every bit of paraphernalia you make. (Make it as big as you can on a single sheet of paper.)

■ You may not be able to locate a graphic that truly represents your team name if it is something like The Banana Slugs. So turn to emblems of the game itself, such as the one shown in Figure 6.27 for soccer.

Figure 6.27 *Image from ClickArt from Broderbund.*

■ Create a series of pages with text approximately 288 points (four inches) high.

Typical rallying phrases are "We're Number One!" and "Go, Team, Go." You may come up with something original; just remember you want the text big enough so that as you drive by, opponents can read your phrases and wince.

■ Attach the graphic at both ends of the text banners, as shown in Figure 6.28.

Figure 6.28

■ Yes, use masking tape or duct tape to attach these literary and artistic masterpieces to your car.

■ Make a smaller version (half the height) of the banner and tape that to your bumper.

Making mini-posters

When you get into a sport, you may want to put up reminders around your room or office. Certainly kids do. But no one has a lot of space on the wall, what with those full-color glossy photos of Michael Jordan, Mark McGwire, and so on.

The computer is perfect for miniature posters — the size of one sheet of 8.5" × 11" paper. You can easily tack them up and, if they get stained or yellowed, toss'em away, because you can always print another — or make a new one in a few minutes.

1. Start with a photo of your favorite sport — your own or clip art you have taken from a collection or off the Web.

   The photo should mean a lot to you, even if it isn't going to make professional photographers nervous. For instance, a picture of the beginner's slope like the one shown in Figure 6.29 might inspire a young skier more than snow blowing off of the peak at Zermatt, in Switzerland.

Figure 6.29 *Photo from ClickArt from Broderbund.*

2. If the picture shows something familiar, but in a boring way, select the whole image and apply whatever distortions you can find in your application.

   You might, for instance, invert the colors, as shown in Figure 6.30. The eye struggles to figure out what before seemed so recognizable, a distortion that often intrigues the eye, and pleases kids who have grown bored with standard photos. You might transform selected areas by dragging them out of shape, or changing their tint; you can even use strange brush shapes to break up the skyline, as shown in Figure 6.31. Just don't obliterate the original subject matter, even in its distorted version.

Figure 6.30 *Manipulated in ClarisWorks*

Figure 6.31 *Manipulated in ClarisWorks*

3. Add a slogan (see Figure 6.32).

4. Keep experimenting, making a set of posters, as shown in Figure 6.33.

Figure 6.32 *Manipulated in ClarisWorks*

Figure 6.33 *Manipulated in ClarisWorks*

You could line one wall with a whole series of posters, leading the eye from one to the other. Ask for slogan suggestions from your young athlete and refine the imagery based on that input as you go.

Exploring Neighborhood

Using your skills at digital imaging, you can get more involved in your neighborhood, advertising your garage sale so everyone knows about it, setting up a treasure hunt through the area, mapping your block, or learning a new neighborhood by creating a board game.

Advertising your garage sale

You'll enjoy putting out these signs. No more of those crummy cardboard signs with "Garage Sale" scrawled on top and an address that's too small to read. Signs like that don't inspire anyone to check out your used chairs and old board games out on the lawn.

You can use your computer to draw people to your garage or yard sale with a set of colorful signs — even a whole series of signs. Put the first one up long before a driver has to slow down to make a turn into your street or driveway. Put the next sign up a little farther along. And the next after that... leading people, sign by sign, right to your sale. Your neighbors will get a kick out of figuring out where the trail leads. Who knows? Maybe you'll sell out by lunchtime. Here's how to make your inviting roadside signs:

1. Collect electronic pictures of six items you are selling.

   You can snap electronic pictures of these sale items, scan old photos, make sketches in a paint program, or use clip art. If you make photos, set the items against a plain background such as a cement walkway or your lawn — so the bird feeder and the salad bowl really stand out. And get as close as you can, so that old basketball fills the frame. You're in advertising now!

2. Open an application that lets you put text underneath your pictures. A word processor like Word, or the modules in Microsoft Works or ClarisWorks will do fine.

3. At the top of the first page, insert whatever picture you think a fast-moving driver could recognize right away.

4. Grab the handles to shrink the picture so it leaves a few inches at the bottom of the page.

5. Press Return, and type the word DO in capital letters, about 144 points high (two inches), as shown in Figure 6.34.

6. Insert a page break.

Figure 6.34

Figure 6.35

7. Repeat, putting one picture at the top of each page and one word at the bottom of each page, finishing the question you just began: DO YOU BRAKE FOR GARAGE SALES?

The idea is that you will have one picture and one word on each sign, as shown in Figures 6.35 and 6.36.

Figure 6.36

8. On another page, put a big arrow that will point to your house.

Most clip art collections offer good arrows — or use a simple paint program to cook one up.

9. Print out each page, mount it on a piece of cardboard, and then duct-tape it to a stick.

10. Plant the sticks along the street so drivers can read one after another, as shown in Figure 6.37 — until they turn into your driveway.

Separate the signs by 40–50 feet, if you can, but however far apart you put the signs, keep the rhythm regular so once someone has read the first two they get the idea and pick up the other signs in sequence.

Figure 6.37

Setting up a treasure hunt

Kids love following the trail of clues until X marks the spot, where you have hidden gold — or at least some candy. To give the kids the clues, you can use pictures that suggest where to look for the next clue, and the next, and so on, around your house and yard, or the neighborhood. Images work better for the younger set, who can't read too well; and the older kids find the pictures just as challenging as verbal hints.

The clues can be 8.5" × 11" sheets of paper — good for beginners; or cutouts, which are harder to find because they are smaller.

1. Collect electronic pictures of the places to which you're going to send the kids for the next clue — or the gold.

   Consider eight or ten places. Check them out to make sure you can hide a clue in, under, or on top of each spot.

   If possible, take electronic pictures of parts of the locations — the arm of a chair, not the whole chair. That way, the kids have to figure out what the picture shows, and then guess where it might be. Or do a wide shot, so the kids have to probe the whole area. For instance, taping a clue under one wooden beam of a fence, you could show the solid pile the wood fits into, as shown in Figure 6.38.

Figure 6.38

If you're snapping a small object, put it against an unfamiliar background before taking its picture so the surroundings don't give its location away (see Figure 6.39).

Figure 6.39

If photos won't work for you, collect clip art — that will definitely make the challenge tougher, because the images won't look exactly like anything at your house or in your neighborhood.

2. Plan the sequence of clues so the searchers have to run from one end of the yard to the other.

   You might make a rough map for your own sanity.

3. Print the images, fold them up, and tape them out of sight on the locations you have chosen.

   We've found that we need to place the clues in exactly the order the kids will follow them to make sure we don't accidentally leave one out.

4. At the end of the trail, put a pot of gold. If you don't have enough gold bars for everyone, try party favors or chocolate for the hunting party!

Making a map of your block

If you've just moved into your block and your youngest is still feeling a little disoriented, you might make a visual map of the neighborhood together. This activity focuses your child on learning what the houses look like and what is next to what — stretching the "known" from your house to include nearby houses, and perhaps the trees and playground farther down, if you feel it's safe for your child to go there alone.

1. Go out with your child and take pictures of whatever landmarks you encounter as you walk along.

    You can use a regular camera and have the pictures digitized if you don't have a digital camera. Encourage your child to indicate what you ought to photograph. If a house has an interesting or unusual entrance, like the one shown in Figure 6.40, snap that.

Figure 6.40

Consider whatever is closest to the sidewalk, so the pictures will reflect what your child really sees. For instance, take a snapshot of a fence if the house is set far back, as shown in Figure 6.41.

Figure 6.41

If there's a place to play, like a mini-park, or a basketball hoop set out for neighborhood kids, capture that image (see Figure 6.42) so you can talk about meeting and playing with the other kids on the block.

2. In your imaging software, reduce each picture to about 4" × 6", and then print them.

3. Lay out one or two sheets of cardboard or foamboard and glue or tape the pictures down in order, starting at your own door.

If you're in the middle of the block, the pictures will extend to the left and right. If you took photos of the other side of the street, put those images there. You are making a visual map — it's not to scale, and it leaves out a lot, but your child can rehearse the walk down the street with it.

Figure 6.42

4. Discuss each picture with your child to help build a mental model of the neighborhood.

Tell your child what you know — who lives where, what a certain tree is (see Figure 6.43), what a fence is made out of. Find out what questions occur to your child and try to answer them.

After you and your child have discussed your local tour a few times, you may both want to go out and take a new set of pictures, focusing on one subject, such as front doors or windows. Great! That's a way to explore the neighborhood, discovering its patterns, like the Unifix™ cubes teachers use.

5. When your child feels more secure, cut up the map into big, clumsy "cards," and make a game out of shuffling them and then laying them out in order.

Figure 6.43

Making a game out of local real estate

If you get a kick out of board games, maybe it's time to make one yourself, using the computer to make the game board and funny money. Use LEGO people to run around the board. You can pretend you and your family are all realtors, buying and selling the houses, barns, stores, and vacant lots in your area.

Making a gameboard

1. Start by taking lots of pictures of places around your neighborhood.

   Because this game is economic, think in terms of communities. You need "undesirable" areas with buildings like those in Figures 6.44 and 6.45.

Figure 6.44

Figure 6.45

Include some places with gardens, as shown in Figure 6.46, and expansive gates, as shown in Figure 6.47, to represent a well-off cul-de-sac.

Figure 6.46

Figure 6.47

Collect a few public monuments, such as the school shown in Figure 6.48, for the corners, or to put between communities.

2. Group the pictures in twos and threes to make little communities.

3. In a word-processing program, insert each picture, and then shrink it to about wallet-size; then add the community name, and a price, as shown in Figure 6.49.

Figure 6.48

¶
The·Big·Mean·Dog·House¶
Aristocratic·Acres¶
$2.5·million¶
$1,000·a·day·rental¶

Figure 6.49

If your kids are just beginning to be able to keep track of numbers and prices, keep these simple. But if you will be playing with older children, or adults who really care how much everything costs, put real prices on each structure.

If you like complexity and want to keep the game going for a while, add rental fees, so that anyone who lands on the property has to pay a night's lodging.

4. Print two copies of each property, and then cut out each image with its text so that each takes up about the same amount of room.

5. On construction cardboard or foamcore, lay the communities out around the outer edges of the board, in a continuous sequence. (Keep the second copy of each property as a proof of ownership).

If you have two run-down shacks, put them together as Fleabag Flats. Mansions go in Aristocratic Acres. Put schools and post offices at the corner, as places where nobody has to pay.

The idea is that you are making a series of panels for players to navigate.

6. Cover the whole board with laminating plastic, if possible, to keep everything in place.

Now you have a gameboard that reflects your own town and you are almost ready to wheel and deal to take over the prime properties. But first you need some cash.

Making a bundle

You need some crazy money, to buy (and rent) all these properties. Make the bills in ones, fives, and tens for the elementary school kids, and switch to thousands, tens of thousands, and so on for teenagers and adults, who want to imagine they have a pre-approved mortgage at the bank.

1. In a painting or drawing program, invite several partners to swap turns drawing as freely and colorfully as possible.

2. Using the selection rectangle, grab and then make a copy of a section that has approximately the shape of a bill—whether it's an American dollar or bigger, such as a Japanese yen or French franc.

3. Start a new painting or drawing and paste in your artwork, as shown in Figure 6.50.

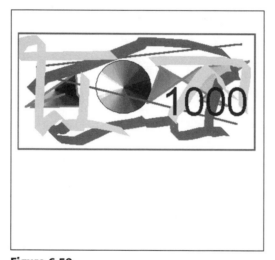

Figure 6.50

4. Paste as many times as will fit on a page.

5. Save and print (several copies).

6. Cut out your counterfeit money and stack it up.

7. Make yourself several more denominations, so you can make change.

Establishing the rules

Make the rules up to suit your players. Here are some fundamentals:

- Hand out lots of money to each player.
- Roll dice to move around the board.
- You can buy any property that isn't owned by someone — except for public buildings (at the corners).
- If you land on someone else's property, you have to pay rent. (So make sure you have made money that matches the rent payments!)
- Invent further obstacles, such as a stack of Bad News cards, to slow players down.

Troubleshooting

We can't cover all the incredible variety of trouble you may get into, thanks to multiple conflicts between vendors, between hardware and software, between one application and another, between one operating system and another, and, really, just stupid internal conflicts within whatever application you happen to be using. You would like your computer to have the reliability of a refrigerator, but the system is so complex that really, truly, no one human being can ever hope to diagnose the reason for some crashes, blow-ups, collapses, and messes.

If something goes wrong, ask yourself:

- What's different this time? Did I just hook up a new piece of hardware, or install a new piece of software? Suspect the new. Try uninstalling the latest gizmo to see if all returns to normal. If it does, take the darn thing back to the dealer, and get something else.

- What exactly did I do before disaster fell? Write down the actual actions you took, because after you wait an hour to talk to someone at customer support, that person will want to know, step by laborious step, what you did to mess up their lovely software or hardware. If you can't recall what you did, even an expert may have trouble helping you.

Having reconstructed the moments before disaster, try the following:

- RTFM. Read the fine manual. Yes, if you buy from companies that care, they may actually have put the answers in the manual. Of course, manuals are written on the assumption that everything works fine, and most leave out a troubleshooting section, on marketing's theory that if you do not admit problems, no one will have any problems.

- Have patience. By this we mean take the time to read the canned answers that the companies put up on their Web sites, or on their phone menus. Odds are that nothing there is exactly like your situation. But you may get a hint of what to do. Definitely spend an hour on the Web before abandoning yourself to the black hole of customer support.

- If you can't stand it anymore, call customer support. But try not to break down in tears, or start yelling when you finally get a human. Despite much evidence, the person at the other end of the phone line is actually human, too. That person cannot see your computer, does not know what you were doing, and needs your help in order to help you. Just expect that this process will take two to six hours, and you won't start screaming when the first fifteen attempts at diagnosis fail.

In this section we discuss some of the most common problems that afflict users of digital cameras, scanners, and printers, and the associated software. We can't cover everything, but these are the biggies. Remember that 80% of the problems people encounter stem from an unusual combination (this printer with that scanner, this software with that file, this action followed by that action), in which case your problem is so unusual that no one else would find it helpful to get the solution. If you don't find an answer in this section, or in the manual, then try the Web site for the vendors.

Using a Digital Camera

Q: Why are there different levels of quality, and how can I adjust the quality?

A: Quality, here, means detail. Unfortunately, the more detail you want to capture and store, the more memory each picture takes up. So you have a choice of good, better, best, or basic, fine, and super-fine, because even the lowest setting is pretty good. You choose quality by purpose. If you intend to post your pictures on the Internet, the basic quality gives you enough detail for small, but good-looking images on the Web. At this setting, you can take a lot of pictures before running out of memory.

On the other hand, if you want to blow pictures up to 8" × 10" or poster size, though, you need as much detail as possible, so that your lines will look superfine, and the resolution will be the best possible. In that circumstance, you need the best quality, which sops up tons of details, and expands the size of each electronic file so that you can only take a few pictures before you run out of memory, and have to offload the pictures to your computer.

Example

There are three photo quality settings on the HP PhotoSmart Digital Camera C20, C20xi, or C30: Basic, Fine, and Super-fine.

- Basic Photo Quality. Produces good-quality photos and is the most memory-efficient, making it ideal for photos that you plan to send via e-mail or store on your disk or in a database. You can store 40 photos on a 4-MB memory card when using Basic mode.

- Fine Photo Quality. Produces high-quality pictures and uses less memory than Super-fine mode. In Fine mode, you can store 20 photos on a 4-MB memory card.

- Super-fine Photo Quality. Produces the highest-quality pictures and uses the most memory. You can store eight Super-fine photos on a 4-MB memory card.

The Photo Quality setting determines how many photos can be stored in the camera's memory (Table A-1). For example, using an HP digital camera with a 4 MB or 10 MB flash memory card, you can store more pictures with lower "quality," although the images will be just fine for the Web, or printed on an inkjet in small sizes.

Table A.1
Photo Quality Settings

Photo Quality	Status Icon	4-MB card	10-MB card
Basic	one diamond	40 images	100 images
Fine	two diamonds	20 images	50 images
Super-fine	three diamonds	8 images	20 images

You can use different photo quality settings on the same flash memory card. Decreasing or increasing the photo quality just changes the number of additional photos that can be stored on the memory card.

Q: How do I download photos to a PC?

A: To download images to your computer to print or use in all types of creative projects (such as greeting cards or calendars), you can either hook up to the computer using a cable, or, if you are using a flash memory card or computer disk inside the camera, you may be able to take that card or disk and slip it into the computer.

1. Connect the camera to your computer, if you have a cable.

    a. Plug one end of the connection cable into the PC serial port.

    b. Plug the other end of the cable into the camera.

Note

Most cameras connect to a 9-pin serial port. If you do not have a 9-pin serial port available, you can use a 9-to-25 pin adapter (available at most computer supply stores) to connect to a 25-pin serial port. See your computer user's guide or contact your computer manufacturer if you have problems locating an available serial port.

2. Connect the AC power adapter, so you do not use up the charge in your batteries.

    a. Attach the plug to the adapter. If your camera came with multiple plugs, select the one that matches the power outlet for your country.

    b. Plug the adapter into a power source (such as a wall outlet or power strip).

    c. Connect the flat end of the adapter cable to the camera.

3. Open the lens cover to turn the camera on.

   On the computer, the camera's software should start automatically as soon as the PC detects that the camera is connected. Once the software opens, you begin to see thumbnail versions of each picture.

4. If the software does not start, launch it yourself, then choose to get the images from the camera.

5. View your photos.

Note

If you have a computer (such as a laptop) that has a PCMCIA slot, you can read photos directly from the CompactFlash memory card using a compact flash adapter. See the adapter manufacturer's instructions for details. When you use a compact flash adapter, the photo-finishing software inside the computer reads the memory card as an additional disk.

Q: Can I connect my digital camera to a television to view pictures?

A: Usually, yes, but you have to fiddle with cables to do so. When you connect the camera to your TV, the TV displays your pictures. The TV is like a giant version of the LCD display on the back of your camera. With some software, you can even use your television to view a slide show, making it easy to share your photos with family and friends. If your camera comes with the option of connecting to a TV, your vendor's manual will give you the details, but basically it works like this:

1. Connect the AC power adapter to the camera, so you are not using up your batteries.

   a. Attach the plug to the adapter. If your camera came with multiple plugs, select the one that matches the power outlet for your country.

   b. Plug the adapter into a power source (such as a wall outlet or power strip).

   c. Connect the flat end of the adapter cable to the camera.

2. Connect the video cable.

   If you are using an NTSC connection (U.S. and Japanese), plug the input (yellow) end of the video cable into your television set's video-input connector (on most televisions, this is also yellow).

   If you are using a PAL connection (German), plug the input (yellow) end of the video cable into the adapter (supplied with your camera), and then plug the adapter into your television set's video-input connector.

3. Plug the other end of the video cable into the camera.

4. On your television, set the video input to be the video input connector where you connected the camera.

    Usually this means tuning to channel 2 or 3—whatever you use to view stuff from your VCR. See your television owner's manual for specific instructions on how to set the video input.

5. Turn on your TV.

6. Press the button that brings up the LCD display on your camera.

    The same menu appears on the TV.

7. Use the Menu button and the arrow buttons on your camera to view photos.

    No, your remote control will not affect the camera. You have to run any slide show from the camera itself.

    Photos taken in vertical format (with the camera turned sideways) appear sideways on the TV set. You can rotate the photos after you download them to your PC.

8. To disconnect, turn off the TV and camera, then unplug.

Q: What cleaning and maintenance should I do on my digital camera?

A: First, make sure you are storing your camera in a dry, clean spot that is not too close to a heater or air conditioner. Beware of:

- Direct sunlight
- High humidity
- Extreme dust
- Close proximity to an air conditioner, heater, or moisturizer
- Areas of high vibration
- Hot houses, hot cars, windows in summer

To keep the camera clean, wipe the entire surface of the camera using a clean, dry, soft cloth. Then clean the lens.

Cleaning the Camera Lens

Keep the lens clean because dust particles can show up as dots on your photos.

1. Use a blower to eliminate dust.

2. Use a lens cleaning tissue to wipe off the lens if necessary.

Dealing with Condensation

Condensation can occur if a your camera is subjected to sharp temperature changes, which can create enough condensation to cause damage. To avoid condensation, carry the camera in a pocket, or close to your body when outside in the cold. Avoid going from hot environments directly into cold ones.

Tip

Should condensation occur, removed batteries and leave the battery door open for several hours.

Q: What should I do if I am using the photo software and the computer crashes, or the software disappears after starting, or I get a message warning me of Fatal Exceptions or Illegal Operations?

A: Somehow, your computer may have run out of disk space or memory while trying to run the program, or the program illegally tried to write some data to an area that already held information crucial to the system, or the programmers didn't follow the standards the computer expected. There are a number of possible causes you can look into to make a little more memory available.

- Your hard drive may be almost full, in which case the computer cannot use parts of it to park information briefly, until needed again (virtual memory). One cause of that may be something worse than dental plaque: excessive temporary files build up.

- During start up, there may be a bunch of unnecessary programs getting started, each taking room in the computer's memory, without your knowing about it.

Clearing out some space for virtual memory on your hard disk

The amount of free space on your hard drive (usually your C drive on a Windows machine) is critical because your computer parks information there briefly, until needed (treating the hard disk as if it were its own memory); if the computer cannot find a space for this information, processing collapses.. As free space approaches less than 200 MB free, you may experience problems while installing software, your computer may freeze or crash, and you may see threatening messages taking a fatal exception to your ways, or accusing you of illegal operations. Really, none of this is your fault. Programmers just designed the operating system sloppily: for instance, why doesn't it diagnose the problem and tell you to clear out some space on the hard disk.

An additional hard drive may not solve the problem because the operating system puts the temp directory on the c: drive by default. (the one with the rest of the operating system living on it). However, this setting can be changed in the Virtual Memory dialog box, which can be accessed from the System panel of the Control Panel. If you have a second hard drive, you can also move non-critical files to the new hard drive to free up space on your main hard drive.

Discovering how much free space your hard disk has left If you are using a Macintosh, select the hard drive and look at the amount of space free, in the window. If you are using a PC, open Windows Explorer and select the drive. You'll see the amount of free space on the Status bar at the bottom of the window. Windows can also show you a graphical picture of disk free space. Here's how:

1. Double-click My Computer.

2. Right-click the icon for the C drive.

   You see a list of options.

3. Click Properties.

   In a moment you see a diagram of the hard disk's available space, with a colored section indicating what amount is currently used. Look above the diagram for an exact number indicating the amount of free space in bytes. You hope to see a number higher than 200,000 bytes.

4. If free space is less than 200 MB, clear the hard disk.

Clearing some room on your hard disk To make room, do the following:

- Delete programs that you no longer use.

   Make backup copies of old documents, data, pictures, then remove the files from the hard disk.

- Clear out whatever directory stores files collected during your tour of the World Wide Web. Look in the Windows directory for Internet temporary files. If you have not specified in the Internet settings that only a few days' worth of these files be kept, this folder could eventually swell to fill the hard drive.

- Find and delete temporary files. Start by clearing out c:\windows\temp directory.

In Windows, click Start, then Find, and choose Files and Folders. Type ***.tmp** to find temporary files no matter what their name, then click Find Now. Then delete those files and restart the computer. On the Mac, look for any folder called Temporary, particularly inside the folders devoted to your Internet browser and word processor.

Shutting down background activities that may have been launched during startup

Many Windows programs start behind your back every time Windows loads. These background activities may slow the speed of the computer, reduce the system resources, or cause lock ups, fatal exceptions, illegal operations, or other memory problems. The quickest way to check out what's going on here is to right-click the Start menu, click Open, select the Programs folder, and then open the StartUp folder. Programs such as virus checkers usually park themselves here when you install them. To see if any of these programs are causing the problem, create a new folder within the Programs folder (call it temp or something), move the contents of StartUp into the temp folder, and reboot the computer. If this fixes the problem, move an icon from the temp folder back to StartUp and reboot. Continue until you've found the responsible program.

A general rule of thumb is that if programs are acting flaky, or freezing, to shut down all activity in StartUp.

1. At the Windows Desktop, press the Ctrl, Alt, and Delete keys, all at the same time. (But just press this combination once!)

The Close program window appears.

Note

If you happen to press Ctrl, Alt, and Delete keys twice, the computer shuts down, then restarts. Only press once.

You see a list of activities the computer is running.

2. Click on any activity except Explorer, then click End Task.

3. If a second window pops, up click End Task.

4. Repeat Steps 1–3 until all activities, except Explorer, have been ended.

5. Try the activity that originally was causing the issue.

Note

Each time you restart the computer, all these activities come back. This step may need to be repeated if the computer is restarted. A long term solution might be to call PC manufacturer to clear StartUp.

Q: Why do pictures look patchy or garbled in my photo software?

A: When you run photo software in a display of less than 800 × 600 High Color, a message may appear prompting you to increase your resolution and color depth. You have to go to the Control Panel and change the settings to a higher resolution with more colors for the picture to come out looking right.

1. Choose Start, Settings, then Control Panel.
2. Double-click Display.
3. Choose Settings.
4. Choose any combination higher than 256 colors at 800 × 600 resolution.

   The more colors, and the higher the resolution, the better your pictures will look.

Scanning

Q: When using my scanner to scan a color image or save an image to a file, the error message "Not Enough Memory to Complete Operation" appears. What should I do?

A: You need to clear up some memory by closing down other applications, and expanding virtual memory (make-believe memory that uses your hard disk as if it were part of the random-access memory or RAM the computer uses to do its calculations and store your current work). Here's how.

1. Close any applications not being used.
2. Try scanning again.
3. If that doesn't work, clean unnecessary items off your hard disk, so that virtual memory has a little more room to play.

   If you don't have a utility to clean up your hard disk, discard all the files in your temporary folders (such as c:\windows\temp) and those kept by your Internet browser with all the pages you have viewed for the last century. Uninstall applications you no longer use. Run a disk defragmenter utility on your hard disk, so that you have each file in its own place, rather than lying around in bits and pieces all over the hard disk (making it hard for the computer to put all the pieces together with any speed).

4. Restart your computer with a little prayer.

Q: I just hooked up my scanner, but the computer can't see it.

A: Your SCSI Card must be properly configured and installed before your scanner will be found on your system. To check this, choose Settings on the Start menu, open the Control Panel, and go the System tab, to see if the SCSI card shows up. (If not, you may need to reinstall it.) If the SCSI card is visible, make sure that you haven't inadvertently assigned the same card to two different devices, both of which you have turned on at the same time; their arm-wrestling could bring both of them down. Oh, and really check that cable: just a little shaking may have loosened the connection. One other possibility: your scanner may have to be turned on before you start your computer, to ensure that the computer sees it is there.

Q: Can I connect my HP PhotoSmart Scanner and flatbed scanner together on one card?

A: Yes. You need to verify that both scanners are using different addresses, and that the termination has been configured correctly, before they will work together.

Q: When I scan an image into an application like Microsoft Works or Corel Photo-Paint, the image is either smaller or larger than the original scanned image. What can I do?

A: The image size actually is unchanged, but your display is limited to 72 dpi. So if you scan an image at, say 144 dpi, it will appear twice as large on the screen than it will print. If you are preparing an image for on-screen presentation, there's no point scanning at a higher resolution than 72 dpi, unless you intend to use an enlarged area of the image. For example, suppose you have a photograph of two dogs and only want to use one of them. You can scan the image at 144 dpi, select the dog you want to use, and crop out the rest of the image. Then, resample the image to 72 dpi, keeping the image *size* unchanged. (In Corel Photo-Paint, this command is found in the Image/Resample dialog box.) If the final output is going to be hard copy, just zoom the image to a comfortable working view and don't be fooled by the on-screen size.

Printing

Q: How can I print a picture in different shades of gray?

A: There are times when you may want to take a picture that you created in full color, then print it in a range of grays, so you can easily see what it looks like without taking the time and toner ink to print in color. You may want to use grayscale (the range of grays from black to white) if you intend to photocopy the printout using black ink, or if you intend to make the image fit into a document that already has other images in black and white.

1. Choose Print from the File menu.

   In a moment you see the Print dialog box. Look for a button with a name such as Properties, Setup, or Printer (the name varies from one application to another).

2. Click Properties (or Setup or Printer) to change the way you print.

   You may see a dialog box with a series of tabs; if so, click the Color or Printout tab.

3. Choose Grayscale, and click OK twice, to confirm that choice.

   From now on your color documents will print in shades of gray until you change the setting. For faster draft printing in grayscale, use the black print cartridge, not the photo cartridge (if you have a choice).

Q: Why don't the colors on my printout match those on the screen?

A: There are a lot of reasons why there will be only an approximate match, even when all is going well. First of all, the screen makes color by shining light through a screen, so anything on screen appears brighter, more vivid, and glowing. Your printer makes colors by mixing inks on paper, and you pick up those colors when light bounces off the page.

And behind these two ways of displaying color are two technologies, one that started out modeled on televisions, which generally have three guns shooting out red, green, and blue, in just the right combinations to create all the other colors, the other beginning with the printing press of Gutenberg. There is no way these two technologies can produce images that give you exactly the same impression.

On the other hand, professional designers calibrate the screen so that they can always, or often, predict what colors will emerge in print, for each color on the screen. You don't want to know how this works, but the gist of it is a kind of mental jiujitsu, in which the designer can predict — but not actually see on-screen — a specific color emerging from the printer.

Still, you should be able to see a real similarity between the color onscreen and the color on paper. If you don't, there may be several different reasons, and therefore several solutions. We'll look at those in the following sections.

What if the colors on paper are OK, but just not as vivid as they usually are?

You may be printing on the wrong side of the paper. If turning the paper over makes no difference, look for the Properties, Setup, or Printer button in the Print dialog box, press that, and change the print quality to Best. If you are using a special paper, change the Paper Type setting (in the same dialog box) to match the paper.

Make sure that you have a fresh color cartridge installed. If it's been a long time since you printed in color, the toner may have dried up; if you have been printing a lot in color, the toner may be depleted. Generally, the sign that you are losing toner is that your pictures begin losing their reds, and turning greenish yellow, or light blue. Time to replace the toner cartridge.

If you have tried refilling the print cartridge on your own, the toner may have jammed; time to buy a new cartridge and start over.

Why has my printer begun to print wrong colors (for example, red looks like brown)?

In rare instances, you may be suffering from screwed-up settings in the software program that you are using. Another possibility: accidental mixing of colors inside the print cartridge; or the cartridge may be empty.

Software settings Settings for "configuration" (that is, what printer the program expects) inside the program that you are using can affect the way that colors print. Suspect this cause if the colors print correctly in another program. If all of the programs print wrong colors, configuration settings are not the cause.

Accidental mixing of colors inside the print cartridge You can print a self-test page to determine if the colors in the cartridge have mixed (see your owner's manual for step-by-step instructions). If the self-test page does not print with the proper colors, check the print cartridge for color. Some color print cartridges have three separate chambers, one for each of its three ink colors (cyan, yellow, and magenta). The colors become mixed when ink from one chamber finds its way to another chamber. Now this color mixing can happen in several ways:

- Any nonporous material placed in contact with the nozzle area can cause the inks to mix through a phenomenon known as "capillary action." Generally, color mixing happens when you reapply tape to the nozzle area of the cartridge, in an attempt to prolong its life. Instead, the tape encourages the inks to spread out and come into contact with each other. (The tape was never designed to be reapplied once you remove it from a new print cartridge).

- Color mixing may also occur when you place the entire print cartridge in a resealable plastic bag in an effort to keep the print cartridge from drying out. If the nozzle area comes into contact with the plastic bag, the inks can start oozing toward each other.

If color mixing is the problem, the print cartridge is probably permanently damaged. However, if the mixing did not occur over a long period of time, the output might improve with use. When the color mixing occurs only in the printhead portion of the cartridge and does not contaminate the ink in the reservoir itself, the print quality may return to normal as you use the printer.

If the print cartridge is new or if the color mixing has occurred even though nothing was allowed to come into contact with the nozzles, the tape placed on the nozzles during manufacture may have caused the problem. The tape over the nozzles occasionally lifts slightly during shipment, thereby providing a path for the inks to mix.

Perhaps the cartridge is out of ink, or broken Usually your printer comes with a utility or toolbox program that lets you run a test sheet of paper through the printer, to see if colors are coming out right.. Often you are asked to compare the printout with the dots on the cartridge.

- If the colors do not match, replace the color cartridge.

- If the colors do match those on the cartridge, you have enough ink, so you should explore the next possibility.

Maybe you selected the wrong printer Verify that the correct printer model is selected as the default printer in Windows.

FOR WINDOWS 3.1X:

1. Open Main, Control Panel, and Printers.

2. Check: Is the correct printer model selected as the default printer?
    - If the correct printer model is not selected as the default printer, highlight the appropriate printer model and choose Set As Default or install the appropriate printer driver by following the steps in the printer User's Guide.
    - If the correct printer model is selected as the default printer, try the next possible solution, below.

FOR WINDOWS 95/98 OR WINDOWS NT 4.0:

1. Choose Start, Settings, then Printers.

2. Right-click the appropriate printer icon and verify that there is a check next to Set As Default.
    - If the appropriate printer icon is not listed in the Printers window, install the appropriate printer driver by following the steps in the printer User's Guide.
    - If there is not a check next to Set As Default, choose Set As Default and try printing in color again.

3. If there is a check next to Set As Default, select Properties.

In Windows 95/98, choose the Details tab and verify that the correct printer is listed next to "Print using the following driver." In Windows NT 4.0, choose the General tab and verify that the correct printer is listed next to "Driver." For example, if the HP DeskJet 870Cse or 870Cxi printer is being used, the printer icon and printer driver will be labeled "HP DeskJet 870C Series."

- If the correct printer driver is listed, proceed to the next possible cause below.
- If the correct printer driver is not listed, delete the printer icon by right-clicking the printer icon and selecting Delete. Then, install the appropriate printer driver by following the steps in the printer User's Guide.

Maybe you have a conflict with the software that runs the display (the video driver) Change the video driver on the computer. Contact the computer manufacturer to change the video driver.

Maybe the computer needs more memory to do color printing. Verify that there are enough system resources available for color printing.

FOR WINDOWS 3.1X:

1. Select File, exit Windows, and choose OK.

2. At the MS-DOS prompt, type MSD and press Enter to run the Microsoft Diagnostics utility program.

3. Press M for Memory and verify that the Total Extended Memory meets or exceeds the minimum system requirements listed in the printer User's Guide.

   If the Total Extended Memory does not meet or exceed the minimum system requirements listed in the printer User's Guide, more RAM will need to be added to the computer.

4. Press Enter to return to the Microsoft Diagnostics utility main screen.

5. Press D for Disk Drives and verify that the Free Space on the C: drive is at least 10 to 20 MB.

   If the Free Space on the C: drive is not at least 10 to 20 MB, more disk space needs to be created on the C: drive.

6. Press Enter to return to the Microsoft Diagnostics utility main screen.

7. Press F3 to return to DOS, type WIN, and press Enter to return to Windows.

FOR WINDOWS 95 OR WINDOWS NT 4.0:

1. Right-click My Computer and choose Properties.

2. Click the General tab and verify that the amount of RAM meets or exceeds the minimum system requirements listed in the printer User's Guide.

   If the amount of RAM does not meet or exceed the minimum system requirements listed in the printer User's Guide, more RAM will need to be added to the computer.

3. Choose OK and then open My Computer.

4. Right-click the C: drive and choose Properties.

5. Select the General tab and verify that the Free Space is at least 10 to 20 MB.

   If the Free Space on the C: drive is not at least 10 to 20 MB, more disk space needs to be created on the C: drive.

6. Choose OK and close My Computer.

Q: How do I prevent black ink streaks on the paper when I print?

A: Small quantities of dust, hair, fibers and other debris can build up inside your printer to produce streaks or smears on your output (Figure A-1). To prevent this from happening, occasional cleaning of the printer is recommended. The following is a quick and simple process that will clean debris and fibers from your printer to ensure clear, sharp output every time. You should perform this process at least every three months.

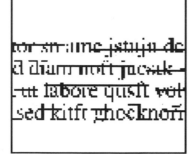

Figure A.1 Example of black streaks.

Before you start, make sure you have the following:

 8–10 cotton swabs or any clean pieces of soft, lint-free material that will not come apart when wet or leave fibers behind.

Enough distilled, filtered or bottled water to moisten the swabs. Do not use tap water because it might contain contaminants that could damage the print cartridges.

 Sheets of paper or paper towels to rest the print cartridges on while you are working.

Warning

Keep the print cartridge out of reach of children.

Remove the Print Cartridge

To remove a print cartridge, follow these steps (Figure A-2):

1. Turn the printer on and lift the top cover and wait while the print cartridges move to the center of the printer.

2. After the print cartridges have moved to the center of the printer, unplug the black power cord from the back of the printer.

3. Remove both print cartridges and place them on their sides on a sheet of paper.

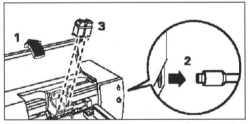

Figure A.2 Sample diagram of a typical printer (may not exactly match yours).

Note

Do not leave the print cartridges outside the printer for longer than 30 minutes. If a cartridge is left uncapped for too long, the ink will dry out and the cartridge will become unusable.

Clean the Print Cartridge

To clean the print cartridge, follow these steps (Figure A-3):

1. Dip a clean cotton swab in water and squeeze out any excess.

2. Hold the black print cartridge by the colored cap.

3. Use the swab to wipe clean the face and edges of the print cartridge as shown by the arrows. DO NOT wipe the nozzle plate.

4. Inspect the cartridge to see if any debris has been left behind.

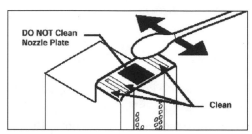

Figure A.3 How to clean a print cartridge (may not exactly match yours).

To do this, hold up to the light and tilt it at an angle. If you see any traces of dust, dirt or fibers, repeat Steps 2 and 3 to remove them.

5. Now repeat Steps 1–4 to clean the color print cartridge.

Always use a fresh cotton swab for each cartridge to avoid transferring debris from one cartridge to another.

Clean the Print Cartridge Cradle

To clean the print cartridge cradle, follow these steps (Figure A-4):

1. Locate the cradle that held the print cartridges.

2. Locate the three black, hook-shaped arms on the base of the cradle. If you lift the front of the printer slightly, you will be able to see these more easily. Lower the printer before proceeding to Step 3.

3. Using clean, moistened swabs, wipe the flat surfaces (the shaded area shown in the diagram) underneath each arm, from back to front.

4. Repeat the process until no ink is left on a clean swab.

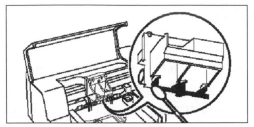

Figure A.4 Cleaning the cradle (may not look exactly like yours).

Clean the Service Station

The Service Station is located behind the on/off switch on the right side of your printer, (Figure A-5). You will need to reach back behind the casing to clean it. To clean the service station, follow these steps:

1. Using a clean, moistened swab, wipe the rim of the sponge holder.

2. Remove any built-up ink and fibers from the top of the sponge. If the sponge is higher than the rim, use the cotton swab to push it down below the rim.

3. Using a clean, moistened swab, clean Wiper 1 and the top surface of Cap 1.

   Always use a light touch when cleaning the print cartridge caps. Rubbing may unseat the caps which could eventually damage the print cartridges.

4. Now take another clean, moistened swab, and clean Wiper 2 and the top surface of Cap 2.

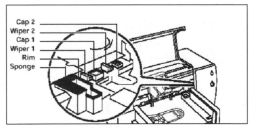

Figure A.5 Diagram of a typical service station. Remember, your printer may not look like this.

Reinstall the Print Cartridges

1. Re-install the print cartridges and close the printer's top cover.

2. Re-insert the black power cord into the back of the printer.

3. Run a test page through the printer.

   Most printers have a utility that allows you to print a self-rest. If not, print an image that has a wide range of colors, so you can see if they all come out correctly.

Note

Careful cleaning will usually be enough to remove any streaks. However, it is possible that fibers or debris may have been missed which might interfere with print quality. To remove them, simply repeat the cleaning procedure until the test printout is 100% clear and sharp.

For trouble-free printing with your printer, remember to clean the cartridge, cradle and service station every three months.

You can find other useful tips about how to maintain an HP printer on their website at:

`http://www.deskjet-support.com`

Q: My paper keeps jamming, or not getting picked up at all. What should I do?

A: Try any or all of the following:

- Make sure the Paper Tray (tray with the handle for the HP) is pushed in all the way.

- Check for overloading. If too many sheets of paper were loaded (20 sheets *maximum* for photo media, 40 sheets for plain paper); remove some paper. [This may vary, depending on your printer.]

- If the paper is damaged, ragged, wrinkled, or curled, replace the paper.

- Make sure all papers in the paper tray are of the same type, size, and weight.

- Clean the pick rollers inside the printer.

- Using a lint-free cloth, slightly moisten with water, wipe the rollers by turning the black plastic rod that they are attached to.

- Turn off the printer using the power button, then unplug the power cord from the printer and remove the paper tray. Power the printer back on without the paper tray installed.

- The printer should come up in the ready mode (green LED on steady) this should put the paper pick mechanism back into the correct state. Remove any media from the paper tray, put 5 to 10 sheets of plain paper in the tray (adjust paper guides tightly against the paper edges but do not crimp the paper) and install the paper tray. If your printer offers a diagnostic test, run that now.

- If you are having troubles only with glossy paper, and plain paper works OK, load no more than twenty (20) sheets in the paper tray, and adjust the paper guides so they are not too tight — you should be able to move the media slightly as it sits in the tray: Front to back, leave about 1/4 of an inch and on the sides, leave about 1/32 of an inch so that the guides are not binding the glossy media.

Q: Sometimes the prints come out slanted. What can I do about that?

A: Try some of these fixes:

- Remove the media from the paper tray, straighten up the stack and then reload it back into the tray.

- Make sure the paper width and length adjusters/guides fit snugly against the left and bottom edges of the paper stack so the paper is being fed "squarely" into the printer.

- Check that there are no more than 20 sheets of media loaded in the paper tray.

- Check to make sure that only one size and type of paper is loaded in the paper tray.

- Make sure that your paper weight falls between 16 and 64 lbs (and is not more than 9 mil in thickness), for most printers.

- Try a different type or brand of paper.

- Make sure you are following the paper vendor's directions carefully. (Are you putting the paper in right side up, and with the right end in?)

- Clean the pick rollers inside the printer. Remove the paper tray. Open the top access door, looking inside toward the front of the printer. Using a lint free cloth, slightly moisten with water, wipe the rollers by turning the black plastic rod that they are attached to.

Index

A

Adobe, fonts from, 196
advertising postcards, 15
airbrushing, 10, 38
albums, 120–122
    of pets, 144–147
    of sky observations, 125–127
Alfred Hitchcock stamp, 114
America Online
    e-mailing images with, 55
    genealogy area, 169–171
analog images, 7
ancestors, 157. See also genealogy
    articles on, 170
    image and information collection,
        167–171
anchor spots, for art, 263
announcements, 200-202
AppleWorks (Apple), 41, 56, 63
aprons, 15
arrows, on signs, 85–86
attachments, images as, 55
auctions, pictures at, 169
awards, 212–213
    fonts for, 212
    for good behavior, 223
    landscape orientation for, 212
    layout of, 212–213

B

backgrounds, editing, 180, 285
balance, of text and graphics pages, 205
banners, 15, 46, 89–92
    cut sheet paper for, 89
    font size for, 90
    for game-day decorations, 288
    for holidays, 74
    margin settings for, 90
    revising, 92
    for Valentine's Day, 186–187
bead projects, 89
Bettmann Archives, 69
big league players, morphing into,
    285–287
birthday party invitations, 78–79
bitmap (BMP) images, 28, 36
    e-mailing, 55
bitmap programs, 37–38
bits
    for color data recording, 28
    scanner use of, 20
Bitstream, fonts from, 196
black-and-white pictures, reducing tint for, 28
board games, local real estate, 301–307
book assignments, advertising, 227

book covers, 229–231
    theme images for, 229–231
borders, 146
    for stationery, 192-194
boxes, 98–101
brightness, 20
    adjusting, 10, 26–27, 41
brochures, project software for, 46
brush tips, 94
Burns, Robert, 179
bushes, photographs of, 103
business cards, 51, 199
bytes, 28

C

calendars, 136–139
    multi-weekly or multi-monthly, 138
    personalized, 136–138
    pictures and clip art on, 137
    project software for, 46
campaign posters, 277–279
    emotional appeal of, 279
    goal illustration, 279
    listing supplies on, 278
    pictures on, 278
Canvas (Deneba), 41, 45, 62-63
car game-day decorations, 287–288
    clip art for, 287
    text size for, 288
cards. See greeting cards
Casa de Toad, free fonts from, 196
catalogs, 260–268
    columns, 261
    cover, 263
    margins, 261
    order form, 263
    page layout, 261–262
    professional printing of, 260–261
    text area, 263
    trim size, 261
census records, 164–165
certificates, 212–213
chat sessions
    archived, 172
    on genealogical topics, 171
Cheap Sheets, 199, 212
children
    card-making process, coaching through,
        62–67
    chores checklists for, 138–139, 224-226
    experimentation of, 63
    major-league players, morphing into,
        285–287
    Operating Room tour booklets for,
        218–219

painting programs for, 62–63
paper activities for, 221–222
personal calendars for, 136–138
sports cards of, 281–283
chore boards, 224–226
    clip art for, 224
chore checklists, 138–139
    pictures on, 139
Christmas decorations, 74
Christmas tree ornaments, 75
Church of the Latter Day Saints, research
    by, 170
ClarisWorks, 56, 62–63
ClarisWorks for Kids, 62–63
class newsletters, 245–246
    font size for, 246
    parent photographs in, 246
    student photographs in, 245
classroom projects, 223–246
    book assignments, advertising, 227
    book covers, 229–231
    classroom chore reminders, 224–226
    cultural diversity cutouts, 231–232
    flash cards, 238–239
    newsletters, 245–246
    number lines, 232–234
    one-fact-a-day sheets, 227–229
    planets cutouts, 239–240
    rain forest cutouts, 234–237
    rewards, 243–245
    science fair projects, 240–243
clip art, 46
    coloring, 70
    fonts, 196
    for holiday cards, 70
    labeling containers with, 122
    for wrapping paper, 92–94
    writing inside, 194
collections, labeling, 122–124
color, 19
    experimenting with, 250
    importance of, 190, 249
    inverting, 289–290
    for marketing purposes, 249–254
    scanner recognition of, 20
color printers, 7, 8
    dots per inch of, 57
    functionality of, 50
    loading, 52–53
    manual feed, 54
    multiple, 54
    paper types for, 51–52
    setup of, 53–55
    small formats, working with, 53
color wheel, 28

columns
  art in, 206, 207
  for newsletters, 206–207
  for product catalogs, 261
  separating, 206
  for stationery art and text, 192, 194
community spirit
  appeals to, 274
  and profit, 274
Complete Publisher (Sierra and Micrografx),
    45, 46, 56
compression of image files, 29, 35
computers, 8
  drawing with, 7
  early images on, 18
  graphics on, 18
  professional artist use of, 19
  video jacks or cards, 35
contrast, changing, 10
Corbis collection, 69
Corel Draw (Corel), 39, 40
Corel PhotoHouse, 165
corporate identity, inventing, 190
coupons, 185
Crayola Magic 3D Coloring Book, 63
Crayola Print Factory (IBM), 46, 63
cropping images, 24–26
cultural diversity cutouts, 231–232
customers, awarding prizes to, 200
Cyndi Howell's list of genealogical sites, 167

D

darkness, adjusting, 27
databases, 166
della Femina, Jerry, 247
Deneba, 62–63
DesignJet (HP), 52, 187, 221
diet warnings, 132
digital cameras, 7, 8, 29–30, 47
  deleting mistakes, 32
  distances, choosing, 30–32
  erasing images, 34
  exposure control, 33
  functionality of, 30–36
  image manipulation with, 30
  image quality settings, 33
  images from, 30
  picture preview, 30
  preserving images, 34
  shadows, overcoming, 32–33
  slide show, 34
  timers, 32
digital images, 7. See also electronic imaging
  accuracy of, 7
  copyrights of, 12
  display of, 13
  integration of, 9
  professional appearance of, 11
  publishing, 13
  uses of, 14–15
dinosaur flash cards, 238–239
  poster size, 238
direct mailers, 266–268
  back page, 266
  personalizing, 267

  photographs on, 267
  pitch page, 266
donations
  honor role of, 276
  recognition for, 275–276
Donne, John, 178
dots per inch (dpi), 50, 57
Draw a Story (Orly), 41
drawing programs, 36, 39–41
  coaching children through, 62–67
  editing in, 39, 40
  for landscape mapping, 108
  large font sizes, 90
  objects, placing and removing, 108
  scalloped edges, creating, 116
DVD (digital video), porting to computer, 36

E

e-mail
  for genealogical research, 167
  image attachments to, 69
  pictures, 55
Egyptian projects, graphics for, 156
8-bit color, 20, 21
Einstein, Albert, 6
electronic images
  cutting holes in, 71
  layering, 71
electronic imaging, 8–14. See also digital im-
    ages
  advantages of, 8
  costs of, 8
  creation, from scratch, 36–47
  flexibility of, 10
  hardware and software requirements, 47
  with Macintosh, 18
  speed of, 9, 30
  tools for, 8
emotions, evocation of, 5
engravings, online collections of, 69
eraser tool, 285
  children's use of, 64
ethnic diversity cutouts, 231–232
ethnic groups, information on, 171
event announcements, 272–274
  graphics for, 274
Expert, fonts from, 196
exposure, adjusting, 26–27

F

faces, on invitations, 78–79
Family Heritage and Generations software,
    166
family history, 157–175
  dramatizing, 164–167
  images for, 166
  map of origins, 160–164
  newsletter on, 171–172
  pictures for, 158
  requests for information, 172
  software for, 164–167
  tape-recording interviews, 157–158
  transcribing interviews, 158
  Web pages, family, 172–175
family newsletters, 171–172

family tree cutouts, 231–232
Family Tree House, 171
Family Tree Maker (Mindscape), 165
Family Tree Maker Deluxe (Broderbund),
    164–165
family trees, 164–165
family Web pages, 172–175
fax cover sheets, 199
file formats
  lossless, 29
  for saving scanned images, 28–30
FileMaker, 56, 267
filled shapes, 95
finger puppets, 222
flash cards, 238–239
FlashPix, 29
flea markets, pictures at, 169
The Floral Collection, 175
flower bed designs, 105–108
  images, capturing electronically, 107
  plant criteria, Web search for, 105–106
flowers
  capturing electronically, 107
  romantic images of, 175
flyers, 245–246
  digital images for, 14
  for fund-raising events, 275
  for lost pets, 153–154
  project software for, 46
foam-core boards, 240–241
fonts
  for business stationery, 194, 196
  for company name, 252
  consistent use of, 253
  experimenting with, 196, 197
  for large letters, 90
  for marketing materials, 253
food labels, 133–136
  for friends, 134–135
  listing ingredients, 136
  for sale items, 135–136
food wrappers, 181–184
  images for, 182
  sizing , 182
Fractal Painter, 38
FrameMaker for catalog pages, 260
Freehand Selection tool, 95, 110, 154, 285
Front Page (Microsoft), 56
fund-raising, 275–277
  recognition for donations, 275, 276

G

gameboards, for local real estate game,
    301–305
  crazy money for, 306
  laminating, 305
  layout of, 305
  pictures for, 301, 302
  prices on, 304, 305
  public monuments on, 303
  rental fees on, 305
  rules for, 307
garage sale advertisements, 292–295
  arrows for, 294
  font size for, 292
  pictures for, 292

planting signs, 294–295
text for, 292
garden design, 101–105
design area, gridding, 108–110
design area, visualizing, 110–114
flower bed designs, 105–108
garden features, photographing, 102
images, combining, 105
landscape design software for, 112
mapping area, 108–110
pasting objects on plan, 110, 111
planning area, 109–110
vegetable garden plans, 105–108
GEDCOM, 169
genealogy, 157–175
on America Online, 169–171
conferences on, 170
dramatizing, 164–167
online classes on, 170
software for, 164–167
Genealogy Forum, 169–171
chat sessions, 171
History message board, 170
Message Board Center, 170
quick-start guide, 169
Surnames Center, 169
Generations Deluxe Family Tree Software
(Sierra), 166
geometric shapes, company names around,
252
gift bags, 96–97
gift boxes, 98–101
art for, 100
design of, 98
flaps, 100
gift tags, 72
paper thickness for, 72
reusable, 72
Glossy Calendar paper (HP), 138
Glossy Photo Greeting Cards (HP), 177
Glossy Photographic Paper (HP), 156
graphic files, availability of, 12
Graphic Image Format (gif) files
e-mailing, 55
for Web images, 57
graphical user interfaces, 19
graphics, artistic styles, 210
graphics programs, 47
image creation with, 36–47
gray, degrees of, 20
greeting cards, 51, 62–77
automating creation of, 68–69
for holidays, 69–76
invitations, 78–101
messages, disguising and hiding, 70, 71
for Mother's Day, 62
personalizing, 62
poetic lines on, 178–179
project software for, 46
scents on, 184–185
sending online, 69
sentimental, 175
for Valentine's Day, 187

H

Halloween masks, 72
Hanukkah decorations, 74

health-care industry projects, 213–223
instruction sheets, 216–218
Operating Room tour booklets, 218–219
paper activities for the waiting room,
221–222
patient anxiety, lessening, 219–221
personal reminders, 213–216
rewards for good behavior, 223
hieroglyphics graphics, 156
hobbies, 114–129
albums of successes, 120–122
collecting, 114–119
holiday banners, 74
holiday cards, 69–76
for Mother's Day, 62
Valentine's Day cards, 69–73
holiday decorations, 73–76
stuffed objects, 75–76
home business projects, 190–213
awards and certificates, 212–213
business cards, 199
fax cover sheets, 199
marketing, 246–268
newsletters, 202–213
postcards, announcements and thank
you's, 200–202
stationery, 190–199
Home Page (FileMaker), 56
home towns, maps of, 162–164
homemade papers, 92–96
Howell, Cyndi, genealogical site of, 167
hues, 20

I

icons, 19, 130, 251
Illustrator (Adobe), 40
images. See also digital images; scanning
adjusting, before scanning, 22–29
attraction of, 5
background editing for, 180
and computers, 7
cropping, 24–26
digital, 7
digitizing, 34–35, 47
distorting, 289–290
exposure, adjusting, 26–27
for expression, 6
flipping, 128
information from, 5
labeling collections with, 122–124
layering, 130
mirroring, 23, 128
period, 168
printing, 29, 47
recall of, 5
romantic, 175–187
rotating, 22–23
sentimental, 273
series of, 131
shrinking to icon size, 130
size of, and download speed, 57
and thinking processes, 6
tinting, 28
inkjet printers, for printing graphics, 47
instruction sheets, 216–218
as contracts, 218
formality of, 218

numbered steps, 217
patient photographs on, 217
practitioner photographs on, 216
text size, 217
Internet/Intranet Design Shop Gold
(Boomerang), 56
invitations, 78–101, 186, 200
for birthday parties, 78–79
waving hello with, 83–85
Iron-On T-Shirt Transfers (HP), 181

J

journalists, digital camera use by, 30
JPEG (Joint Photographic Experts Group)
format, 29
e-mailing images, 55
for Web photographs, 29, 57

K

KidPix (Broderbund), 40, 63
kisses, images of, 180–181
kitchen, using images in, 129–144
diet warning signs, 132
preserves labels, 132–136
recipe cards, 139–143
shopping lists, 129–131

L

labels, 51, 77
for collections, 122–124
for food preserves, 132–136
positioning, 124
landscape design software, 112–114
and shadow movement, 112
landscape orientation, 26, 54
for awards, 212
for banners, 89
for calendars, 137
landscaping. See garden design
laser printers, 50
The Learning Company, 164–165
letters, digital images for, 14
Library of Congress's American Memory
site, 168
line art, 210
for coloring, 229
logos, 190–194, 251
saving in word processing program, 191
selecting one, 190
shrinking, 206
size of, 253
love, expressing, 175–187

M

Macintosh, 18-19
screen captures, 36, 107
MacPaint, 18, 38, 62–63
Magic Artist, 63
mailers, 51
maps, 80–83
of family origins, 160–164
landmarks on, 80, 81, 298, 299
local scenery on, 162
major streets, 80

continued

maps *(continued)*
  natural or geological background on, 164
  of neighborhood blocks, 298–301
  of landscapable areas, 108–110
  written directions on, 82
marketing brochures, digital images for, 14
marketing, digital, 246–268
  budget for, 249
  catalogs, 260–268
  colors for, 249–254
  company positioning, 248
  design process, 247
  direct mailers, 266–268
  fonts for, 249–254
  marketing plan, 249
  organization name, 247
  portfolios, 263–266
  posters, 255–258
  product or service quality, 248
  report and proposal covers, 258–260
  symbols for, 249–254
masks, creating, 72
Mattel, 164–165
meeting notices, 281
  agenda of, 270, 271
  font size for, 271
  graphics on, 271
memories, evocation of, 5
MGI Photo Suite (MGI), 45
Microsoft
  fonts giveaways, 196
  graphical user interface use, 19
Microsoft Encarta's Atlas 97, 162
Microsoft Paint, 38
Microsoft Word
  Landscape orientation in, 137
  stationery border creation, 193
  stationery creation in, 192
mini-posters, 289–292
  distorting images, 289–290
  as personal reminder, 213
  photo or clip art for, 289
  slogans for, 290
mirroring images, 23
Monotype, fonts from, 196
Mormons, genealogical research by, 170
Mother's Day cards, 62
  by adults, 65–67
  by children, 62–67
  electronic photos, importing, 64, 65
mottos, 206
mousepads, of famous stamps, 114

N

Neferchichi, 156
neighborhood activities, graphics for,
    292–307
  garage sale advertisements, 292–295
  local real estate game, 301–307
  mapping the block, 298–301
  treasure hunt clues, 296–297
neighborhood maps, 298–301
  images for, 298–299
  layout, 299
newsletters, 202–213
  art for, 280–281
  audience for, 203

boxing art, 210
  colors for, 204
  columns for, 206–207
  contributors to, 203
  enlivening, 279–281
  family, 171-172
  folding, 211
  fonts for, 204
  graphics for, 208–211
  information in, 202
  layout of, 205
  logo on, 206
  mailing address box, 207, 211–213
  mottos on, 206
  name placement on, 204
  nameplate area, 206
  naming, 203–206
  photographs for, 208
  picture captions, 210
  postage on, 212
  project software for, 46
  school publications, 245–246
  shading behind text, 207
  size, length, and frequency, 202–203
  table of contents, 207–208
  text for, 279, 281
  topics in, 203
number lines, 232–234
  images for, 232–233
numbers, mirroring effect on, 23

O

objects
  color and pattern fill adjustments, 40
  copying and pasting, 40
  creation in drawing programs, 39
  flipping, 40
  grouping, 40
  moving, 40
  shape adjustments, 40
  size adjustments, 40
office wall decoration, large prints for,
    219–221
one-fact-a-day sheets, 227–229
Operating Room tour booklets, 218–219
  pictures for, 218
oral history, 157–160
Outlook 98, e-mailing images with, 55

P

PageMaker, for catalog pages, 260
PageMill (Adobe), 56
Paik, Nam June, 124
Paint, 62–63
paint bucket, 38
paint programs, 36, 37
  children, experimentation with, 63–64
  for chores sheets, 138
  coaching children through, 62–67
  frames, creating, 66
  large font sizes, 90
  scalloped edges, creating, 116
  wrapping paper design in, 94
paintbrush, 38
paintings, online collections of, 69
PaintShop Pro (Jasc), 41, 63

paper, 50–52
  bright white, 51
  business card, 51
  calendar, 51
  dimensions of, 54
  felt, 175
  glossy, 177
  greeting card, 51
  heavyweight, 51, 52
  labels, 51
  loading, 52–53
  mailer, 51
  manual feed, 54
  note-size photographic, 51
  orientation of, 89
  photo, 51
  plain, 51
  postcard, 51, 76, 200
  premium, 51
  T-shirt transfer, 51, 181
  transparency film, 51
  Tyvek®, 51, 255
paper activities for the waiting room,
    221–222
paper airplane, 221
paper bags
  colors for, 96
  printing on, 96
Paper Direct, 195, 199, 212
paper prints, scanning, 12
parties. *See also* invitations
  craft projects for, 89
  signs to, 85–89
party favor bags, 96–97
Party Friends, 89
patient anxiety, lessening, 219–221
patients, rewards for good behavior, 223
patterns, projects for, 233
Pencil tool, 180, 285
personal reminders, 213–216
  art or calendar graphics on, 214
  authority of, 214
  images on, 216
  patient photographs on, 214
pets, 144–156
  albums of, 144–147
  on imaginary flights, 147–151
  lost pet flyers, 153–154
  on pedestals, 154–157
  show animal posters, 151–153
Photo Creations (Creative Wonders), 68
photo editors, 47
  contrast and brightness adjustments, 27
  and JPEG images, 29
  text capabilities of, 67
Photo LandDesigner™ (Sierra), 112
photo-finishing software, 36, 45
Photo-Paint, 63
PhotoCreations (Creative Wonders), 45
PhotoDeluxe (Adobe), 45
PhotoDraw 2000 (Microsoft), 45
photograph enlargements
  of digital camera images, 33
  from digitized 35mm film, 34
  digitizing photographs from. *See* scanning
photographs
  brightness adjustments, 41
  color adjustments, 41

combining, 10
copying, 41
cutting, 41
digitizing, 12. *See also* scanning
edges, softening, 41
framing and bordering, 41
manipulating, 41–45
of landscape items, 102, 103
online collections of, 69
pasting operations, 41
printing, 50
quality of, 208
rotating, 41
sharpness adjustments, 41
tinting, 41
tracing, 41
transparency adjustments, 41
unidentified, 169
PhotoMagic (Micrografx), 45
PhotoShop (Adobe), 27, 41, 45
PhotoSmart Photo Scanner (HP), 22
PhotoSmart printers (HP), 47, 50, 156
PICT (Picture) files, e-mailing, 55
pictures. *See also* images
e-mailing, 55
frames for, 66
importing, to greeting cards, 64, 65
morphing, 285–287
posting on Web sites, 56–57
printing, 50–55
pictures, existing, scanning, 19–29
pillowcases, transferring images on, 15,
180–181
pixels, 38
planets cutouts, 239–240
hanging, 240
labeling objects, 239
plastic bags, food labels for, 133
portfolios, 263–266
After pictures, 265
Before pictures, 265
binder for, 265, 266
challenge description, 264
constraints description, 264
dividers for, 265
headers and footers for, 264
page sleeves, 265
personalizing, 266
project situation page, 264
solution description, 264
table of contents for, 266
portrait orientation, 26, 54, 176
postcards, 76–77, 200-202
dimensions for, 76
graphics for, 156
margin adjustments for, 77
online, 69
of pet attractions, 156
posters, 15, 177, 219, 245–246
borders for, 257, 258
for campaigning, 277–279
costs of, 275–276
for fund-raising events, 275–277
image styles for, 255
images bleeds on, 258
key facts on, 152
logo on, 258
for marketing , 255–258

for meetings, 271
mini-posters, 289–292
printers of, 221
project software for, 46
sentimental imagery for, 273
of show animals, 151–153
slogans on, 255
text on, 256–257
for upcoming events, 272–274
for Valentine's Day, 187
PowerGoo (Kai), 45
Premiere (Adobe), 35
preprinted papers, 195
preserves, labeling, 132–136
Print Artist (Sierra), 46, 191-193
Print Artist Craft Factory (Knowledge
Adventure), 46
Print Artist Platinum (Sierra Home), 69
Print Setup dialog box, 53, 54
Print Studio (Disney), 46
Printable Expressions (Hewlett-Packard),
46, 68, 175
printer companies, large prints production
at, 221
printers
and bringing art to edge, 195
HP Design Jet, 52, 187, 221
logo printing, 191
print area of, 90
printing greeting cards, 70
T-Shirt transfers, loading, 181
prints, large, for office walls, 219–221
PrintShop (Broderbund), 46, 89
PrintShop Signature Greetings
(Broderbund), 69
prizes, for customers, 200
professional artists, computer use by, 19
professional postcard makers, 201
profit, as motivator, 274
project software, 36
clip art in, 46
printing with, 46
templates in, 46
Properties dialog box, 54, 55
proposal covers, 258–260
images for, 14, 259
logo on, 260
page division for, 258
printing, 260
purpose of, 258
speaker photograph on, 260
text color, 260
title, 259

Q

quilts, 127–129
enlarging or shrinking images, 128
size of squares, 128
theme pictures for, 128
transferring image, 128–129
washing, 129

R

rain forest cutouts, 234–237
animal images, 236
background for, 236

bush, fern, and flower images, 236
leaf images, 234
pasting to background, 236
tree trunks, 234
real estate games, 301–307
recipe cards, 139–143
photographs for, 141, 142
rectangle tool, 282
report covers, 258–260
images for, 14, 259
logo on, 260
page division for, 258
printing, 260
purpose of, 258
speaker photograph on, 260
text color, 260
title, 259
resolution, 20
setting, 24
rewards
child's photograph on, 245
images for, 244
personalized, 243–245
romantic expressions, 175–187
with flowers, 175
food wrappers, 181–184
invitations, 186
kisses, 180–181
pillowcase iron-ons, 180–181
poems for, 178–179
scents, using, 184–185
special moments memories, 176–178
Valentine's Day banners, 186–187
Roswell, New Mexico, 274
rotating images, 22–23
rules (horizontal lines), 206

S

sales advertisements, postcards for, 201
scanners, 7, 8, 19, 47
bit-depth and colors of, 21
capabilities of, 21–29
color functionality of, 20
resolution of, 20
scanning, 19–29
adjusting images, before scanning, 22–29
how it works, 20–21
printing images, 29
resolution for Web images, 57
saving scanned images, 28–30
science fair projects, 240–243
chronological sequence of, 243
Conclusion section, 243
Hypothesis section, 241
layout, 243
Materials Used section, 241
Methods section, 241
physical evidence display, 243
presentation of, 240
Purpose section, 241
report for, 241
Results section, 243
text size for, 241
screen captures, 107
seasonal decorations, 73–76
seasonal images, 73
Seattle Filmworks, 34

self-mailers, 263
Self-Seal Mailer paper (Avery), 266
Send to Back, 130
shopping lists, 129–131
show animals, posters of, 151–153
signs, 15, 85–89
    arrows on, 85–86
    graphics for, 87–88
    text on, 88
16-bit color, 20, 21
slides, scanning, 12
Snapshot Digital Imaging Software (Sierra
        and Micrografx), 45
Social Security Death List, 170
software
    capabilities of, 10, 11
    for electronic imaging, 8
    for graphics. *See* graphics programs
solar system project, 239–240
speech balloons, 79, 146
sports cards, 281–283
    award or honors on, 283
    laminating, 283
    line widths for, 282
    name, position, and jersey number, 282
    printing, 283
    statistics and bio, 283
sports projects, 281–291
    car game-day decorations, 287–288
    mini-posters, 289–292
    sports cards, 281–283
    team rosters, 284–285
spraycan, 38
Spraypaint tool, 95, 180
spreadsheets, for calendars, 137
stamps, 116–119
    scalloped edges, 116, 117
    text for, 118
stars, recording observations, 125–127
stationery, 190–199
    borders, 192-194
    font selection, 194, 196, 197
    graphics placement, 192, 194
    homemade graphics for, 193
    logo for, 190–194
    name and address on, 194–199
    preprinted, 195
    preprinted papers for, 195
    printing, 191
    saving, 199
stuffed objects, 75
Surnames Center, 169, 170

T

T-shirt transfers, 51, 119, 127–128
    for pillowcases, 180–181
    washing, 129
T-shirts, 15
tables, 125
tape recorders, for recording interviews,
        157
team rosters, 284–285
    graphics for, 284

names and jersey numbers, 284
    team member pictures, 284
team spirit, building, 284
Tesla, Nikola, 6
text
    for banners, 89
    mirroring effect on, 23
    versus pictures, 5, 6
    for stamps, 118
Thanksgiving decorations, 74
thank you's, 200-202
thinking processes, visual image use of, 6
35mm cameras
    versus digital cameras, 30
    digitizing photographs from, 34–35, 47
3D Landscape (Sierra), 112
thumbnails, 29
tic-tac-toe game, 222
TIFF (tagged image file format) format, 29
    e-mailing, 55
tiling, 74
tinting images, 10, 28, 41
The Tomb of the Chihuahua Pharaohs, 156
toolbars, 19
treasure hunt clues, 296–297
    clip art for, 297
    pictures for, 296, 297
    sequence of clues, 297
    treasure, 297
trees, photographs of, 103
TV
    digital camera image slide show on, 34
    electronic picture files from, 12
    screen captures from, 36
24-bit color, 20, 21
Tyvek®, 51, 255

U

Ultimate Family Tree Deluxe (Palladium
        Interactive), 165

V

vacation memories, 176–178
Valentine's Day cards, 69–73, 187
Valentine's Day posters, 187
Valentine's Day banners, 186–187
van Rijn, Rembrandt, 6
vector graphics, 39
vegetable garden plans, 105–108
    images, capturing electronically, 107
    plant criteria, Web search for, 105–106
video
    editing, 35
    importing, from video recorders or cam-
        eras, 35–36
    storage space requirements, 35
video cameras, porting to computer, 35–36
Visio Home, for map creation, 80
Visual Page (Symantec), 56
volunteering, 270–281
    campaigning, 277–279

event and work session announcements,
        272–274
    fundraising, 275–277
    meeting notices, 270–272

W

weather observations, recording, 125–127
Web
    fonts from, 196
    genealogical research postings on, 165
    genealogy information on, 157, 166–171
    images, gathering from, 12
Web browsers, for genealogical research,
        167
Web Easy (Ixla), 56
Web Express (Microvision Development), 56
Web pages, 15
    background for, 173
    buttons on, 174
    digital pictures for, 33
    download time warnings, 174, 175
    family, 172–175
    FlashPix images for, 29
    JPEG images for, 29, 57
    menus on, 173
    pictures on, 173–174
    site name, 173
    submenus, 174
    text, 175
    thumbnails on, 174
Web sites
    creating, products for , 56–57
    download times, and number of images, 57
    posting pictures on, 56–57
Web Studio (Sierra), 57
Windows Draw (Micrografx), 39, 40
Windows programs
    printer settings in, 54
    screen shots in, 36, 107
Word for Office 97/98, 57
Word for Office 2000, 57
word processing programs
    boxing art in, 210
    for calendars, 137
    for gameboard text, 304
    stationery creation in, 191
work session announcements, 272–274
    humor for, 273
    sentimental imagery for, 273
wrappers, for food items, 181–184
wrapping paper, homemade, 92–96
    clip art for, 92–94
    coloring gaps, 94
    copying and pasting images, 93
    margin settings for, 92
    picture size for, 92
    with "scribble-scrabble," 94–96

Y

yard designs, 101–105
yard sale advertisements, 292–295

Keep it simple.

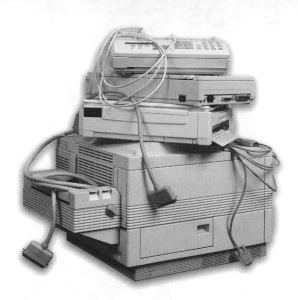

Print, fax, scan and copy with HP's All-in-One.

When you choose one of HP's reliable OfficeJet All-in-Ones, you'll have all the tools you need for colorful, professional-quality printing, scanning, copying and faxing, in one compact unit. Now you can create exciting brochures, posters, flyers and other printed pieces that will get the attention they deserve! Using HP's All-in-One, your projects can come alive in wonderfully realistic color when you use the built-in color scanner. Add colorful photos and artwork to your projects — then print them quickly and easily.

Let an All-in-One simplify your life with the reliability and convenience you've come to expect from an HP product.

It's that simple!

(hp) HEWLETT
PACKARD

Expanding Possibilities

Take a look! Go to Printsville at www.hp.com/go/printsville for the newest ideas in town for colorful calendars, business stationery and more. They're **free**. And, once you're there, go to the Town Map to learn how you can get *HP Idea Kits* chock full of how to's and graphics for business and fun use!

Printsville

Asbestos shirt sold separately.

This tie gives new meaning to the phrase "hot under the collar." Don't worry, you don't need any fancy graphics software. The design is ready-to-print from our Web site. You'll need a color inkjet printer, an HP Iron-On T-Shirt Transfer and a plain, white necktie. Just follow the instructions below.

Step 1: Go to *www.hp.com/go/printsville*. Click on *Town Map* and then *Flaming Tie*.

Step 2: Download and print the design onto an HP Iron-On T-Shirt Transfer.

Step 3: Follow the on-screen directions for ironing the design onto a tie.

(For more project ideas, look for free HP Idea Kits on Printsville.)

HP Idea Kits. If you can imagine it, you can print it.

HEWLETT®
PACKARD

Expanding Possibilities

Quality HP products *for* the home, *direct* to your home!

Find what you're looking for at the HP Shopping Village:

Printers, Scanners & All-in-Ones
Printers, scanners, and All-in-One products for completing the perfect home office.

Computers
PCs, monitors, Palmtop PCs, calculators and computer accessories to meet your every need.

Printing Supplies
All the ink and paper supplies for your printer - as well as Printable Expressions® Greeting Cards.

PC Photography
Everything you need to create your own home digital photo lab.

FREE
2-Day Delivery with Printing Supplies Purchases†

† Your purchase must be $25 or more to qualify

- New and refurbished HP products

- Select supplies for your printer quickly and simply

- Easy-to-use product comparison charts

- Next morning and Saturday FedEx® delivery options available

- Online order tracking

- Order online or call 1-888-774-6847

Copyright 1998-99 Hewlett-Packard Company

HP Shopping Village
www.hp.com/info/hppress3

HEWLETT PACKARD
Expanding Possibilities

my2cents.idgbooks.com

Register This Book — And Win!

Visit **http://my2cents.idgbooks.com** to register this book and we'll automatically enter you in our fantastic monthly prize giveaway. It's also your opportunity to give us feedback: let us know what you thought of this book and how you would like to see other topics covered.

Discover IDG Books Online!

The IDG Books Online Web site is your online resource for tackling technology — at home and at the office. Frequently updated, the IDG Books Online Web site features exclusive software, insider information, online books, and live events!

10 Productive & Career-Enhancing Things You Can Do at www.idgbooks.com

- Nab source code for your own programming projects.

- Download software.

- Read Web exclusives: special articles and book excerpts by IDG Books Worldwide authors.

- Take advantage of resources to help you advance your career as a Novell or Microsoft professional.

- Buy IDG Books Worldwide titles or find a convenient bookstore that carries them.

- Register your book and win a prize.

- Chat live online with authors.

- Sign up for regular e-mail updates about our latest books.

- Suggest a book you'd like to read or write.

- Give us your 2¢ about our books and about our Web site.

You say you're not on the Web yet? It's easy to get started with IDG Books' *Discover the Internet,* available at local retailers everywhere.